University Management, the Academic Profession, and Neoliberalism

University Management, the Academic Profession, and Neoliberalism

JOHN S. LEVIN,
MARIE C. MARTIN,
ARIADNA I. LÓPEZ-DAMIÁN

Published by State University of New York Press, Albany

For information, contact State University of New York Press, Albany, NY
www.sunypress.edu

Library of Congress Cataloging-in-Publication Data

Names: John S. Levin | Marie C. Martin | Ariadna I. López Damián.
Title: University Management, the Academic Profession, and Neoliberalism /
    John S. Levin, Marie C. Martin, Ariadna I. López Damián
Description: Albany : State University of New York Press, [2020] | Includes
    bibliographical references and index.
Identifiers: ISBN 9781438479095 (hardcover : alk. paper) | ISBN 9781438479118
    (ebook)
Further information is available at the Library of Congress.

Library of Congress Control Number: 2020937135

10 9 8 7 6 5 4 3 2 1

Contents

Preface

Background and Acknowledgments

This is the work of three compatible people with decidedly different backgrounds who found each other at the University of California, Riverside. Ariadna from Guerrero, Mexico, Marie from Utah, the United States, and John from British Columbia, Canada, took separate paths but all developed a curiosity for the behaviors and experiences of postsecondary education academics and administrators. They brought to the subject their experiences as students in the three countries and as scholars in the United States. Ariadna had a particular interest in the work and experiences of part-time faculty, especially those who were engaged with organizational life and their work. Marie was attracted to the development and work of administrators, especially university deans and their managerial roles. John gravitated toward full-time tenure track faculty and their professional identity, with attention to the ways in which they represented themselves as professionals. All three were dissatisfied with the state of scholarly knowledge about their areas of interest.

U.S. scholarship has neglected not only the work and professional identities of academics and academic managers, collectively, but also the management of the academic profession. This neglect included scholarly knowledge of university faculty both full-time and part-time and academic administrators in their roles and interactions. We decided to remedy some of the deficiencies through attention to the management of the academic profession in U.S. universities. Management of this profession includes the ways in which academics in their role as administrators, such as vice presidents, or provosts, deans, and department chairs, or heads—by policy and regulations—direct the behaviors of faculty. It includes as well direction and influence by administrators and self-regulation of faculty according to institutional norms. These norms are derived from what we refer to as institutional logics.

The doctoral dissertations of Ariadna and Marie and our investigations of faculty and department chairs at public universities, as well as the immense quantity of reading on academics, academic managers, and universities, served as sources for this project. Analysis of interview data from dozens of interviews of faculty and academic administrators conducted from 2010–17 and the production of conference papers and journal articles furthered our understanding and knowledge of the two twin populations. We traveled to Denver, Washington, Budapest, Calgary, Columbus, Ohio, Dublin, Toronto, Houston, and New York to present our work at scholarly conferences. We were aided by Virginia Montero-Hernandez, Evelyn Morales Vázquez, Raquel Rall, and Tiffany Viggiano, who worked with us on one or more of these presentations and papers or with our analysis of our data. In addition, we became fluent in the concept of neoliberalism and presented papers and published work on this topic related to higher education. We worked with Michael Hoggatt, Evelyn, Tiffany, Laurencia Walker, Aida Aliyeva, and Raquel in this area. We also ventured into the area of academics internationally and Siqi Wang was a research assistant for us. As well, with Jianxiu Gu in China we researched faculty evaluation policies in China and the United States, and John interviewed academics in a UK university to determine their altered identity as their institution underwent sectoral change from college to university status. We investigated the social psychological domain of identity and specifically professional identity and the role of emotions, with Evelyn as our guide and our interviewer. Finally, we completed an investigation of university department chairs and their managerial and academic roles—a topic without much adequate supporting literature—and again Evelyn worked with Ariadna as an interviewer. Siqi complemented our work with explorations of entrepreneurial faculty, her dissertation topic. We are grateful to those who contributed to our work and in some part influenced what we have to say in this book. Vicky (Virginia Montero-Hernandez) was the person (then a post-doctoral fellow) who helped John to initiate a project on faculty at three California public institutional types—community college, comprehensive university, and research university. Vicky interviewed faculty, along with the assistance of Sarah Yoshikawa, a doctoral student at University of California, Riverside, and then Vicky, Sarah, and John began initial analysis of data of the approximately fifty interviews. That project was the foundation for this book.

Although the initial interest in this project focused upon public higher education faculty work and the academic professional identity of faculty in research universities, comprehensive universities, and community colleges, the question of who manages these academic professionals and their work and how they are managed became a central concern. In part, this concern was a consequence of the growing body of literature we had consumed on neoliberal policies and practices in higher education. This body of literature suggested or claimed that the autonomy of academic professionals was eroding or indeed had disappeared, a condition that undermined the academic identity of faculty. This condition of erosion or disappearance pointed toward an ideology that favored practices inimical to academic professional values. But, who or what implemented this ideology and practiced its preferred behaviors in higher education organizations? What specific neoliberal and managerial behaviors were enacted? These questions sharpened our focus and guided our examination, which led to our discoveries.

Our Approach and Sources

In this book, we go beyond traditional scholarship on the management of academic professionals, including professional identity of academic professionals and the context that shapes their work, particularly the organizational management of their work. We look at traditional understandings of institutional and organizational management and governance and the place of academic professionals within universities. We offer a wide array of perspectives on organizational management of universities and the condition and identity of academic professionals. We attempt to provide new understandings of academic management, academic professional identity, and the implications of academic management for academic professionals.

We rely upon several theoretical perspectives for our analysis and discussion. Institutional theory (Scott, 2014) points us to the deep structures and values as well as to the patterns of behavior of the university. Relatedly, we turn to institutional logics (Thornton, Ocasio, & Lounsbury, 2012) to specify the presence and dynamics of values and assumptions that shape and direct university behaviors. Furthermore, we rely upon identity theory (Burke & Stets, 2009; Gee, 2000–01) to capture and explain the professional identity of faculty and academic managers. As well, we follow Mintzberg's theory of power (Mintzberg, 1983, 1989) to guide us and enable us to explain the systems of authority and power within the university. Finally, we turn to neoliberalism (Harvey, 2005) and the critique of this ideological system (Olssen & Peters, 2005) to provide us with concepts and categories that describe and explain the context of the university, the practices of universities and their academics, and the values that underlie these practices (Campbell & Pedersen, 2001). These values point toward the quantifiable, economically productive worth of human behaviors and humans themselves.

The public university in the United States is one prominent venue where neoliberalism has become or is becoming institutionalized. The assertion that the public university is a neoliberal institution has come from a number of prominent scholars, either directly (Slaughter & Rhoades, 2000; Ward, 2012) or indirectly (Bok, 2003; Gould, 2004).

We take a blended approach to the understandings of contemporary behaviors of academic professionals and academic managers. That is, we blend understandings and behaviors of the university and their academic managers and faculty with market liberalism or neoliberalism. To accomplish this, we focus upon the narratives—the descriptions and explanations—of the two populations—academic professionals and academic managers. We look for and identify troubling and incongruent narratives as well as narratives that are counter to conventional wisdom and scholarship. Through these narratives, we connect observations, descriptions, and explanations to concepts and theories, an inductive process. We interrogate these narratives, in order to explain them in their variety and in their different contexts. We rely upon interviews to reconstruct and then project academics' narratives of their professional selves.

In the construction of our explanations, we use interviews that we have conducted beginning in 2010 and extending to 2017. We include two extensive series of interviews with faculty at a public research university and a public comprehensive university in California, one set of interviews with academic deans in four public research universities, one set of interviews with part-time faculty in three comprehensive universities, one set of interviews with department chairs at six universities in three Western states at public research and comprehensive universities; and, finally, interviews, in 2016, with faculty at a UK university that had recently attained university status. These data sets are conveyed in a table in the Appendix. We are as well informed by the interviews of full-time non-tenure track faculty conducted by Genevieve Shaker (2008) for her doctoral dissertation, the analysis of these interviews in Levin and Shaker (2011), and the interviews of distinguished tenured faculty conducted by Evelyn Morales Vázquez (2017). Finally, we pay attention to the narratives referred to and discussed in scholarly literature in Australia, Canada, New Zealand, the Netherlands, the UK, and the United States that address the experiences of academic professionals in universities.

We subscribe to the view that knowledge is both undergirded by story (Harari, 2014) and that story conveys the beliefs or understandings of individuals or groups of individuals. These stories, collectively, form the mythos, the belief system, of a social structure (Campbell, 1968). In our case, the stories of faculty and academic administrators, coupled with the stories conveyed or explained by other scholars in their work, point to contemporary understandings and beliefs about the academic profession and the management of the academic profession.

Our chapters include narratives from four categories of academics, including academic managers: part-time faculty, full-time faculty (non-tenure track, pre-tenure, tenure, distinguished faculty), and department heads or chairs and deans. Through these narratives, we connect concepts such as management, administration, and academic professional identity, and the academic profession. We interrogate the meanings of the management of academics. For example, in our explanation of part-time faculty, we note the administrative management of this population by department heads or chairs, as well as the emotional and professional support provided by department chairs to part-timers.

Our Limitations

There are two striking limitations to our discussion: one includes our data sources; the second, the content that is absent. Of course, to borrow from poet Andrew Marvell, "if we had world enough and time," and included more data sources and data and extended the discussion to include other pertinent topics, the book would have been much longer, and likely unacceptable to our publisher. Our data sources are, primarily, from Western U.S. public universities—research and comprehensive universities. Dozens of interviews, several lengthy and some second interviews of participants, comprise our data set, which spans eight years and several Western states, although the large majority come from California. We acknowledge, then, that although we speak broadly about academics and academic managers in the United States and our literature sources cover this population, our interview data cover a minority of states in the U.S.

A second and perhaps more controversial limitation includes the topics omitted in this book. Both internationally and in the United States, differences in the experiences of faculty based on their gender, race, and ethnicity are not only a rising area of interest with respect to research on faculty and administrators but also a major focus in the United States because these are profoundly significant conditions (or variables) in both daily and professional life. We do not disagree with the importance of these identities in the academic profession and in the management of the profession. We did not address this topic, in large part because the interview data did not support such a discussion and in part because of constraints upon us in the writing of this book. Although we have written on this topic elsewhere (Levin, Haberler, Walker, & Jackson-Boothby, 2014; Levin, Walker, Haberler, & Jackson-Boothby, 2013), we acknowledge that there is much more to be done in this area and that the topic deserves attention.

No doubt, there are other limitations to and within this discussion of the management of the academic profession, and dutiful scholars can rely upon these to further understandings of the topic. As none of the authors are experts in such disciplines as sociology, psychology, or anthropology, or certainly philosophy—disciplines from which we borrow established knowledge—those well-versed in theory from these areas can build upon and indeed refute our observations and conclusions. We trust that we are setting a direction for the further examination of both the profession and its management.

The Management of the Academic Profession

For all academics, we note that academic life, whether in the form of teaching or research, concerns learning and stimulating others to learn. We note as well the idealization in narratives about the academic profession, which is combined with omission or forgetting by narrators. But forgetting also pertains to the researcher, the interviewer who is caught up in the narrative and omits to ask questions, as well as the researcher who during analysis makes connections that are not there or fills in blanks in narratives in order to establish a coherent story. In such cases, we rely upon the scholarly literature and theory to reframe and enhance the content of the interviews. Department chairs, for example, discuss at length the duties and tasks they undertake, but in the main, they neglect to discuss faculty interactions within their departments and their role in those interactions. Tenure track faculty, in the main, neglect to discuss their department chairs or their deans in their enactment of their professional identity, as if faculty function in a vacuum. They do discuss pressures for performance but, generally, they do not locate specific sources of these pressures (e.g., department colleagues, or chairs, or deans), and there is only minimal or vague reference to administrative pressures.

For academic managers, narratives indicate both divided identities—between academic and administrator—and, in most cases, rejection or dismissal of the managerial identity. We include here both deans and department chairs or heads. Narratives of deans associate these deans with, on the one hand, their academic backgrounds as researchers and, on the other hand, with their unit (school, college) as the senior or lead academic. Narratives of department chairs connect chairs to other faculty, particularly the community of faculty within a department, and note that chairs are not necessarily career administrators but good citizens who are doing their duty for their community. In both populations—deans and department chairs—the label *manager* is most often not used and when referred to is dismissed as not applicable. The literature indicates that there is a gap between what academic managers profess as their actions and how they are viewed and judged as acting by their subordinates. Narratives indicate that both ideal or traditional concepts of academic managers, and projected preferred identities of managers, shape descriptions and explanations of managers' behaviors. Deans indicate that they are scholars or researchers first; department chairs elaborate on their role as mentors, sometimes illuminating the work of their faculty colleagues by reference to these colleagues' research or teaching. Rarely does either population assert that they are decision makers, or strategizers, or managers of personnel—actions that are central to managerial work in the university.

Thus, for both groups, academic professionals and academic managers, management is, if not an alien concept and term in daily professional life, then, a fuzzy notion that does not apply to them. Academics deny or omit the presence of management in their professional work, as well as their actions as managers in the form of managing academics, with perhaps the exception of organizing and supervising the work of part-time faculty. This incoherence and lack of acknowledged connection between the state of higher education (now permeated by market behaviors and managerial logics) and academic professionals and academic managers' conceptualization of academic life serve as the starting point of this book.

The Book's Chapters

There are five chapters in this book, and four cover the major populations of the academic profession: tenure track faculty, non-tenure track faculty, department chairs, and deans. While these chapters can be treated in isolation as separate examinations, they do speak to each other as the populations and topics intersect.

In the Introduction: The Management of the Academic Profession, we offer a first approximation of our main argument: New managerialism and neoliberalism have been adopted by universities, and U.S. higher education has a blended academic/neoliberal logic that contextualizes academic work. Scholarly literature, national reports, and theory are the primary sources for this chapter. This chapter presents the theoretical foundation of the book.

In chapter 1: Full-time Tenure Track Faculty: Academic Professional Identity and Managerialism, we focus on the traditional professoriate. In this chapter, we argue that neoliberalism and managerialism have negative effects on tenure track faculty's academic professional identity. For this chapter, we explain academic professional identity as a theoretical framework for our discussion. As well, we explore the role that faculty play in the negotiation of academic and nonacademic values in their work and workplace.

Chapter 2: Non-tenure Track Faculty: Professionals with Commitment and Self-Worth in an Exploitative Environment focuses on both part-time and full-time non-tenure track faculty. The argument of this chapter is that the negative working conditions of this faculty group push them to become ideal neoliberal workers, and that although non-tenure track faculty may attach themselves to academic values, they are conceptualized institutionally and expected to behave as labor rather than as professionals.

Chapter 3: Department Chairs: Dual Roles; Dual Identities focuses on this population of academic administrators, the consequences of managerialism for them, and their role in the adoption of managerial logic. We argue that department chairs are both managed (by their deans and central administrators) and are full-blown managers (of tenure and non-tenure track faculty) in denial of their role in the reinforcement of managerialism, academic capitalism, and neoliberal ideology.

In chapter 4: Academic Deans: Double Agents of Two Institutional Logics and Two Institutional Domains, we focus on the highest level of academic administrators. In this chapter, we advance the argument that academic deans enact neoliberal and managerial behaviors in response to an audit and performance-driven culture in higher education institutions but that, simultaneously, deans act as a line of defense against the full infiltration and takeover of neoliberal and managerial values in U.S. universities.

Chapter 5: Higher Education Management in the U.S. University explores the implications of the arguments developed in the previous chapters and offers conclusions for the book. In this chapter, we point out that managerialism and neoliberalism have entered U.S. higher education; however, neoliberal logic and the accompanying managerial mechanics manifest differently than they do in other developed countries.

Our Concerns

Our concerns and thus our rationale for the writing of this book, *University Management, the Academic Profession, and Neoliberalism*, rest with the values we hold for the university and the knowledge both developed and disseminated in the university, as well as with the academic actors within the university. We are concerned that a condition of colonization by a neoliberal state of the university and academic actors has taken shape and threatens the autonomy of academics. We are concerned that these actors have internalized the rhetoric and values of a neoliberal regime (or state), a rhetoric that appropriates the terms or tropes of academe (e.g., shared governance, the value of research to the nation, state, and internationally, and the public mission of the university) and rationalizes economic and competitive behaviors as both necessities for and compatible with the academy. The neoliberal state appropriates the language of liberalism—tolerance, diversity, individual freedom, and progress (through measurable productivity)—as a strategy to seduce, recruit, and ultimately capture subjects, colonize or control them so that these subjects reproduce neoliberal values in their organizations. With this comes anxiety and guilt for those who cannot keep up or conform, given that the personal rewards (money, job security, promotion, and acceptance) and the punishments (isolation, shaming, and denials) are considerable.

The political economic environment for higher education organizations in the United States is referred to variously as market liberalism, neoliberalism, or hypercapitalism, among several terms, all of which suggest economic and private interests' influences upon institutions. We use *neoliberalism*, in large part because this term is in accord with the scholars we follow.

In higher education, the influences of neoliberalism are evident in administrative practices in the academic areas of organizations as well as in the behaviors of faculty. Academic administrators rely upon particular behaviors and actions aligned with characteristics of neoliberalism in order to fulfill not only their roles but also their organization's mission and aspirations, or projected organizational identity. Faculty respond and react to these administrative behaviors and actions in concert with their academic values and professional norms and aspirations. Administrators' behaviors and actions are shaped both by governmental and organizational policies and by organizational cultures, including the demands of students and faculty. In some cases, administrative behaviors are congruent with neoliberal values and antagonistic toward academic values; in other cases, administrative behaviors are resistant to neoliberal initiatives and values; and, yet, in other cases, administrative behaviors combine neoliberalism and academic values, or at least reflect neoliberalism but support academic values. This is the essential view that arises from our discussion; it is our judgment.

Therefore, we attempt here to present our analysis that is on the one hand critical of neoliberalism in the university but on the other hand explanatory of the ways in which academic values can and do coexist with neoliberal-oriented behaviors. Rather than a call to expel neoliberalism from the university, we recognize that neoliberalism has entered the university and is not vanquished easily or without serious consequences, such as loss of revenues for universities and loss of legislators' (and thus the public's) support for the public university. Scholars who have given up on the university (Giroux, 2014; Readings, 1997; Ward, 2012) have been unable to reconcile neoliberalism with the university or conceptualize the university as in the marketplace. We are sympathetic to this approach but are not ready to abandon this public institution. Although we are critical, we strive for a golden mean.

Personal Acknowledgments

We recognize others who have supported us along the way on our path to the completion of this book.

ARIADNA

Writing is a collective task, one in which multiple individuals participate even without knowing about it. Indeed, this book would not have been possible without the interesting discussions, conversations, and collaboration with other graduate students and scholars. Dr. Omar García Ponce de León was the first scholar who invited me to discuss and analyze critically the academic profession. My participation in a research project he led fed my interest in this topic, and our discussions were in the back of my mind when writing this book. Dr. Virginia Montero-Hernández has always been willing to discuss and analyze current and past research on the academic profession, as well as her own experience as a Mexican and American scholar. Her insights have been a useful guide to my understanding of U.S. scholarship and practice.

The conversations I had with my classmates, Evelyn Morales Vázquez and Siqi Wang, doctoral students at University of California, Riverside, enabled me to further explore the personal consequences of neoliberalism and the entrepreneurial activities of faculty. My co-authors enabled me to continue thinking analytically and critically about the academic profession, higher education, and the state of the university. I thank you all who pushed my thinking and writing.

Writing is an enjoyable task that nevertheless may take a toll on the writer, if the act is not balanced. There are people whose support and companionship make this work possible and more enjoyable. I thank my parents, Professors Manuel López Rosas and Ma. Judith Damián Arcos, whose constant inquiries helped me put complex thoughts in words and go back and forth between the world of words and the world of thoughts. Thank you Mom and Dad. My husband Luis F. Hernández Ventura always supported me to do what I love and also helped me to keep a foot in the "real world." His unconditional love and his constant reminders that food, sleep, and movies are basic needs of life kept my brain and my heart working. Thank you, Luis.

MARIE

I would like to thank my co-authors who challenged me to think about the data in new ways and who made the process of writing this book less daunting and more enjoyable. I want to express my gratitude to the five deans (John Levin, Douglas Mitchell, Sharon Duffy, Sarah Sharp-Aten, and Kevin Vaughn) I have worked with over the last eight years in my professional roles at the University of California, Riverside, who not only supported me in my academic pursuits but also served as daily examples and counterexamples of the academic and managerial values, logics, and behaviors of deans. Although my observations of your management were never formal, they were nevertheless informative and useful in the development of my dissertation on deans, which is the basis for one of the chapters in this book. I must also acknowledge my parents, Diane Parisi and Michael Robinson, for their encouragement and for instilling in me at a young age a desire to ask big questions and think critically. I want to thank my sister, Gina Robinson, for keeping me grounded and providing comic relief when I needed it most. Finally, I want to thank my husband and the love of my life, Adam Martin, both an entrepreneur and a community college professor, who provided endless support, allowed me to bounce ideas off him, and who encouraged me to continue to write and chase excellence in all that I do in life.

JOHN

I want to express my debt to various academic scholars, who, perhaps unwittingly, influenced my thinking, guided my scholarly and research directions, and served as models for me in the ways that I thought about the profession. Sheila Slaughter, Larry Leslie, Gary Rhoades, and Doug Woodard were my first U.S. mentors and guides. Terri Seddon and Simon Marginson were my Australian role models for deep thought and for international understandings. Brian Pusser was my sounding board for years during periods when I needed a U.S. academic in the area of higher education who could use theory and push the boundaries of mainstream thinking in the United States. Manuel F. Aguilar Tamayo and Omar García Ponce de León, from Universidad Autónoma del Estado de Morelos, in Mexico, two of the finest men I have known, gave me through our mutual student, Virginia Montero Hernandez, opportunities to observe Mexican university academics. Manuel and Omar both shared their professional experiences with me in detail and helped me to gain some understanding of the academic profession in Mexico. Pete Boyd in the UK gave me an unadorned picture of UK universities and the professoriate as he guided me up a Lake District peak, and Paul Cammack and his family gave me a delicious glimpse of a UK academic's home life. Jianxiu Gu and Yingzi Luo from Nanjing Agricultural University have given me a window through which to understand the academic profession in China, and Jianxiu has offered me insights into aspects of management of the profession in China.

As for practice, Jeff Milem has over the years shared his views with me about the management of full-time tenure track faculty at two universities in two states—Arizona and California. Kathryn Moore at North Carolina State University during the early part of the 2000s welcomed me into some of the inner workings of a university dean's role and behaviors. Dallas Rabenstein, provost at the University of California, Riverside, along with other UC Riverside deans, shared experiences, views, and incidents with me during my period as dean at the university. Steven Bossert confided in me on numerous occasions while he was dean and revealed behaviors of deans and faculty in day-to-day workings of an academic unit. But my initial experiences with university academic managers goes back several years to my doctoral work at the University of British Columbia, when I worked as a graduate research assistant for the provost and V.P. Academic, Daniel Birch. At that time, I was a community college administrator on educational leave, and I served Dan as the staff of a university–community college committee. In that capacity, I gained insight into the political acumen required of an academic administrator in their dealings with a senior group of university faculty: In Dan's case, he had to convince this group to follow his lead in negotiations with community college leaders. One of Dan's main attributes was his ability to give credit to others and to enable these senior faculty to provide direction for outcomes that Dan thought were in the best interests of both the university and the community colleges. He managed by both acknowledging the autonomy of academic professionals and by stepping back so that they could step forward.

I would be remiss if I did not acknowledge the several graduate students at UC Riverside with whom I have worked during the buildup to and during the project itself. I noted them above as contributors to this book in one way or another. I am grateful for their exuberance and willingness to participate with me and even to push related projects farther than I expected.

Lee Levin has talked through aspects of this project and this book with me over several years. She brings to bear a critical perspective and a demand for explanation and evidence. As well, she dragged me away from my computer in order to save my mental and physical health, often with, "Are you coming home from work?" or "It's cocktail time." She ensured that at least one day a week, Saturday or Sunday, I took a break. This was important because it gave my poor brain a rest and a chance to think a little differently when I resumed my work. For decades, Lee has traveled with me from university to university, and enabled me to carry out my research, teach, and serve my profession. She has never encouraged me to stop, give up my research, or even to retire from the profession. Like a good manager, she has left that up to me.

Finally, I am grateful to my co-authors, Ariadna and Marie, who were my former PhD students at the University of California, Riverside, beginning in 2012. They are hardworking, smart, and humanitarian, with an ecological-environmental value system. This book was a collective effort and product, and through the writing process I learned a great deal from both of them. That is magic when the former students can teach the teacher.

Introduction

The Management of the Academic Profession

Over the course of the past several decades, universities and colleges in the United States have adopted neoliberal practices that are manifest in the management of the academic profession, in the actions of both academic managers and faculty. Yet, simultaneously with these neoliberal practices, the academic traditions and practices of universities and colleges continue and the values that underpin these traditions and practices are robust. The context of academic management—the contemporary U.S. public university and its qualities and characteristics—forms the organizational social structure for roles, behaviors, and identities of the actors: the faculty, or academics, and academic administrators. We argue that university values, and what we refer to as academic logic, are to a large extent antithetical to neoliberalism and managerialism; that is, the influence of managers whereby organizational management is the primary system of authority within a university is incompatible with the traditions of faculty autonomy and faculty governance. Yet, in this apparently incompatible condition, academics—both faculty and managers—are able to function in, and rationalize, their roles and maintain an academic professional identity. This professional identity of academics and academic managers is both verified and countermanded by the context of the university and the practices of academic management. As a result, academics construct understandings of themselves as both resistors of and contributors to neoliberalism, as well as victims and promoters, including what is termed managerialism (Gumport, 2000). That is, academics both participate in and counteract neoliberal and managerial practices. To advance our argument, we offer a critical review of the scholarly literature with attention to neoliberalism in the university and academic logic.

1

We draw in large part on the scholarship of non-U.S. countries (e.g., Australia, Canada, New Zealand, the Netherlands, and the UK), and include U.S. scholarship that can help us make our explanations both lucid and valid. Our specific focus is the U.S. university, but international scholarship and examples help us clarify our arguments. For example, we note that while U.S. scholarship speaks to alterations in the academic profession, which are sometimes the consequence of revenue-generating behaviors, sometimes the consequence of the rise of a managerial class in the university, and sometimes the result of prestige-seeking behaviors, unlike in the UK, U.S. scholarship is not focused upon the "isms" of social behaviors (e.g., neoliberalism, managerialism) or the effects of managerial practices upon individual academics. U.S. scholarship concerns itself with outcomes relevant to the academic profession (e.g., diminution of a faculty role in governance, percentages and consequences of a part-time workforce), and addresses general faculty (community college, four-year college, university) as a whole (e.g., workload pressures). Rarely does this U.S. body of scholarship examine underlying conditions or ideologies, such as new managerialism (Deem & Brehony, 2005). Here, we try to correct this omission. We conclude this Introduction with an elucidation of our position on this dynamic: The U.S. university is neither an idealized community of scholars organized as an academic bureaucracy nor solely a neoliberal, corporate, or enterprise institution. Universities are sites where multiple logics (neoliberal logic and academic logic) coexist, alter each other, and blend with one another. In this context, members of the academic profession (faculty and academic managers) have adopted managerial behaviors, and academic management in the U.S. university combines both traditional values of the university, such as academic freedom, peer review and evaluation, and the pursuit of knowledge, and values of the economic marketplace, such as efficiency, resource and financial acquisition, and personal or private benefits. In subsequent chapters, we develop this argument and focus upon tenure track faculty, non-tenure track faculty, department chairs, and deans.

Academics and Authority in the University

Few recent scholarly pieces address the source or locus of university management, and those that do address university management depict it as ambiguous and contradictory. David Labaree (2017) relies upon Weber's three categories of organizational authority: traditional, rational, and charismatic.

He sidesteps or excludes Slaughter and Rhoades' (2004) academic capitalist knowledge regime, Marginson and Considine's (2000) liberal market authority, and Ward's (2012) neoliberalism. Labaree argues that all three of Weber's types are present in the contemporary U.S. university. Traditional authority is associated with what we refer to as academic institutional logic, although Labaree stresses the guild-like characteristics of university academics. There is, however, no specific inclusion of department chairs, associate deans, deans, and provosts into this guild, nor is there a differentiation between tenure track and non-tenure track faculty. This guild-like structure, for Labaree, provides faculty with considerable authority in the university. The lack of categorization of faculty (e.g., academic professional and managerial professionals and tenure track and non-tenure track) obfuscates the claim of traditional authority in the hands of faculty.

The rational system of authority, while not specific or clarified in Labaree's discussion, is likely a rational bureaucracy or a bureaucratic organization configuration consistent with Mintzberg's (1983,1989) organizational power configuration. Yet, this rational bureaucracy is not the same as Mintzberg's professional bureaucracy (1991). Labaree equates this system with hierarchical positional authority, absent ideology or values or subjectivity but rather focused upon efficiency. This system is what associates the university with a bureaucratic organization such as a government department or a corporation (minus the focus upon profit).

Charismatic authority for Labaree rests with faculty, particularly prestigious faculty: renowned scholars, revenue generators, and endowed chairs. Although this categorization of authority in the university has appeal, it is not supported in the scholarly literature. Indeed, for scholars such as Finkelstein, Martin Conley, and Schuster (2016), the profile and position of faculty in the university have deteriorated since the 1980s, and their role in governance and decision making, whether as a group or as individuals, is limited. Certainly, their authority as individuals is negligible or nonexistent. A case could be made that individual faculty have authority over curriculum and instruction but that is debatable given university policies that prescribe rules and regulations. For major university functions (e.g., budget and finance, community relations, facilities), individual faculty have, at best, advisory roles (e.g., through a senate). Indeed, for Birnbaum (1989), faculty authority is symbolic, neither legal nor enacted in practice.

Unlike Readings (1997) who despairs over the state of the U.S. university and Ward (2012) and others who castigate the institution for its acceptance of liberal market values, Labaree praises the U.S. university's embrace of the market, its ambiguous, and sometimes contradictory, purposes and goals, and its multiple authority systems. Similar to Readings and Ward, and others, Labaree wants a summative statement or concept to serve as a truth for the U.S. university. For Labaree, it is a "fine mess," a work of achievement and accomplishment even though it suggests March and Cohen's (1974) "organized anarchy."

Our view differs from these and other scholars in that definitive statements about the university and particularly about the academic profession might provide a conceptualization of the characteristics of an entity but do not explain how or the way in which the entity behaves and acts. Our view is that behaviors and actions are consequences of management within an organization, and we align our views with Mintzberg's on power (Mintzberg, 1983). Both internal and external systems of influence shape the exercise of power, carried out in the university largely by administrators, faculty, staff, and, indeed, students. The management of the academic profession is enacted by academic professionals or faculty and academic managers. The academic logic, or systems of ideology and expertise (Mintzberg, 1983), that influences the behaviors of faculty also affects the behaviors of managers, although faculty and academic managers are dependent upon and follow in their actions systems of authority. When these systems break down or prove to be inadequate, then a system of politics may take over (Mintzberg, 1983).

Traditionally for universities, particularly in the latter half of the twentieth century, a dominant view, belief, or assumption held among faculty and administrators, and this view persists to the present in the form as an expectation or norm, is that management is collegial, with the underlying view that academics are responsible professionals and that academic managers rely upon faculty for academic decisions (Haviland, Alleman, & Allen, 2017). Faculty, it is assumed, do not have to be accountable, at least to administrators, for their professional activities and their duties of teaching, research, and service. Management in the non-collegial sense plays a more important role for activities that are not in the center of the academic profession, such as budgets, human resources, facilities, and marketing and publicity. In those cases, nonacademic managers have responsibilities and authority to act. In the academic domain, it is department chairs and deans, as academic managers among a larger group of administrators, who are expected to manage academic matters and ensure that others are doing their part. In service that is more aligned with the academic function of the university, committee chairs, who are likely faculty, are expected to manage the business of the committee, and assumed, because they are faculty, to perform in a collegial manner. If management then can be collegial, the term *collegial management* (Tight, 2014) carries with it the assumed identity of professionals, and includes both faculty and academic managers. When administrators do not perform to the expectations of faculty and fail to consult with or depend upon faculty for decisions, then they are charged with lacking in collegiality. This notion goes back in the literature to John Corson (1960) and Paul Goodman (1962), is reiterated much later by Robert Birnbaum (1988), and reinforced into the twenty-first century (Finkelstein et al., 2016; Schuster & Finkelstein, 2006). The legacy of collegiality, shared governance, the community of scholars, and even collegial management (often equated with academic values, or what we term academic logic) persists.

In some contrast to this persistent view, the pervasive encroachment of neoliberalism and its ethos have resulted in the remaking of C. P. Snow's (1961) *Two Cultures*, from a Traditional culture, or culture of Humanities, and a Scientific culture to two new worlds in the contemporary university. One is a culture of nostalgia (Ylijoki, 2005), aligned with an academic logic and a practice of collegiality, and associated with a professional bureaucracy (Mintzberg, 1991); the other is a culture of competition (Ball, 2012; Ward, 2012), aligned with neoliberal logic, including values of efficiency, surveillance, and productivity. The presence of neoliberal logic in the university is viewed as detrimental to academic logic by numerous scholars, both in the United States and internationally (Archer, 2008; Ball, 2012a, 2012b; Clegg, 2008; Davies, 2005; Giroux, 2014; Gonzalez, Martinez, & Ordu, 2013; Gould, 2003; Ozga, 1998; Ward, 2012). Martin Finkelstein, Ming Ju, and William Cummings (2011) report that during the period of 1992–2007, faculty influence at research universities diminished in areas of governance and management of their institutions. This diminution, they conclude, corresponds to the rise of middle managers (this includes deans and department chairs) in governance, especially in budget decision areas. Moreover, they add, this research university phenomenon is evident, although to a lesser extent, at all other higher education institutional types.

The claim from one quarter is thus of growing managerialism in U.S. universities and colleges (Levin, 2017). That is, that the influence of managers, including their policies, goals, and objectives for universities and colleges, has become the ascendant system of authority. When these managers' actions are aligned with neoliberal policies, or policies associated with economic market ideology (Collini, 2013), management of universities and colleges takes on a corporate, business-like approach that values economic goals, including efficiency and measurable outcomes of work, which are managed. As a result, what is understood as surveillance in critiques of neoliberalism, or the monitoring of behaviors, becomes institutionalized in universities and colleges. Thus, the university possesses, and in some cases is, an "audit culture" (Levin, 2017; Shore, 2008). This condition as well is claimed to undermine U.S. universities (Ward, 2012). According to the critics of an audit culture in U.S. universities, these institutions have become businesses and corporations (Gould, 2003) driven by a managerial class (Gumport, 2000) or regime (Slaughter & Rhoades, 2004) and have lost their traditional, primary role as disseminators and creators of knowledge (Readings, 1997).

Yet, there is little empirical evidence, from research investigations, aside from the perceptions of U.S. faculty in the Finkelstein et al. (2011) study, to support the claims of growing or advancing managerialism in the U.S. university. Indeed, in the United States, there is little literature compared to the UK (and other nations such as Australia, Canada, and New Zealand) that points to changes in faculty's role in management and governance. In UK literature, a new cadre of academic managers is targeted as the responsible party that has unseated faculty from institutional governance and management (Locke & Bennion, 2011; Whitchurch, 2006). As Locke and Bennion point out, the literature of the 1990s and early 2000s on the UK's academic profession and their place in institutional governance and management has "a thesis of loss, alienation, and retreat" (2011, p. 194). More specifically, "academics have been proletarianized, their work industrialized, their autonomy eroded, and themselves have been de-skilled. The result . . . is that the profession is demoralized and disaffected, and disengaged" (p. 194). Although Finkelstein et al. (2011) concur that U.S. faculty have increased their disaffection and disengagement, U.S. scholarship has yet to go as far as Locke and Bennion (2011) or other European scholars (Lorenz, 2012) to suggest a hollowed-out profession of academics.

Nonetheless, even though managerialism has not become a negative discourse in the United States, the signs are present to indicate that academic professionals face a daunting task if they are to maintain their professional influence upon institutions of higher education. Furthermore, as noted in at least one recent empirically based U.S. publication (Levin & Aliyeva, 2015), the professional identity of academics in the United States is threatened by neoliberal practices and initiatives. Whereas such initiatives in the UK and other democracies, such as Australia, Canada, the Netherlands, and New Zealand, emanate from governments (Lorenz, 2012; Shore, 2008), in the United States there are no similar statist interventions, for example, where a government department would monitor research output of faculty, as in the UK. Instead, in the United States the institutional leaders—presidents, chancellors, provosts, deans, and department heads or chairs—may be the carriers of neoliberal values, which are reproduced in the actions of faculty. Thus, in the United States, these managers, particularly those who manage academics, may hold the key to the perpetuation of an academic logic in their university.

The University as a Problematical Place

The infusion of neoliberal values and practices into the U.S. university (and universities worldwide) has, unquestionably, if not altered the functioning of the academy then provided a number of tensions within individual university organizations. The university, for our purposes, is the setting in which the behaviors and actions of academics and managers play out. The traditional and long-held assumption is that the university is a sovereign place that possesses legitimacy and authority as an institution, and is free to act, within legal and legislated limits, in order to fulfill its mission, goals, and aspirations. Indeed, the notion of academic freedom is tied to this sovereignty. But sovereignty is not an empirical fact; rather, it is manifest through artifacts, texts, and actions, including rituals and individual behaviors (Davies, 2014b). In the university, sovereignty can be seen in the actions of an academic senate, in the interactions between faculty and students in a classroom, and in the written texts or oral articulations of administrators, such as deans and department chairs when they inform their faculty of a decision, a project underway, or a policy. Central to this sovereignty is trust: on the one hand, the participants trust each other that what they say and do is in good faith, carried out or conveyed with integrity, and legitimate; and, on the other hand, that there is trust among the participants for the organization (Tierney, 2008).

> The individual relationship two parties build with one another differs from the relationships individuals have with their organization. At the same time, individuals create relationships with one another in an organization, and individuals develop attitudes towards the organization based on the myriad of personal relationships that occur in that context over time. (Tierney, 2008, p. 29)

Organizational trust enables individuals to trust one another, in part because individuals can be assured that their organization has integrity and legitimacy, can act to fulfill its goals, and can establish and enforce order (Davies, 2014b).

Because neoliberalism, including its multivariate and not always compatible or consistent values (e.g., state intervention and free market), and its projects rely upon institutions to alter the social and political foundations upon which liberal democratic institutions sit (Ball, 2012a, 2012b; Bourdieu, 1998; Shore, 2008; Ward, 2012), organizations are hard pressed to maintain their sovereignty. Critics of neoliberalism claim that sovereignty and trust have been replaced by surveillance (Lorenz, 2012) and an audit culture (Shore, 2008). It is the economic-rational foundation that measures the quantitative outputs of organizations, such as universities, that neoliberalism favors and seeks to institutionalize in organizations. Performance of the organization and its members, measured and tracked by both organizational agents and by the state (including state and federal governments, corporations, financiers, and other powerful groups and individuals), becomes the key and central marker of the organization's worth (Ball, 2012b; Shore, 2008).

In that part of this economic-rational foundation is tied inextricably to performance, or what Ball (2012b) and others have referred to as "performativity," competition has become, not only in the economic marketplace but also in universities, the central behavior that results in the production or actualization of value. In the university, faculty compete for grants as well as quantity in publications; both faculty and their organizations compete with other faculty and organizations for prestige; and, of course, universities compete with others for students as well as for faculty to hire. Thus, as Davies (2014b) notes, competition leads to unequal results: quantitative differences of outcomes are the goal so that what is assumed to be merit or talent or quality will prevail. Survival of the fittest, Hobbes's state of nature, where everyone is against all, and Social Darwinism apply to the competitive organization where measurable outcomes are standard ways to legitimize worth of either the organization or the individuals within it. Trust in this context, therefore, between individuals is simply an act of the establishment of allies, and trust for the organization is contingent upon the organization's ability to support and advance individual ambitions. Within this condition, the audit culture has replaced the academic culture of the university in various nations (Shore, 2008), including the U.S. (Ward, 2012). The view that a corrosive managerialism has and continues to undermine academic culture in the United States is held by a select number of U.S. scholars, from Readings (1997) to Ward (2012), and is embedded in critiques of the neoliberal university (Slaughter & Rhoades, 2000), the corporate university (Gould, 2003), and the striving university (Gonzales et al., 2013).

But, the critique of neoliberalism (Giroux, 2014) not only targets the university, it extends to both academics and academic managers. The principal focus is upon managerialism or new managerialism (Deem & Brehony, 2005; Lorenz, 2012), or a regime and ideology that not only value economic rationality but also conceive of a managerial class as the dominant decision makers and operatives within a university (Gaffikin & Perry, 2009). Neoliberal ideology conjoined with new managerialism has affected universities, including the work of faculty and the dynamics of the organization, in fundamental ways. Generally, in the scholarly literature there are several dual views related to the influences of neoliberalism and managerialism. Those views directed at administrators conceive of this population as controlling of others, agents of a corporation that rewards and punishes (and monitors, surveils, and evaluates) employees, and promotes and reinforces not only an ideology of corporatism but also intolerance for difference in and resistance to dominant organizational thinking (Ward, 2012). The corporation demands compliance. It seeks to maximize outcomes toward two goals: revenues and prestige. Thus, economic rationality is preeminent as it leads to financial gain and competitiveness. Indeed, a fundamental activity in the managerial university is competition: university against university; unit against unit; and, employees against employees (Davies, 2005). Ultimately, this competition becomes individual self against individual self: "Am I improving? Am I doing enough? Where do I need to work harder?" This form of self-management or surveillance of the self is a goal of the neoliberal state (Ball, 2012a). For the individual academic professional, the result is a high level of insecurity as these professionals are unable to meet the expectations of the organization, or their peers' expectations, or their own expectations (Davies, 2005; Gill, 2009; Gonzales et al., 2013; Knights & Clarke, 2014).

In order to cope with insecurity, individual professionals act (1) to meet some expectations, such as work productivity and thus underperform with other expectations, such as family and personal life, or (2) reject expectations and lose rewards, or (3) meet some expectations and reject others, or (4) play act with expectations and take on the appearance of meeting them but reject them in action (Knights & Clarke, 2014; Levin 2018b). Yet, whatever the actions, these cannot satisfy expectations for the self or reduce anxiety because, even in rejection of expectations, the individual lacks security.

In most cases, at least evident in research and scholarship in the UK, the Netherlands, and Australia, academics do comply with managerial expectations

(Alvesson & Spicer, 2016; Lorenz, 2012), and, as a result, academic autonomy erodes. For academics who undertake managerial work as managers, such as associate and assistant deans, department chairs, and project or unit heads—and even deans who claim a role as researchers/academics because they continue to conduct research—they serve as the organizational voice of academics and pressure other academics to conform to official university decisions. These academic managers maintain their academic legitimacy and have formal authority as managers. Overall, managerialism co-opts academic professionalism by reducing professional autonomy and authority (Winter, 2009). For some scholars (Davies, 2005), autonomy, a hallmark of a profession (Brint, 1994; Freidson; 2001), is an illusion.

Along these lines, the research university has developed into a neoliberal, managerial, corporate university while simultaneously maintaining critical characteristics of the traditional university, with an academic logic grounded in academic values. Foremost among these is collegiality (Tight, 2014), a seminal concept applicable to academic professionalism that contains several assumptions: a management structure with elected leaders; peer review of work, including testing of knowledge; and critical dialogue among academics (Sahlin, 2012, in Tight, 2014). But, as managerialism advances, scholars argue, collegiality diminishes. Trust, too, is a component of collegiality for some scholars, and trust includes respect for the expertise of other academic professionals (Tierney, 2006, 2008).

Yet, the twin logics of the university as a corporate entity and the university as a collegial organization sit together uneasily. Managerialism undermines collegiality through its focus upon measurable efficiency and productivity-centered behaviors; it rewards entrepreneurial research that is transferrable and applied but not necessarily for knowledge advancement; and, it emphasizes goals that are labor market–oriented, revenue-generating, or prestige-yielding but not sociocultural (Ozga, 1998; Tight, 2014). For some scholars, neoliberal regimes distort academic work. Davies (2005) argues that academic work is no longer the life of the intellect and imagination, and that neoliberal discourse has colonized academics. Goals of academics are shaped and determined by practices of a neoliberal state, which become institutionalized within universities (Ball, 2012a, 2012b). Neoliberal discourse infiltrates the daily work of faculty, and neoliberal values become accepted by professionals (Davies, 2005). Thus, academics become neoliberal subjects: The self is defined through economic worth (e.g., income, revenue generation); it is both vulnerable and competitive (Scharff, 2015); and, it is detached from meaningful, personal values: That is, emotional inner life is unanchored (Davies, 2005), a view consistent with Richard Sennett's (2006) conception of the state of occupations in new capitalism. Trust is no longer relevant, and surveillance of self and others is the norm. The autonomous self is an illusion in that universities manufacture conditions of turbulence and dynamic states or contexts, which demand responses that are framed as necessary reconceptualizations and reorganizations of both institutions and daily life (Davies, 2005; Kok, Douglas, McClelland, & Bryde, 2010).

The insecurity and fragility of academic identities (Knights & Clark, 2014) are brought about and increased by controls and performance demands in the face of an idealized profession where demands exceed capacity for individuals to meet those demands. To reduce anxieties, academics will conform to managerial demands, but, in conforming, academics face a threat to the meaning of their profession. Thus, academics become colluded selves (Ozga, 1998) as they surrender to the corporation and are victims of their academic professional identity, an identity that drives their aspirations for an esteemed and valued career.

This grim and almost inescapable plight for academic professionals in the contemporary university (Alvesson & Spicer, 2016; Davies, 2005; Knights & Clarke, 2014; Koh et al., 2010; Lethabo King, 2015; Martinez Alemán, 2014; Ozga, 1998; Winter, 2009; Ylijoki, 2005) offers few if any self-critiques or alternatives. Tight (2014) ponders over, but not convincingly, whether collegiality—the essence of the academic profession—is or is not compatible with managerialism. Mountz et al. (2015) offer an alternative through collective action to adopt "slow scholarship" as an act of resistance to a metrically oriented university. As time is one of the major variables of academic capitalist and managerial regimes (Walker, 2009), control over time may provide one avenue of relief for academics. Yet, this slowing down may also lead not to reduction in overall professional work but to the production part of research. Thus, academics through slow scholarship cannot control all of the demands of and expectations for their work. Ylijoki (2005), from an alternate perspective on the preservation of academic professional identity, discovers that nostalgia is pervasive among Finland university faculty and that this nostalgia for a former academic professional identity is a coping mechanism that manifests underlying tensions between the present and the idealized past. Nostalgia, thus, points to core values that continue to exist in the present, such as academic freedom and personal autonomy. While some scholars may view nostalgia as conformity to and acceptance of present conditions, others view nostalgia as resistance both to colonization and to normalization and standardization of changes in the academy (Ylijoki, 2005).

Among the discussions of the presence of managerialism, new managerialism, and neoliberal values and projects in U.S. universities, there is no reference that suggests these are benign or beneficent conditions in the university. Nor is there an implication that new managerialism has any value to the purposes of the university in traditional understandings of the university as a knowledge creator or disseminator. Yet, in spite of the pervasiveness of neoliberal values and practices, the presence and acceptability of academic capitalism, and the control exercised by managerial regimes, academics continue to express devotion to, or idealized love for, their academic work (Alvesson & Spicer, 2016). At the same time, academics express suspicion of academic work and disdain for the control system that guides and assesses their work (Alvesson & Spicer, 2016).

In new managerialism recognized in the UK (Deem, 1998), a goal for organizational leaders and elites is to reduce identity plurality and manage outlier identities; thus, a unitary perception of organizational life—conveyed through organizational narratives—becomes or is in the process of becoming the dominant, taken-for-granted understanding. We see this in a recent UK project that addresses faculty identity alteration within a context of university sectoral change (see Appendix) (Levin, 2018a). One social scientist faculty member at a predominantly teaching university referred to organizational structures.

> I think there's structures that help nurture those feelings (competitive pressures). . . . [W]e're all vulnerable, and we're all susceptible to unpleasant feelings and envy and jealousy and the whole repertoire of human emotions. But, I think when we live under very repressive and oppressive structures, we prioritize things like the flow of capital over wellbeing and health and humanity and being a human being. And then, I think that creates very, very toxic working conditions, particularly in organizations like higher education. (senior lecturer, social sciences, teaching university)

Another faculty member in Education referred to managers who have lost focus upon the educational and research function of the university, and, more importantly, on human feelings.

> The problem is where they [managers] have taken on so much that they . . . have lost sight. No, I mean actually if you take on the neoliberal agenda to such an extent that you actually lose

sight that you're dealing with people as others, individuals, as teachers, but also the students. It is a business but it isn't actually just selling. You're not selling beans off the shelf. . . . There's a whole lot of emotion and other stuff tied to it. The problem is where you get people who go too far. It's about going too far, I think, to the extremes, losing sight of people's emotional reactions. (principal lecturer, education, teaching university)

A Humanities faculty member at a new university in the UK, one that evolved from colleges and specialized institutes, reflected upon her changed environment. This new environment of a university lacked the collegial qualities of her former college, and manifested the characteristics of a university under new public management or new managerialism.

One of the things I didn't like about [my present] institution was its kind of sense of self-importance and one of the things that I did like about [my former institution] was the very collegiate atmosphere that I felt very strongly in place both as an undergraduate and as . . . a teacher. . . . I really felt very strongly that there wasn't a clear sort of hierarchy among academics and that we're all very collaborative and we're all very interested in each other's work in a very positive way. We had a very friendly relationship with our students. (senior lecturer, humanities, teaching university)

These faculty members identify changes in organizational priorities, a decreased interest in the human side of academia, and an increased hierarchy within universities as consequences of managerialism.

Autonomy, central to professionalism (Freidson, 2001), as well, is central to academic identity, and suggests that whether individual autonomy or collective academic autonomy, academics, according to academic logic (Levin, 2017), set their own agendas and are the producers of knowledge (Henkel, 2005). But, the ideal of autonomy is not realized by all. Rather, autonomy requires considerable academic capital, more often possessed by senior, well-established faculty (Henkel, 2005). Even at the more advanced academic levels, faculty autonomy is constrained by managerial interests of control. A senior lecturer at a teaching-oriented university in the UK notes that his work is determined by quantitative measures: the number of hours and days he has for research and scholarship.

> We are given one hundred eighty-five hours a year, and that's an odd number—it equates to twenty-five working days, that's the nearest way it can be worked out—for scholarly and research activities. It's our time. And I designate twelve days of that for my editorship of the journal. . . . So, that's enough, but that's just about sufficient. We don't actually take twelve days. . . . So, those twenty-five days are for those sorts of activities. That's where we do our research; that's where we do our writing; it's where we go to conferences out of those days, and so on and so forth. Then, for the rest of the academic year, our academic year works on sixteen hundred and eleven hours. (senior lecturer, UK, teaching university)

For those 1,611 hours, this senior lecturer is not autonomous and is scheduled by his superiors (who are themselves academic professionals) to teach and evaluate, confer with students, work on curriculum, and carry out school-site visits. His colleague, a professor, has more latitude than the senior lecturer.*

> I'm supposed to have a third of my work just for my own personal research, but I mean I'm just under pressure just like everyone else. I wouldn't say this year I've had a third of my time on my own work. My own work gets blurred you see, because those projects are bringing in income so, really, they are normal work. . . . I think I'm squashed for research time, not as much as other colleagues obviously. . . . I'm in a privileged position where I'm a research coordinator and that means I'm working for the research office in graduate school and I can shape policy. . . . I have a lot of freedom and I can shape policy and my own work very strongly. And so, I'm really lucky compared to many of my colleagues who are not in that situation. (professor, professional learning, UK, teaching university)

There is thus variability in autonomy for academics. Yet, within a larger context of a managerial or audit culture (Deem, 1998; Shore, 2008),

---

*In the UK, in general, faculty rank in the teaching and research career is organized as follows: from higher to lower rank, professor, reader, senior lecturer, principal lecturer, lecturer or clinical lecturer, and assistant lecturer.

academic professionals are controlled by neoliberal regimes, either at the institutional level (Lorenz, 2012) or state level (Ball, 2012). The UK professor, with his privileged position, nonetheless, is vulnerable in the same way as his less privileged colleagues. He is subject to the same evaluation system as his colleagues; his work is monitored; and, he has expectations from his university to produce. His university, similar to others in the UK, directed by a neoliberal state (Ball, 2012a), is both an object of neoliberal policies and a perpetuator of neoliberalism. His autonomy is in actuality pared down to his actions of resistance. "Neoliberalism is fully central to all UK education from K-12 to unis. There is no way to ignore it; the only option is to work within the system and reform it; resist where possible; and, speak out when necessary" (professor, UK, teaching university). Consequently, academic professional identity for the professor is fluid and autonomy is constrained. "Identity is understood . . . as part of the lived complexity of a person's project and their way of being in those sites which are constituted as being part of the academy" (Clegg, 2008, p. 329). Academic professional identity even undergoing change processes is expected to be both authentic and legitimate (Archer, 2008). Yet, authenticity is undermined in a new managerial environment as is legitimacy (Archer, 2008).

The former unidimensional organizational conditions of the university of the 1960s to 1980s (conditions present in the United States and internationally) were assumed as what was fundamental or central, unique, or distinctive, and persistent or enduring about the organization (Humphreys & Brown, 2002). Stories or narratives that suggest congruency or isomorphism and contain those defining values and norms of the organization led to or supported legitimacy. This legitimacy contributed to or reinforced the self-esteem of members who in turn regarded their organization in a positive light (Humphreys & Brown, 2002). This academic logic, based upon elite sponsored identity narratives, however, was not congruent with individuals' self-authored narratives, beginning in the era of Reagan and Thatcher (Shore, 2008), originating in the late 1970s. Thus, there were conflicting discourses of organizational identity, followed by negotiations to determine which discourse, or logic, dominated and whether or not the other discourses were accepted or adopted, or isolated, and whether or not they were attacked or shunned (Scharff, 2015). Indeed, the academic professional identity was in flux. We argue that this flux continues in the United States in the present as faculty members negotiate their identity every day in a multilogic institutional environment (we extend this topic and our theoretical standpoint regarding academic professional identity in chapter 1).

The neoliberal university, the corporate university, and the enterprise university were among the appellations for research universities internationally (Marginson & Considine, 2000; Slaughter & Rhoades, 2000) that conveyed the new logic of neoliberalism that not only entered but also commandeered the university. The questions that surround this new logic is whether or not it replaced or was amalgamated with the existing academic logic of the university.

Institutional Logics

The link between the academic professional and the institution of higher education, specifically the university, is symbiotic and indissoluble. The university, as an institution, sustains the academic profession and the academic profession sustains the university. Academic professional identity is formed within the university and structured by the institution. In addition, faculty are both actors and reflectors and producers and reproducers of the university's institutional logics. Thus, there is an interplay between the institution's logics and the individual's academic professional identity.

Organizational actors adhere to institutional values based upon a dominant institutional logic or logics (Thornton, Ocasio, & Lounsbury, 2012). These logics are entrenched within an organization and give meaning to organizational life. Institutional logics underlie and sustain the purposes of the organization, and they shape organizational identity in the ways in which the actors embrace and enact these logics. Through these behaviors, stability in an organization is reinforced (Scott, 2014). These logics define the meanings attributed to organizational context and actions (Hinings, 2012). Institutional logics are "rule-like structures that constrain organizations or a set of cultural toolkits that provide opportunities for change in the existing structure and practices" (Thornton et al., 2012, p. 81); however, institutional logics are structures that can be altered.

New logics can enter the institution and give rise to a condition where multiple logics coexist, even collaborate, or compete.

> The rise of new logics, or the existence of multiple logics, can create ambiguity and the concomitant need for sensemaking about the implications of logic change. Subsequently, action is taken to somehow cope with or resolve tensions or ambiguities linked to plural institutional logics. (Thornton et al., 2012, p. 142)

Institutional theorists claim that the presence of multiple logics in organizations is widespread (Besharov & Smith, 2014). Furthermore, these multiple logics coexist in various arrangements, including separation or amalgamation, or blending. "*When competing logics co-exist in an organizational field actors guided by different logics may maintain strong separate identities and engage in collaborations that result in mutually desirable outcomes and thus sustain the co-existing logics*" (Reay & Hinings, 2009, p. 646; italics in original). Furthermore, the mixing of logics, through amalgamation or blending, can lead to hybrid institutions (Thornton, Jones, & Kury, 2005), as a result of individual actors' and organizations' adoption of the logics of multiple sectors. For coexistence of two or more dominant logics within an institution, theorists note the necessity for compatibility of these dominant logics and that two logics together have low or non-centrality to the organization's core features; that is, taken together they are not central to the organization's functioning (Besharov & Smith, 2014). However, in cases where competing logics cannot coexist, one dominant logic replaces another.

For the contemporary university, logic compatibility or competition pertains to neoliberal logic and academic logic, what is understood as the foundational logic of the university. The entry of a market or neoliberal logic into the university, particularly through its vehicle of implementation, new managerialism (Deem, 1998), has challenged and indeed threatened the institutional logic of a university.

Academic Logic

Accounts of the effects of new managerialism, particularly in countries such as Australia, the UK, and Canada, and to some extent implied in those of the United States, rarely acknowledge the power of the traditions, historical values and practices, and taken-for-granted assumptions within the university. These we refer to as academic logic, the dominant value and meaning system, and its associated practices in universities. That is, universities contain a dominant logic, an academic logic, that through a common meaning system unites actors (Hinings, 2012).

There are numerous and distinctive characteristics of traditional universities, both ideals and norms. The ideals include the concept of collegiality: the "idea that university decisions can be made collectively by the academics affected, with the assistance and support of the administration" (Tight, 2014, p. 294). Clegg (2008) and other scholars add the exercise of professional autonomy to the ideal of universities. Distinctive characteristics of universities generally include judgments based upon merit, academic freedom, professional and institutional autonomy, and bicameral governance (Levin, 2017). These are at the core of academic logic.

University values are an explicit topic in U.S. literature on higher education institutions, although there is no definite agreement on the main values or the number of values. The term *values* is used instead of institutional logic, although logic is more comprehensive and encapsulates values. Finkelstein et al. (2016) identified three "traditional core values central to faculty identity: academic freedom, autonomy, and shared governance" (p. 292). They broaden values to include those that pertained to academic work and careers, gleaned from Gappa, Austin, and Trice (2007): academic freedom and professional autonomy; collegiality and consensus; merit; opportunities for professional growth; and, flexibility in work arrangements. These values are components of academic logic but not the whole. Collegiality continues as an acknowledged or at least articulated core value in U.S. universities: the central value that characterizes the social and intellectual culture and provides for professional organizational cohesion (Haviland et al., 2017). This value reflects one of the main mechanisms in the operation of the professional bureaucracy (Mintzberg, 1991).

In the professional bureaucracy, or what Mintzberg also refers to as a meritocratic power configuration in organizations, management is symbolic (Mintzberg, 1983) and authority is meritocratic; that is, there is an internal coalition of experts, and power is centered internally and diffused among the experts on the basis of skills and knowledge (Mintzberg, 1983). Administrative power is limited; managers have "weak authority" (Mintzberg, 1983, p. 399) and serve at the discretion of the experts as liaisons between the internal professionals and external influencers—such as donors (Mintzberg, 1983). In the professional bureaucracy, any managerial attempts to intrude on the experts' domain or manage their work are rejected. It is in the conditions of the professional bureaucracy that the values and academic logic of the university (autonomy, collegiality, academic freedom, and the like) thrive.

Academic logic forms and guides the ways these institutions function, administer, govern, and organize themselves: from their organization in units (e.g., departments, centers, schools, colleges, faculties), to the subjects of their curricula, to their emphasis upon research and the topics of their research, and to their policies and practices for admission of students. The university's assumptions of its intellectual purpose and of its dissemination of knowledge, both to students and the public, are taken for granted, but comprise its institutional logic.

Neoliberal Logic and Academic Logic

The logic of neoliberalism and academic logic are not compatible, certainly not in the view of most scholars. In neoliberalism, market principles are reinforced by the state: the state defines and regulates "social life through principles that come from the market" (Gane, 2012, p. 613). The neoliberal logic of competition, commodification, and performativity (Ball, 2012b) has entered the university in order to modify academic logic. At the most extreme limit, neoliberal logic threatens to replace academic logic, and this is the basis of the claim of scholars who articulate a world lost, even for those who did not label the cause neoliberal ideology (Readings, 1997; Wilshire, 1990). At a more modest level, neoliberal logic has entered the university through integration or segregation—that is, either neoliberal logic has integrated with academic logic or neoliberal logic occupies the university, segregated from academic logic. New managerialism, documented in the UK and in European countries (Deem & Brehony, 2005), is one manifestation of neoliberal logic; academic capitalism (Slaughter & Rhoades, 2004), noted in the United States, is another.

Academic actors (faculty and academic administrators such as department chairs and deans) who live out these logics and their conflicts in U.S. universities recognize alterations in university expectations and in their practices. Indeed, faculty act in accord with neoliberal principles (Levin & Aliyeva, 2015) in efforts to acquire research grants that provide financial support to their university, in self-monitoring their own performance in areas of productivity, and in taking on more work, including more students in classes (Finkelstein et al., 2016). Department chairs at both research and comprehensive universities articulate the demands placed upon them for efficiency, revenue generation, and productivity for their department members (Levin, López Damián, Martin, & Morales Vázquez, 2017). Deans at research universities acknowledge the imperatives for them to produce outcomes consistent with their universities' goals, such as national and international prominence, research grant acquisition, and private financial donations (Martin, 2018). Yet, simultaneously, academics extol the merits of their academic professional identity: for faculty, their autonomy and academic freedom; for department chairs, protection of the academic values of their departments; and, for research university deans, the importance of maintaining their own research, in the face of demands for increased managerial work.

The Managerial University

In contrast to the notion of the professional bureaucracy is the managerial university, a manifestation of neoliberal logic. Features of the managerial university include the elimination of (or efforts to eliminate) professional bureaucratic processes and procedures and the pursuit of teamwork, flexibility, efficiency, effectiveness, accountability, financial targets, audits, performance indicators, and benchmarks (Deem & Brehony, 2005). These behaviors and goals are driven by managers with a "right to manage" (Deem & Brehony, 2005, p. 220) who elevate the activities of management to a level of supremacy "above all other activities" (Deem & Brehony, 2005, p. 220). The managerial university implies and emphasizes a "myth of a community of scholars" (Levin, 2000, pp. 32–33), that such a collegial environment was an illusion. In the managerial university, managers have primary authority over decision making and usurp power from the professional experts (the faculty) through increased surveillance of faculty work, audits of teaching and research, the introduction of devolved budgets and cost centers, and outcomes-based reforms (Deem & Brehony, 2005). The managerial model is in direct contradiction to the professional bureaucratic model, as it redefines the structure of power, dissolves both trust and autonomy, and reorients professional experts into "marginalized" and "overly managed" (Deem, Hillyard, & Reed, 2007, p. 49) individuals. The managerial model is a manifestation of a managerial regime that goes hand in hand with neoliberal ideology.

In the managerial university, the goal is to shape academics into entrepreneurial subjects and all organizational members into managers. "[E]ntrepreneurial subject[s] relate to themselves as if they were a business, are active, embrace risks, capably manage difficulties and hide injuries" (Scharff, 2015, p. 2). Academics are expected to ensure that the university increases its revenues, status, and prestige, that is, its marketable image. For individuals, "social critique is transformed into self-critique, resulting in a prevalence of self-doubt and anxiety" (Scharff, 2015, p. 2).

At the level of serious critique of the managerial university and its ideological home of neoliberalism, there is no remedy to or justification for the subordination of academic logic, either at the organizational level or the personal or professional level. The university, at least the idealized view and version of the university, is in ruins, as Bill Readings (1997) claimed more than twenty years ago. Furthermore, the academic professional is not just managed in Gary Rhoades's (1998) terms but is imprisoned in an intellectual and personal cul-de-sac: there is no relief. Even though academics can claim that they love their work and that they have freedom in the profession, the critique of the managerial university indicates that academics are both subjects of neoliberal projects and instruments for managerial goals (Ward, 2012).

Through the practice of new managerialism (Deem, 1998), the technology of the managerial university, the ideal is for everyone to be a manager—engaged in managing others or the self, or both—and an extension of the corporate university (Davies & Bansel, 2010; Ward, 2012). The academic self is subordinate to the managerial self, but the academic self is called upon to narrate (or pointedly interpret) individuals' personal values and professional meanings. Academic managers, especially, possess both an inner and outer professional self (Winter, 2009), with the inner self aligned with the academic profession, and the outer self aligned with neoliberal values. Yet, the inner self is servant of the outer. Academic managers have dual roles and dual identities (Lorenz, 2012), including divided loyalties. These divided loyalties, fraught with tensions and conflicts in the form of multiple roles, occur not only between academic managers and faculty but also within the individual academic manager. Although such divisions have been characteristic of universities since the rise of an academic administrative body—academic vice president, academic dean, and department chair—it is with the introduction and growth of managerialism that the role dualities have become prominent. Deans and department chairs are subject to discursive dualities (Lorenz, 2012): they hold almost paradoxical views of the purposes of the university if they operate within a managerial regime and claim identities as academic professionals.

For those who are technically faculty but occupy an administrative role, such as department chair, they can be in a futile position where there are efforts to "corporatize the university," which are not in the interests of the faculty. A research university department chair narrates a situation in which she has no way to resist and certainly no power to influence those who are her superiors, to alter what she calls "new space that we are in."

> I . . . [am the] administrative person that represents the faculty. . . . [I]n the chain of command, from faculty to chair, dean, etc. is the chair. I used to think that . . . before becoming

chair, I really thought that the dean was on our side. The dean played favorites, but the dean was on the side of the faculty. And I don't think so . . . especially if they're trying to move up that their best interests are served by being advocates of the faculty. And so, it's like you have to court the dean, but you're at odds with the dean, and I don't know if it's the vision of the current chancellor and current administration, or it's the budget, or it's just this kind of new space that we are in where they are trying to kind of corporatize the university. I don't know what the combination is there, what the drivers are, but we very clearly moved. (department chair, research university)

At an organizationally higher remove from department chairs are academic deans, who, although technically managers and not faculty, at research universities generally consider themselves aligned with faculty. One dean at a research university notes the differentiation between himself and his university's executive level managers—president and vice presidents—as he critiques this group's view of faculty.

For the [research university deans] . . . the presumption on the part of executive administration is that the respect of the faculty is a critical component in the ability to manage them [and] that they are notoriously unmanageable, except by inspiration or intimidation. (dean, research university)

Research university deans identify themselves by their research or disciplinary areas and as members of the faculty community. Most if not all arrive at the dean's position through the faculty ranks, even from within the same university.

I began as faculty in a different department. . . . I've been department chair. I've served on the committee on academic personnel. I've been on almost all of the major academic committees. I began [as] associate dean. . . . [T]he previous dean decided to step down. The position was open; I applied for it. (dean, research university)

Research university deans continue to identify with their faculty colleagues, in part because they originate from that community and in part because they maintain a role as a researcher and scholar, an academic professional. "I have a busy research agenda, like most of the faculty, and I've been publishing my papers and my books" (dean, research university). This is not to say that all research university deans are academics first and managers second. In time allocations alone, deans can devote themselves primarily to management: "I would say [that my time is divided] 95% of administration, 5% research" (Dean, research university). That same dean uses his dual role for practical purposes, including the acquisition of donations for his unit.

> If I go . . . fundraising, it depends on the situation. . . . [F]or some potential donors [it depends on] their experience or what they do related to my research. I will be more willing to say "I'm a faculty doing research related to what you do." . . . [O]n the other hand, if I talk to the alumni, they're looking to see the dean; I will have to present myself as the dean. (dean, research university)

And, although academics prefer the term *leadership* to *management,* deans do ascribe to managerial practices of control.

> [Faculty] will probably describe me as a strong leader, and I'm willing to be pretty bold . . . and you can't make change . . . without being bold. . . . I'm very engaged in what goes on in the departments. . . . I'm not afraid to go down and step in. So, some people who know that I'm working against a tide are delighted that I'm willing to show some leadership and push things. People who don't agree with me would say I'm micromanaging. (dean, research university)

Managerialism, new managerialism, new public management, and *audit culture* are the scholarly terms that are used to identify the practices of university managers in the past decades in developed, industrialized countries (Bleiklie, Enders, Lepori, & Musselin, 2011; Brennan, 2011; Butterwork & Dawson, 2005; Deem & Brehony, 2005; Lorenz, 2012; Shore, 2008). They are not, however, common terms in use or addressed in U.S. scholarship. In the United States, management and managerialism applied to universities have more often than not appeared in critiques of traditional higher education institutions and remedies to bring universities and colleges in line with a market economy (Keller, 1983; Massy, 2016). Although Slaughter and

Rhoades (2004) provide a critique of the economic and neoliberal bent of U.S. universities and colleges, they refrain from attributing organizational behaviors to managerialism. Instead, they underscore the sources of economic behavior as a regime of academic capitalism, which extends beyond the organization to knowledge management.

Managerialism in the U.S. university is not a homogeneous enterprise directed solely or even primarily toward efficiency and effectiveness. Rather, managerialism is multivalent, a many-headed monster that claims rationality but is often irrational. In budgeting, financing, and in financial allocations, the terrain shifts, depending upon several factors, including institutional leadership. A department chair at a research university notes that under one president the university was dominated by the rhetoric of change ("transformation") in order to create economic efficiencies by amalgamation of departments, whereas under the next president the call and response were aimed at accounting for student numbers and thus financing departments rather than restructuring departments.

> We had a previous university president who instituted something called "the transformation." And all the departments were supposed to transform. That was a very bad time. That was quite some time ago now. And still in meetings, where people say: "Oh, that was during the transformation years." And everyone goes: "Yep." . . . [M]ore recently our university has adopted a new accounting or . . . what do they call it? Is it accounting model? Is it a business model? I am not sure. And that is having huge effects on everything. (department chair, research university)

Within this new emphasis (i.e., responsibility-based or centered management), the former imperatives of revenue generation from grant acquisition were replaced by the promise of university and departmental revenues gleaned from student tuition and state funding. "[T]hat's when we made the change from 'go bring in external grants'—external grants or that thing that shows your value—to 'bring in gazillions of undergrads.' That's the only thing that brings in money" (department chair, research university).

"Audit culture" is another term used to refer to the infiltration of neoliberal logic into the university (Shore, 2008), and audit is a practice associated with new managerialism (Deem, 1998). Those faculty torn between the status and privilege of their positions and their distaste for an "audit culture" (Shore, 2008) may rely upon the approach of the UK professor noted above ("the only option is to work within the system and reform it; resist where possible; and speak out when necessary"). Such an approach is rational but not satisfactory. First, it does not enable the academic professional to maintain an identity that matches the standard of the role (Burke & Stets, 2009) of faculty as a professional with autonomy in the pursuit and dissemination of knowledge. Second, the survivalist approach reinforces the academic manager's adoption of neoliberal policies, including the pursuit of resources and prestige, which fosters competition and "performativity" (Ball, 2012b). Third, the pragmatic approach does little to remediate the position of the university as a quasi-market (Pusser, Kempner, Marginson, & Ordorika, 2011) where students are treated as both consumers and commodities, and the university is a marketplace, not of ideas but of knowledge products and symbols (such as diplomas or certificates).

The "audit culture" or the practice and pervasiveness of "audit," although articulated clearly in the UK, as the tool and creation—idea, process, and technique—of *new public management* (Shore, 2008) is missing in the higher education literature of the United States, with some exceptions (Ward, 2012). Yet, audit cultures have some consistency with the values of academics (e.g., self-discipline, pursuit of quality in research and teaching) and are insidious in their infiltration of and institutionalization in universities, internationally (Ball, 2012a; Lorenz, 2012; Shore, 2008). Audit ideas and processes construct environments in order to render them auditable (Shore, 2008). Their presence in U.S. universities through quality initiatives, performance indicators, and student learning outcomes' practices is not out of line with rising expectations in universities for faculty productivity and university prestige. These expectations are shared among faculty and administrators and include aspirations for and efforts to increase university prestige through national and international rankings (Marginson, 2009), as well as personal market value and status.

Yet, it is clear whether in countries such as the UK or the United States that university managers have embraced and practice audit as the model of governance (inclusive of decision making, organizational values, and rewards), legitimacy, and authority (Shore, 2008, Ward, 2012). This audit practice is also viewed as synonymous with data-driven decisions, and even though faculty governance can be acclaimed, faculty's decisions within the context of audit are not legitimate. "[F]aculty continue . . . to serve on senates and budget committees; however, the true decisions [have] already been decided beforehand in the administrative suite by managers" (Ward, 2012, p. 69).

In what is now construed as the U.S. managerial university, neoliberal logic has commandeered the institution, and the conception of the university has either demoted the efficacy of academic logic or ignored it entirely. *Managerialism, new managerialism, new public management,* and *audit culture* as critical terms for the management of the academic profession signal the erosion or demise of academic logic and the practices of academics that have legitimated their academic professional identity

Conclusions

Although the critique of neoliberalism for both universities and conditions of administrators and faculty has validity and considerable relevance to our discussion, it minimizes both resistance to and rejection of neoliberal values and initiatives, and, furthermore, it overlooks, empirically, those views and behaviors that treat neoliberalism as either inconsequential or as not present. Or, in the view of Mark Stern (2012), who does not reject the presence of neoliberalism but tends to acknowledge its all-encompassing pervasiveness and opts for an alternate theory to explain social life, one more compatible with feelings and emotions, lesser, even weaker and more local theory may enable people to act without the shackles or consciousness of neoliberalism.

Whereas the scholarly argument is that universities have altered since the 1970s from the idealization of a community of scholars and a professional bureaucracy to corporations within a higher education marketplace sustained by competition and the drive for legitimacy and prestige, such a condition may be a charge in the extreme, on both counts. The argument on the one hand may be a nostalgic view of the past and a dystopian view of the present. The argument on the other hand may ignore the blending of logics—academic logic and the logic of neoliberalism—that is contained within the contemporary university. Alternately, and consistent with the concept of post-democracy (Schipper, 2017), the trappings of one condition—the ideal university, the collegium—could remain in the university, including the authority of expertise, peer review, and evaluation based upon merit, but the deep structures of authority are embedded in a managerial class, who are extensions of a neoliberal state (Ball, 2012).

The neoliberal state, the neoliberal university, managerialism, and managerial culture form the social structure for roles, behaviors, and identities of the faculty, tenured and non-tenured, and the academic administrators, deans and department chairs. Within this structure, each group (and, indeed, individuals within the groups) adapts to, participates in, resists, and supports neoliberal and managerial practices in different ways and with different results. In the following chapters, we analyze these actors' responses to neoliberal and managerial values, as well as the effects of neoliberalism and managerialism on the professional identities of members in each group. We devote one chapter each to focus on the separate populations.

We begin with a discussion of full-time tenure track faculty (chapter 1), a group of faculty that is in a relatively stable position in the academic profession. Although they are advantaged in comparison to full-time and part-time non-tenure track faculty, they experience anxiety, vulnerability, and self-doubt, as well as pressures for productivity, due to neoliberal values and managerial practices adopted in U.S. universities. The consequences of neoliberalism in the academic profession have been discussed in the scholarly literature; however, the full-time tenure track faculty role as participants in managerial practices and their adoption of neoliberal values as well as the consequences (negative and otherwise) of these values on their academic professional identity have not received adequate description and explanation in the literature. Thus, in chapter 1, we conceptualize faculty as professionals in a complex institutional context. We argue that tenure track faculty are critical of neoliberal values but have adopted managerial practices to a point that their relationship with colleagues and with their work has changed—management and self-management have taken a toll not only on their professional life but also on their personal life. We illustrate and explain our arguments with the use of faculty members' depictions of their own experiences.

Chapter 1

Full-time Tenure Track Faculty

Academic Professional Identity and Managerialism

In the Introduction, we argued that universities in the United States have blended academic logic and neoliberal logic, and, as a result, managerialism guides practices within universities. Academic logic pulls universities toward traditional values such as academic freedom, professional autonomy, and the pursuit of knowledge. Neoliberal logic pushes them toward competitiveness, individualism, financial gain, and quantitative productivity. Thus, management and managerialism in the university take a different form than in for-profit organizations and in nonacademic organizations. We advance the argument here with a focus on tenure track faculty: with contradictory logics blended or coexisting, academics have adopted managerial practices; they both manage one another and manage themselves. They are willing to resist an amorphous managerial class in universities, but they fail to identify their own role in managerialism and the perpetuation of neoliberal logic.

The academy has characteristics of a professional institution: it serves a social function (to develop knowledge and transmit knowledge in the form of teaching), and individuals in the profession have special traits (e.g., expert knowledge, legal legitimacy, and traditional authority). Moreover, autonomy and academic freedom are idealized as central features of the academic profession. However, university attention to performance, or what Ball (2012a, 2012b) calls "performativity" and thus connects the academic profession to neoliberalism, results in insecurity and constraints upon both autonomy and academic freedom of university faculty (Archer, 2008; Enders & Musselin, 2008; Garcia & Hardy, 2007). With the growing use and abuse of new managerial strategies and the pervasiveness of neoliberal ideology to challenge faculty members' professional identity, this academic professional identity is both problematical and questionable. Are faculty part of an integrated community of scholars (Goodman, 1962)? Or are they members of a fragmented professional culture (Clark, 1987)? Do they embrace nonacademic values of the marketplace or do they reject and oppose them (Alvesson & Spicer, 2016)? Are they independent actors or are they neoliberal subjects (Davies, 2005)? Or, are there variations and gradations in academic professional identity for university academics? Does neoliberal ideology in the form of new managerialism disturb or distort academic professional identity? Here, we discuss the evidence that responds to these questions.

In the United States, the critical concern about the condition of the profession is the degradation of the traditional professoriate. The threat to full-time tenure track faculty identity is the neoliberal takeover of, or infiltration into, higher education in the United States. This takeover not only emanates from the state but also from the university itself, overtly in the form of a managerial class, as well as covertly from full-time faculty themselves. Full-time faculty are central to the university but both as objects of neoliberal policies and managerial control and as neoliberal subjects. They are neoliberal subjects (Ball, 2012a) because full-time faculty continue to carry out the central functions of a neoliberal university: They generate resources (e.g., grants) and engender organizational prestige (e.g., rankings); they develop, monitor, and revise the curriculum, and teach the majority of the curriculum at the graduate level, where they reinforce (e.g., socialization) and perpetuate (e.g., future faculty and researchers) the production and revenue-generating function of the university; and, they sell their products (i.e., entrepreneurship) and thus aid in a nation or state or region's economic development (Cantwell & Kauppinen, 2014; Slaughter & Leslie, 1997; Slaughter & Rhoades, 2004; Ward, 2012), as productive citizens tied to the neoliberal state.

With the rise in the exercise of managerial authority in U.S. universities, faculty independence has become attenuated. The role of tenure track faculty in the governance of their universities is viewed, at present, and even in comparison to 2006, as diminished (Finkelstein et al., 2016). As well, their professional selves are highly subject to their social context, or social structures that are shaped by neoliberal ideology (Morales Vázquez, 2019). Their academic professional identity in large part has depended upon their social structures, and one of the structures that has gained considerable attention since the 1990s is the managerial one of their universities

(Gonzales, Martinez, & Ordu, 2014; Rosinger, Taylor, Coco, & Slaughter, 2016; Ward, 2012).

In this chapter, we address academic professional identity, first from a theoretical standpoint; second, as constructed by faculty; and, then, we move on to the management of full-time faculty. Overall, we rely upon both scholarly literature and empirical data from more than 130 interviews collected between 2010 and 2017 in public research and comprehensive universities in the United States to sustain our argument (for more information about the participants in these interviews see Appendix). These in-depth qualitative interviews conducted with both male and female faculty (including deans who were former faculty) from various ranks and disciplines in eight universities in the United States illustrate the discrete and nuanced ways in which academics are managed and manage.

Professional Identity as a Theoretical Tool

We employ the label *academic professional identity* throughout our book; thus, we explain the term here. First, we move from identity to professional identity. Identity has several theoretical roots in the literature, but there is no single definition of identity or professional identity that is sufficient for our examinations and explanations. Consequentially, we draw upon an amalgamation of theories of identity to aid us in a useful definition of academic professional identity, a definition that accounts for both the cognitive and behavioral outcomes of our academic faculty and academic managers within the context of two dominant institutional logics—academic logic and neoliberal logic.

Identity can be derived from various components, including life spheres such as cultural, economical, familial, financial, political, and religious contexts; it may be influenced by life roles, such as "parent" or "breadwinner"; and, it may stem from work facets, such as the workplace environment or social groups in that workplace (Bothma, Lloyd, & Khapova, 2015). Identity is formed through a process whereby the individual adopts "certain meanings, norms, expectations, beliefs, and core values" (Bothma et al., 2015, p. 27) in accordance with a social group (such as the academy). Institutional logics, discussed in the Introduction, are manifest in the meanings, norms, values, beliefs, and expectations that shape an individual's identity within an institution. Thus, the logics of the institution (i.e., academic logic and neoliberal logic) play a role in the construction of an academic professional identity.

Explanations of how identity formation processes occur vary across different identity theories. The outcome of an identity formation process is referred to as either a prototype (Hogg, 2001) or an identity standard (Burke & Stets, 2009), which is a guide for behavior (Bothma et al., 2015). Social identity theory posits that identity is rooted in membership in a specific group where the group members hold compatible views and perspectives (Bothma et al., 2015). Self-categorization theory, an extension of social identity theory, places the determination for membership in a group on the individual. Individuals' self-categorization in a group suggests that individuals behave, think, and perceive phenomena in accordance with the group (Bothma et al., 2015). These group members reject adherence to behaviors and values associated with perceived "out groups" and adhere instead to behaviors and values associated with the "in group" of their self-categorization (Bothma et al., 2015).

Role identity theories differ from social identity theories in that role identity theory places the basis of identity in role-related behaviors; that is, individuals act in accordance with role expectations (Hogg & Ridgeway, 2003; Stets & Burke, 2003). The term *salience* is used in identity theories to explain the activation of an identity as well as the probability that an identity will be activated in a situation (Bothma et al., 2015; Burke & Stets, 2009). A given identity (e.g., academic) will be more salient in one place (e.g., a university) than in another (e.g., a prison). Individuals endeavor to verify their identity through feedback loops, or reinforcement from others, and adjust behavior to maintain an identity prototype or standard within a specific social situation (Bothma et al., 2015; Burke, 1991). When an individual fails to activate and verify the acceptable behaviors and identity, this can result in negative feelings such as personal stress and either a change in behaviors or reduced salience, including abandonment of that identity (Burke, 1991).

Professional identity alludes to the part of a person's identity that is derived through identification with a profession. Professional identity is an "enduring" (Ibarra, 1999, p. 764) "collective identity of a profession and an individual's own sense of the professional role" (Feen-Calligan, 2005, p. 122). We understand professional identity as a self-categorization that involves role expectations and individual and group construction.

Our data reveal that academic professional identity extends beyond the formal role of the professor, the individual faculty member, or the academic manager. Academic professional identity is derived from the personal attributes and history of an individual, their self-categorization as an academic, their adherence to both role expectations as well as socially accepted behaviors, and their membership in a social "in-group" that verifies their identity through both formal (e.g., tenure, merit, and promotion) and informal mechanisms (e.g., norms and expectations).

The academic professional identity of full-time tenure track faculty, those who are in the most stable position in the academic profession, is both complex and ambiguous (Enders & Musselin, 2008). Yet, the scholarly discourse reflects an idealized past for the faculty, when there was less complexity and ambiguity (Schuster & Finkelstein, 2006), and a more homogeneous way to characterize academic professional identity (Becher, 1989; Clark, 1987), with variation limited to institutional type and discipline. U.S. scholars Finkelstein, Martin Conley, and Schuster (2016) assert that the faculty profession in the United States is transformed, compared to the 1960s and 1970s. Yet, this alteration has for these scholars no clear source: They are vague about those at the helm of the transformation; they have little to say about those who manage the profession. Furthermore, Finkelstein et al. (2016) fail to suggest, as do earlier critics (Slaughter & Rhoades, 2004), that contemporary faculty identity is ambiguous, not one condition or another, but a combination of several conditions, such as the managed laborer and autonomous actor, and that those who manage the profession are themselves, in the main, academic professionals.

Academic Professional Identity

As early as the 1950s, faculty in the United States self-identified as independent professionals, with responsibilities dictated primarily by themselves and accountable to themselves and their colleagues rather than to their employers (Jencks & Riesman, 1968). Aside from unionization, as a condition where faculty are categorized as a collective, faculty at a university constitute a legitimate collective body only in governance matters (often through a senate), and even here the role is informal, legally as recommenders. However, faculty in disciplines or departments can be construed as a collective within a university. They function as a guild (Clark, 1987) or tribe (Becher, 1989), in some contrast to enterprise or administrative authority (Clark, 1987), even though the discipline or department has more traditional authority than legal authority over academic matters. Indeed, discipline or program affiliation and the socialization process within that unit have a shaping effect upon not just the cohesiveness of a unit but as well upon the academic professional identity of tenure track faculty at a university (Becher, 1989; Clark, 1987). Research and the associated research culture and epistemology of a discipline are major socializers going back to graduate education of university faculty (Austin, 2002; Becher, 1989).

> If you go to graduate school in a graduate department that has [a] self-concept of itself as a grant-driven research shop that is a research one and is training people to do that sort of work, the rules of the game are very quickly learned and very easy and apparent. Because it is the entire culture. This is very clear. (professor, sociology, research university)

The research function has differentiated and stratified tenure track faculty in "hard/soft and pure/applied" fields or disciplines (Becher, 1989, p. 153), and more recently through productivity measures that include the acquisition of money (Slaughter & Leslie, 1997; Slaughter & Rhoades, 2004) and prestige, as well as funds from sources legitimate to managers (Roisinger et al., 2016). "In the sciences, the culture of evaluation of faculty is really based on how much money is arriving" (professor, sociology, research university). Research as well is a primary activity of university faculty, especially at research-oriented, or research intensive, universities, and is reinforced through faculty activity with external resource providers (Becher, 1989; Rosinger et al., 2016; Slaughter & Leslie, 1997). Moreover, the research role of full-time tenure track university faculty has, traditionally, at least from the 1960s to the 1990s, provided them with an independent role within their universities, and served as a central characteristic of the profession (Schuster & Finkelstein, 2006). Such autonomy is a key marker of a professional (Freidson, 2001).

Traditionally, self-ascribed identity, research orientation, and discipline affiliation are major components in the academic professional identity of tenure track faculty. In identity theory, when an individual categorizes themself as an occupant of a role, they incorporate "the meanings and expectations associated with that role and its performance" (Stets & Burke, 2000, p. 225). That is, "identities are internalizations of role expectations" (Stryker & Burke, 2000, p. 286), which include the meanings attributed not only by the self but also by others. These meanings of roles and the expectations for action shape individual behaviors, which themselves convey meanings and thus reinforce or repudiate identities and what they signify (Stryker & Burke, 2000). If others confirm one's identity through interactions (behaviors), then that identity is verified and reinforced. In contrast, if one's identity is repudiated, then the saliency of an identity erodes (Stryker & Burke, 2000). In the case of full-time tenure track faculty, social and professional contexts are thus salient for academic professional identity. Faculty in departments that they view as "collegial" or "supportive" project positive views of their work and their academic professional identity (Hoyt, 2012). In this way, faculty can and do align academic professional identity with group identity, sometimes a discipline or department, and sometimes a research collaborative group that is either internal or external to the university, or a combination.

Group identity suggests individual commitment to common values, beliefs, and understandings of experience. "[W]hen several persons interacting in a common situation mutually verify the identities held by each, their commitment to one another increases" (Stryker & Burke, 2000, p. 290). These affinity identities (Gee, 2000–01) can be undermined when "persons interacting in a common situation have difficulties in verifying their identities" (Stryker & Burke, 2000, p. 290). When this is the case, "ties are broken and structures dissolve" (Stryker & Burke, 2000, p. 290). Fractious departments can undermine faculty professional identities just as "collegial" departments can validate identities. Faculty in departments classified as "collegial" by their members suggest that their colleagues are supportive and thus their behaviors verify or validate their academic professional identities. A professor of biology at a comprehensive university characterizes her department as "collegial," that is, faculty are engaged in departmental matters and they interact without animosity. Her experiences in this department are without negative experiences that undermine her academic professional identity.

> One of the things that's attractive about this department is we're pretty collegial. I've been in some departments that are slightly dysfunctional, but this particular department is good, and that's part of the attraction of my job is that the faculty in this particular department pretty much all get along, and they all pull their weight, and they—I don't say that they're all easy going—but enough so that we get along. The downside is our faculty meetings sometimes last three hours because they won't go home. . . . Every other week we get together, so things get hashed out. . . . The dynamics [are] fairly loose, and that may be the key to the success of this department. It's more of a democracy. . . . We're not so big that we can't have an effective

meeting, and we're not so small that individual personalities might cause a problem. (professor, biology, comprehensive university)

Faculty in departments where there is limited trust and where there is fear of retaliation for behaviors that are not in accord with group preferences find themselves unable to express their views; indeed, they are unable to enact their professional judgment. An associate professor of sociology at a research university, who is newly tenured, reflected upon his departmental colleagues' behaviors during his tenure process. His academic professional identity was threatened both because the tenure process placed him in a position of vulnerability and because the judgments of his departmental colleagues negated and did not verify his role.

> [W]hen you have to worry about retaliation, when it comes to voting, promotions, files, and so on, then it's hard for me to really feel comfortable as though I can really express what it is that I want to say when I'm worried about retaliation. . . . I actually had experiences when it came to certain times in which my file went up where people voted and said things about my file and my record that were inaccurate. And so, when that happens, then you have validation that this is a group that is not to be trusted; that you're being excluded; that they don't see you as an insider or somebody worthy and so on. And so, I felt like, "Yeah, I didn't trust that I could say anything without there being possible retaliation, and these folks have some power because, if ultimately my tenure is at least partially decided upon by my faculty's vote, and I feel as though I have to watch myself, then I can't feel like I'm a full citizen." And then when that gets validated by things that happen in terms of voting, then you really feel as though, "Yeah, I was right not to trust my faculty." So those kinds of things make me feel that way. (associate professor, sociology, research university)

The strengthening or weakening, or indeed dissolving, of group identity affects individual commitment and the salience of an identity. Such is also the case in disciplinary research.

> [Y]ou get both communities of cooperation, people who are personally supportive, engaged in the same kind of activ-

ity . . . supportive of one another. And you also get an awful lot of individual competitiveness. In many ways, the humanities and letters are more viciously personally competitive than the world of science, although there's certainly an awful lot of that in sciences as well. In science, the science side . . . the individual contributions are also very important, but the products are very often collaborative team projects. (professor, sociology, research university)

The implication, then, is that identities, including academic professional identity, are fragile, subject to social disconfirmation or rejection (Knights & Clarke, 2014). In particular, within the context of a university, there are idealized expectations for academics, where there are both processes of ongoing identity formation (e.g., tenure and promotion) and multiple demands (e.g., teaching, research, and service) that lead to self-exposure and unfulfilled outcomes (Knights & Clarke, 2014). Faculty develop an academic professional identity or their *academic self* through a combination of interpretations or imaginings based upon prior and present socialization, past experiences, and current conditions in their environment (e.g., university) (Billot, 2010). These interpretations and imaginings are intersected by emotions (Burke & Stets, 2009; Morales Vázquez, 2019), which are personal responses to verification or nonverification of identity standards.

In general, professionals are associated with knowledge expertise, judgment, ethics, and self-governance (Freidson, 2001; Spenceley, 2006). More specifically, academics are associated with research and teaching, knowledge pursuit, self and peer governance, autonomy, and academic freedom (Enders & Musselin, 2008; Mendoza & Berger, 2008; Winter, 2009). The academic professional identity rests upon a community of practice, as well as responsibility to peers, autonomy, and self-regulation (Winter, 2009). What follows from scholarly views upon the academic profession as a community of practice is whether or not academic identities necessitate community, in the form of shared values and common experiences. Furthermore, this might entail whether and the extent to which individual academics define themselves through their organization or as a member of a profession. Yet, the two do mix: both the organization (e.g., the university, the college, the department) and the larger profession (e.g., discipline, field) have salience for academic professional identity.

Identities, too, are shaped by contexts, which include sociopolitical environments. These affect both the professional role of faculty, their social role as members of a social group, and their personal identities as unique individuals (Burke & Stets, 2009). For faculty, the intersection of the professional and the personal influences faculty's responses or reactions to neoliberal pressures—policies, norms, expectations, and demands of their university—for productivity. In our examination of faculty and their productivity (Martin, López-Damián, Levin, & Montero Hernández, 2015), we noted the types or archetypes of faculty and their work at public research and comprehensive universities. We found five general archetypes: researcher, teacher, advocate, entrepreneur, and administrator.

> These ideal types responded to and coped with neoliberal pressures on their productivity in different ways. One ideal type rejected neoliberal ideology (advocate); another embraced it (entrepreneur); and another endeavored to survive within a neoliberal environment (researcher). The adoption of one of these identities served as a way to cope with or counteract neoliberalism. Thus, faculty were not solely victims of neoliberal influence and coerced to define and act toward productivity in specified manners and meet institutional, disciplinary, and departmental expectations. Rather, faculty were individuals who worked within an academic environment in a manner to maintain their employment while simultaneously exercising agency to meet their own needs and goals. (p. 20)

This diversity of types suggests that a single academic professional identity for full-time tenure track faculty is unattainable (Enders & Musselin, 2008) and not a sound construct. This absence of singularity or commonality reflects a postmodern condition for professionals (Garcia & Hardy, 2007). That is, university faculty's professional identities are multiple, fragmented, and contradictory (Gornally & Salisbury, 2012).

Generally overlooked in higher education scholarship, the personal is a component of academic professional identity (Archer, 2008; Ball, 2015; Morales Vázquez, 2019), at least to the extent that personal identity and professional identity intersect. The personal, including emotions, shapes, reinforces, or nullifies parts of academic professional identity. Identities "have both cognitive as well as an affective or emotional process" (Burke & Stets, 2009, p. 61). This general absence of consideration of emotions or the intersection of the personal and professional in the scholarly literature constitutes an implicit view of professionals as roles, and more recently as productive beings, disconnected from emotions. They are conceptualized as working beings, or worker bees, not as subjective and reflective individuals.

The Personal and the Professional

Full-time faculty academic professional identity is tied, and for some inextricably, to personal histories and present roles and values. The higher educational literature is not direct or explicit on this subject, but there is scholarship that implies, and from time to time notes, the personal as a component of the professional (O'Meara & Campbell, 2011), including emotions (Bloch, 2002). Yet, emotions are viewed as an anathema within the academy (Bloch, 2002).

The ways in which faculty describe their academic identities are constructed and shaped by personal experiences and professional aspirations, which include their emotions (Gill, 2009; Knights & Clarke, 2014). Work itself within the academic profession and within the university has value to individuals and affects their emotional responses to their profession, which contribute to self-definitions as professionals (Clarke, Knights, & Jarvis, 2012; Morales Vázquez, 2019). A chemistry associate professor at a California comprehensive university reflects on his value to his university and his students, and simultaneously he notes his level of emotional gratification, and lack thereof. He vacillates between the benefits of his work to his lack of career advancement and to his lack of personal satisfaction.

> I've been able to build a pretty good . . . lab. And it's been a terrific thing for students. It's not so much research though. . . . It's kind of low-level stuff. But we're doing important work, but not research. . . . [I]t's been great for the students because the students are getting good jobs. . . . So, for the students, I think it's a great thing. It's been terrific. It hasn't been as rewarding career-wise for me, but I do like the fact that the students are all doing quite well. . . . It hasn't given me the personal gratification, but things are going very well, so I can't really complain. It isn't as exciting as I'd like it to be sometimes because it's a lot of work, and it's like I'm doing a lot of work, and it's not bringing me a lot of personal recognition because I'm not publishing a lot of papers, and I'm not doing things that would advance my career as much. But they [officials at the university] do recognize the

fact that I'm bringing in a lot of money and supporting, paying students that otherwise were working at some other job somewhere. . . . So, it's kind of a mixed bag. I can't really complain. But I would certainly prefer to be at this point in my career both making more money and doing something that I think is just more along the lines of all the training and education that I have. I think I could be doing a lot more. But you take what comes. (associate professor, chemistry, comprehensive university)

This faculty member experiences a mixture of feelings that stem from a misalignment between his preferred academic professional self (i.e., a high research, high publication, student supporting professional) and his de facto professional self (i.e., provider of funds, student supporter only, low status professional). His activities, what he does as a faculty member, define him as a professional but as well provides him with the potential for negative emotions related to lack of recognition and personal gratification. This apparent dissatisfaction with one's status and professional work aligns with Labaree's (2017) explanation of the effects of inevitable stratification of U.S. universities.

For some faculty members, the rewards of the profession and the personal benefits outweigh the financial benefits, and this aids them in the maintenance of positive views and emotions directed toward their profession (Clarke et al., 2012). An assistant professor of psychology at a California comprehensive university balances her positive emotional responses to the nature of her work with not only what she views as inadequate financial compensation but also with the recent results of the Great Recession in the state of California.

We had a ten percent cut in our pay last year. And then we had certain days where we took as furlough days where we didn't work, supposedly. But in terms of the amount of stress, even though that cut into my actual pay, and I wish I was getting paid a lot more, but I'm not, I still wasn't upset. . . . [There are] all these various things they (other faculty) could get upset about for us being in that situation, but I just feel like it's out of my control, and . . . why would I waste time stressing about something like that. I'm grateful to have a job. I love my job. I have so many benefits like freedom. I can work from home if I want and juggle different things. I have summers off, December off. I'm

> just very happy and grateful. So, I didn't see it as a source of
> stress. (assistant professor, psychology, comprehensive university)

This description is an example of those faculty members who are able to rationalize the problems in their profession as connected to the context of their university, in this case the economic context. Such rationalizations enable these faculty to maintain positive views and, thus, emotions toward their profession.

Faculty's emotions are connected to their professional aspirations and their work (Gill, 2009; Knights & Clarke, 2014). The personal can and does intertwine with the professional as an assistant professor of psychology at a California research university makes her personal life subservient to the attainment of tenure.

> I very much hope in the coming five years I'll get tenure. Yeah,
> I would be perfectly happy to visualize my entire career here,
> right here, doing what I'm doing right now. That would be
> very satisfying, in fact, quite good outcome. . . . That's best-case
> scenario and ideally, hopefully feasible. So, I don't envision any
> major changes unless they're forced on me by a failure to get
> tenure, which is really the big turning point. My husband and
> I . . . we're renting a house right now . . . and we think do we
> really want to make some decisions about where we want to live
> more long term. And, it's always, "Wait until tenure. Wait until
> tenure. Wait till we see if." . . . I'm very close to my parents,
> and they live in Florida still . . . are in their late sixties, still
> absolutely healthy and great, and everything's fantastic. But, the
> reality is that probably won't be the case forever. So, I worry
> about that slightly, but when I think about it, I think much
> more in terms of moving them out here than us going anywhere.
> So, we'll see if reality lines up with my expectations. . . . My
> husband and I, we don't really discuss anything except staying
> here even though life is unpredictable. (assistant professor, psy-
> chology, research university)

For faculty, their professional trajectories and their histories in a given university take a central role in their definition of their life choices. The professional and the personal are not independent but influence one another.

Whereas the role expectations for university faculty members organize their work (e.g., teaching, research, service), their academic professional identity organizes their experiences, including the values and meanings they attribute to their work (Castells, 1997), as well as to their career achievements and personal aspirations. It is this internalization of the characteristics of an academic professional identity that establishes and sustains an academic's identity. Thus, there is indeed an "inner" professional self, distinct from an "outer" organizational self (Spenceley, 2009; Winter, 2009).

The outer, organizational self articulates a powerful attraction to the profession, whether the emphasis is upon teaching or research, or both. Indeed, there is the notion that the professoriate is a "calling," an almost spiritual or cultural imperative (Alvesson & Spicer, 2006; Cannizzo, 2018). Those who express adoration or passion or addiction to their job emphasize a form of autonomy, usually personal freedom, and personal satisfaction either in developing students or in discovery or solving intellectual puzzles. "This is not a job; it is a calling," notes a professor of sociology at a research university. "I am . . . like the king of my own little country," articulates a biology professor also at a research university. A psychology professor at a comprehensive university "loves" her job because she "loves the freedom" that enables her to work at home. However, the attraction to the profession is contingent upon personal gratification, or inner satisfaction, and threats to the personal, such as problems with a work-life balance, can affect views of identity (Morales Vázquez, 2019). Time, for some, becomes the enemy of satisfaction. "My only negative experience [in my work] is the time. It takes so much time. . . . [M]y job . . . just takes a lot of time. . . . I wish I had more free time," expresses a psychology professor at a comprehensive university. For others, the negativity is aimed at more external entities that interfere with their professional roles and performance: the bureaucracy of the university, the state government, or the university's administration. "We all work for the state," notes a professor of biology at a comprehensive university, who also criticizes his university's administration who treat faculty as commodities: "[T]hey look at us as interchangeable labor."

Outer and inner selves of the academic professional are connected to and shaped by social structures—the university as an organization and personal histories as individual experiences. Both of these selves—the inner professional self and the outer organization self—are governed and managed by rules and regulations, traditions, norms, and rewards and punishment (i.e., positive and negative reinforcements of expectations). Ideally, the inner professional self is governed by standards of the profession (Freidson, 2001), such as an "ideology that asserts greater commitment to doing good work than to economic gain and the quality of work rather than the economic efficiency of work" (p. 127). The outer self is governed by the organization's policies and the laws of the state, which define and classify work of the academic labor force (Freidson, 2001).

The Academic Professional through the Lens of Neoliberalism

Neoliberalism has led to a chilling effect on academic professional identity and an erosion of professionalism. For Freidson (2001), not only is the free market emphasis upon maximization of profit destructive of professionalism but also the motive of personal gain is an assault on professionalism. Within neoliberal ideology, the market is the basis for social relations, and thus the values of a professional are based upon productivity and the professional is a resource unit (Ball, 2012b). This resource unit within the university is organized to be managed and governed, by others, or self-managed, or both. Academics become "new performance professionals" (Ball, 2012b, p. 19). Thus, managerialism is the extension and arm of neoliberalism within organizations, including universities (Ward, 2012).

In the U.S. context, the scholarly perspective on faculty identity and the effects of managerialism are more muted, constrained, and conservative than in other jurisdictions such as the UK, Australia, Canada, New Zealand, and Scandinavian countries, which are far more statist in their governance of higher education than the United States. However, in the United States, the general signs of identity erosion of faculty (Bowen & Schuster, 1986; Finkelstein, 2017; Finkelstein et al., 2016) are accompanied by more specific examples of loss of autonomy (Levin & Aliyeva, 2015) and fragmented lives (Gonzales et al., 2014). An associate professor of anthropology at a research university articulates the university's extensive demands upon her: Raise money, serve the community, publish, and, for those faculty in her areas who do not bring in money to the university, teach large numbers of students. A professor of chemistry at a research university notes that his university does not "honor" reflection in research and that national funding agencies are moving away from basic research grants. For him, then, research guided by curiosity is disappearing, and a measure for quality research productivity is beginning to vanish in his university's evaluation system. As he is nearing the end of his career, he devotes his energies to reflection and thinking about concepts and problems, even though his university's norms for publishing quantity do not permit deep thinking and reflection.

A principal characteristic of the professional, indeed the defining quality, autonomy (Freidson, 2001), is redefined within the neoliberal context as a form of market-based freedom: choice. For faculty, this appears as choice among many for teaching courses, workplace (e.g., home), and work hours. Whereas autonomy of professionals refers, traditionally, to independence from the state, from the organization, and from the public to exercise one's profession—one's knowledge and skills—for the public good (Freidson, 2001), in the neoliberal context it has been reduced to individual choice, personal preferences, and responsibility to the self (Ball, 2012a; Harvey, 2005).

Management, whether by self or others, in the university has reduced opportunities for and reinforcement of professional autonomy; indeed, performance as production of professional behaviors is the contemporary standard (Ball, 2012a, 2012b). Surveillance, by self or others, serves as a technology to ensure compliance. Autonomy is undermined through surveillance. The observation that a culture of surveillance has permeated universities in countries such as the UK and New Zealand (Kok, Douglas, McClelland, & Bryde, 2010; Lorenz, 2012) is not prevalent in U.S. scholarship. However, the observation does appear in Gonzales et al.'s (2014) investigation of new faculty. Gonzales et al. (2014) extend Bowen and Schuster's (1986) notion of a dispirited or fragmented faculty body, with a specific focus upon particular tenure track faculty who engaged in "constant working, individual self-sacrifice, [and] a constant disciplining of self" (Gonzales et al., 2014, p. 107), while under surveillance as competitive market participants. Furthermore, extensive evaluation of faculty by the university through the mechanism of peer review promotes not only productivity that can be measured but also a form of continual audit, itself a form of surveillance. The competitive process, whether for places in the faculty ranks or for merit pay, instills a culture of monitoring—of others and oneself. The competitive practice is a form of tournament (Gu & Levin, 2016). Through these practices, U.S. full-time tenure track faculty manage themselves for productivity, akin to Ball's (2012a, 2012b) *performativity*.

The Management of Full-time Tenure Track Faculty

A cadre of academics manage full-time university tenure track faculty. Traditional U.S. scholarship refers, in the main, to "administration" not "management" (Dill, 1984; Schuster & Finkelstein, 2006), with some exceptions (Rhoades, 1998), as that body or group that oversees university and college employees, including faculty. Academic managers—the academic administrators (department chairs, assistant and associate deans, deans, provosts)—are those responsible for the administration of the academic domain of the university, and almost entirely come from the faculty ranks or continue to remain in the faculty ranks during their administration tenure (Martin, 2018; Wolverton, Ackerman, & Holt, 2005). Those who manage this profession, which include not just academic managers in administrative positions but full-time faculty themselves—those who share academic professional identities with full-time tenure track faculty—take varying positions and enact various value systems in their practices. This dual role or dual community of interest—the community of scholars and the community of managers—obfuscates the identity of tenure track academic professionals and academic administrators (Whitchurch, 2006; Winter, 2009).

Although there are claims of intrusive managerialism and growth in the managerial class in U.S. universities (Finkelstein et al., 2016; Slaughter & Rhoades, 2004), the effects of the administrators or managers on full-time university faculty—on their academic professional identity and their work—has not been documented in U.S. higher education literature, with the exception of Rhoades (1998) for unionized environments and based upon the text of union-management labor agreements. Yet, the charges are clear, both in other jurisdictions and the United States. Under new managerialism and the neoliberal context, academic professionals are subject to corporate expectations and demands for certain forms of production (Ward, 2012), including the gaining of external revenues and publications in prestigious venues, not just once but continually (Archer, 2008). Through this iterative process, "academic identities are rendered insecure, temporary, and risky within regimes of performativity" (Archer, 2008, p. 392). Thus, stability over time is not possible, and the academic professional identity requires re-formation, conditional upon the expectations and demands of the university. Rhoades's concept of *managed professionals* (1998) in the United States, once confined to unionized higher education institutions, primarily state comprehensive universities and community colleges, now pertains to all universities.

Research universities may emanate more pressures for productivity, especially in research, than teaching universities. Yet, teaching university faculty express stress over workloads and demands from their university for the generation of funds. "Our university is not too supportive of research; they are interested in money, through grants and contracts" (professor, anthropology, comprehensive university). But, it is not a group of managers alone that pushes faculty to perform, as faculty themselves internalize institutional and organizational norms for productivity (Levin & Aliyeva, 2015). "One of the things that maintains productivity is the sense of obligation to your colleagues. . . . [T]hose people too need to have their promotions and their tenure, and their merit raises" (professor, psychology, comprehensive university). Research university faculty as a group or department establish their own norms for faculty evaluation, and this reward structure emphasizes measures of productivity, which can include number of publications, grant acquisition, and prestige of publication outlet, among other measures (Gu & Levin, 2016). This also can lead to research that is driven by economic ends. "It is unwise to do research that is unfundable," notes a professor of psychology at a research university. Managerialism is thus embedded within the faculty themselves (Gonzales et al., 2014; Levin & Aliyeva, 2015).

Those who manage faculty in universities—department chairs or heads and deans—view full-time faculty as a critical resource: for finances, for prestige, and for work production, such as teaching. In conditions of resource scarcity, department chairs look to faculty to generate revenues. In one case, where the state's appropriations for higher education had diminished severely over an extended period, the university changed its approach to revenue generation and focused upon student tuition, and, as well, the accommodation of larger numbers of students.

> Where we've had success is when the university . . . turned to a tuition economy rather than the states' giving the money economy. We grew the number of students we teach and that's how we, we increased the teaching that we do to bring in the teaching budget and we get teaching money from teaching more students. . . . [T]here is pressure to do more. . . . [I]t's the pressure of the age is to do more with less. (department chair, research university)

This department chair thus managed faculty in accord with university policy to increase their teaching productivity. To meet the university's budget goals, the faculty were required to teach greater numbers of students than in previous years. And this department chair is, in turn, evaluated, assessed, and judged by the dean: "[T]he dean evaluates me as a department [chair] in terms of research, teaching, and service. How much research did the department do? How much teaching did the department do?" At the same university in another department, "return on investment" was used as synonymous for faculty productivity.

[W]hat the dean called return on investment: . . . How much SCH (student credit hours) is this person bringing in? How much grant dollars are being brought in? So, for a time, the administration kept showing scatterplots that showed departments plotted against how much revenue was brought in from teaching, how much revenue was brought in from grants, and rating departments on that basis. (department chair, research university)

This department chair noted the outcome for faculty based upon this approach to faculty as resource units. "[T]hose same kind of graphs were generated for individual faculty, and that had a somewhat demoralizing effect on everyone . . . because it seemed that that was all that mattered." These management practices replaced a value system based upon "[t]raditional academic mission accomplishment . . . having educational priorities, research priorities . . . [W]hat you accomplished research side and what you accomplished in terms of educating students seemed secondary" (department chair, research university). Thus, the faculty role identity as researcher and educator was not verified; rather, the "new performance professional" (Ball, 2012b, p. 19) was the role verified. Those who generated resources, in this case, taught more students and gained "grant dollars," received reinforcement as they enacted the new prototype or identity standard in their university.

Deans also manage faculty, particularly in setting expectations and in monitoring performance. A dean in a California research university suggested that revenue generation was the critical element in the preservation of the academy, a social responsibility. This dean's view filters down to department chairs and faculty and signals that resource generation is a priority.

Jerry Brown [the governor] is not giving us any more money. Janet Napolitano [the university president] is not giving us any more money. California legislature is not giving us any [more] money. The chancellor is not going to give us [more money] and we're home alone. If you want to take charge of the destiny, you need to understand what your resources are and you need to generate the kinds of resources that you need. (dean, research university)

Another dean took responsibility for faculty workload: It was " 'the dean's problem to solve' " lack of faculty performativity and to improve the " 'collective productivity of the faculty' " (Martin, 2018, p. 114).

New managerialism (Deem, 1998; Deem & Brehony, 2005), executive power (Marginson & Considine, 2000), neoliberalism (Ball, 2012a, 2012b; Levin & Aliyeva, 2015; Ward, 2012), and academic capitalism regimes (Slaughter & Leslie, 1997; Slaughter & Rhoades, 2004) are all held up as the responsible conditions and practices that have undermined the traditional academic professional identity of university faculty. This alteration of an identity, once dependent upon the norms and practices of a discipline (Clark, 1987), what Finkelstein calls an "integrated academic role" (2017, p. 10), is at present contingent upon several bounded entities (e.g., discipline, department, organization, institution). The organization itself as the principal driver of, or at least the prime responsible party for, professional working conditions (Freidson, 2001) through its systems of control has led to insecurity for academics (Archer, 2008). The university, the organization, in the form of management or through administrative authority, enacts neoliberal policies that undermine the academic professional identity of full-time tenure track faculty.

Stephen Ball's account of his career in the UK, from welfarism to neoliberalism, accentuates not only the considerable change to one's academic professional identity but also alteration in personal identity. "I began working in a 'new' welfare university and now find myself living the life of a neoliberal academic, a neoliberal subject" (Ball, 2015, p. 825). Along the path of self-discovery through self-reflection and composing himself in a journal article, he asks, "What am I?" (p. 827); yet, soon after this question, he moves to his academic professional identity. His question is directed at his place: "[M]y home in the ivory tower is being flattened by neoliberal bulldozers to make way for a fast-fact higher education franchise in which all knowledge has a price" (p. 828). His conclusion is that his academic professional identity is one of process not a destination or place. He characterizes himself, Professor Stephen Ball, Distinguished Service Professor of Sociology of Education at UCL Institute of Education, and a Fellow of The British Academy, as a figure in a text, perhaps a fictional character who offers both himself and his readers just a glimpse of his academic professional identity. He is not there, wholly. If such an esteemed professional academic cannot locate his personal or professional self, then what might that mean for academics in general?

This ethos that combines or includes performativity (Ball, 2012b), competition (Ward, 2012), and surveillance (Gonzales et al., 2014; Lorenz, 2012) tends to undermine or erode the integrity of faculty academic professional identity. Within this social and cultural condition noted by Ball (2015), academic professional identity is fragmented and conceived of as a relative or contingent state (e.g., contingent upon economic worth). A community of scholars (Goodman, 1962), or even an academic tribe (Becher, 1989) at the disciplinary level, is unlikely within this environment, especially one that is competitive, and communal values are scarce in that instability and insecurity are the norm (Archer, 2008).

Stability within an Insecure Academic Professional Identity

Set against the decentering outcomes of neoliberalism that have turned universities into competitive and corporatized institutions, the collective values and beliefs of academics within universities—the institutional logic of the university or academic logic—continue to serve as stabilizers of academic professional identity. Full-time tenure track faculty face two main sets of expectations: First is role expectations that include expertise in a knowledge field and allegiance to disciplinary or subject area practices, as well as professional ethics and institutional commitments (e.g., teaching, research, service). Second, these faculty confront and are coerced to abide by institutional policies and directives that require them to participate in a self-monitoring and surveillance environment (Davies, 2005). These policies and directives often conflict with their role expectations as professionals and result, potentially, in feelings of insecurity and destabilization of their academic professional identity (Davies, 2005; Knights & Clarke, 2014). Identity theorists (Burke & Stets, 2009) call this nonverification of identity standards that can lead to identity alteration.

Yet, there are examples of full-time tenure track faculty at universities who do hold fast to their academic professional identities, and claim to value their professional work at their universities (Alvesson & Spicer, 2016). They maintain their identities as faculty in a number of ways (Humphreys & Brown, 2002). First, they dismiss negative identity demands as minor irritants that they can fulfill on top of their role demands. Second, they integrate these negative identity demands into their role demands by rationalization of the negative into positive or neutral demands (i.e., they are temporary). Third, they ignore or pretend to (and do not) fulfill the negative demands. And, fourth, they resist and protest against the negative demands. A biology associate professor at a public comprehensive university who sees that his university has developed into a more managerial-run institution, with little attention to the needs of full-time faculty, or even to the non-administrative employees of the institution, has rejected his responsibility for administrative work.

> [T]he overall long term strategy of the university is to have a top-down managerial system. . . . [F]ull time faculty numbers have not gone up. Funding has not gone up. In fact, it's gone down. Staff has not increased. There's only two things that have increased: number of students and number of administrators. . . . [I]f that's what they want to do, fine. Then do that. And then just take away the administrative burden I guess. For faculty, it's just getting us to do busy work. (associate professor, biology, comprehensive university)

To some extent, he has altered his role standard: Administrative work is "busy work" and not necessary for him to undertake in order for him to remain as an academic professional.

An anthropology professor at a research university indicates that her university not only "gives mixed messages" about work expectations, such as "raise money, serve community, public, [have] high teaching load" but also is clear that publications are "what counts." She resists and argues that her work as a collaborator with students and with the local community are worthy of recognition. Yet, she is unsupported by colleagues. A professor of environmental science at a research university claims that quality is not recognized in a performance-based system. "Quantity does not necessarily mean good work." He chooses to publish less frequently than expected and aims for quality in his publications. Another research university professor indicates that evaluations of faculty undermine academic professional identity: "[Evaluation for] merit does fragment and encourages fragmentation because of quantitative measures." A professor of psychology at a research university is able to tolerate the service component of his work with what he views as the most gratifying component of his work. With some humor, he acknowledges that committee work is part of his academic professional identity even though he prefers to underscore the researcher role of his identity.

> Probably what I enjoy most is the portion of research where I learn something new, which usually is in the sort of data analysis phase. And at this point in my career, that usually happens with

a graduate student showing me results of analyses. I would say that's the best part. There certainly was a personal decision that it's relatively easy to dodge that kind of work if that's what one wants to do, and a portion of the faculty do just that. And when I first got here, when I was an assistant professor, I didn't do that kind of work largely because I thought it inappropriate for a junior faculty member to do it. But once I had tenure, I suppose, somewhere along the line, I got socialized to be a good citizen. And so, when things were asked of me, I did it. The kind of work where, I guess faculty joke, "No good deed goes unpunished." If you do a good job on a particular committee, you'll be asked to be on another committee, and the only way to avoid that is to do a lousy job. (professor, psychology, research university)

This is not to say that all full-time tenure track faculty hold fast to their academic professional identities. They do alter their identities in order to fulfill and abide by negative identity demands. These faculty may assume roles as entrepreneurs and generate resources not only for their universities but also for themselves. They may also try out administrative roles such as department chairs and heads or associate deans. They may move permanently to other administrative positions and abandon their main faculty roles and identities. A professor of psychology at a comprehensive university occupies a role as assistant dean but teaches at a 50 percent faculty level and has given up research. With retirement in sight, he is no longer attached to his role as an academic professional even though he maintains faculty status.

It may be, however, that academic professional identities are more complex and indeed multiple than conceptualized in the critical literature on the undermining of faculty's identities. Faculty identities rely as well upon life histories, personal circumstances and experiences, and emotional states. An anthropology professor with leukemia devotes much of her time to writing poetry and teaching undergraduates, even though she works at a research university. Her recognition of her health condition and the threat of that to her life expectancy rearranged her priorities and her work, and altered her academic professional identity. In tenure and promotion processes, the personal and the professional can meet head-on. For an associate professor of sociology at a comprehensive university, the tenure and promotion process does damage, emotionally.

> I got challenges in the classroom, of course, but that's nothing in comparison to the brutal tenure system, tenure and promotion system. That's brutal. . . . And I think that ten years between assistant professor, entry level assistant professor, and full professor, I would not want to repeat that for anything in the world. And I actually don't know how I got through that. . . . [P]eople not recognizing your work; people putting your work down; people being very, very subjective. There's no objectivity to the tenure process. . . . [R]ight after I got tenure and associate professor, I got on that committee, the college committee . . . and I saw how subjective it is. And if it hadn't been for me, several people would not have gotten promoted and tenure because of pettiness that I witnessed on that committee because [faculty] don't like somebody; because they're not as good as them. . . . They can be very snarky. It is not an objective process. . . . These are people who are making value judgments. . . . [O]n my particular committee in my college . . . there was one economist, one geographer, and a couple of other people from totally different departments than mine who are judging my sociology work, and looking for numbers. "Where's your r-square. Where's your chi-square?" And you say, "Well I don't do that. I'm a qualitative sociologist." (associate professor, sociology, comprehensive university)

An associate professor of psychology at a research university judges promotion and tenure as entirely different from the sociology professor at the comprehensive university.

> So, tenure is sort of the gold ring at the end of that whole long process. You see, the thing about tenure is it's really a validation of your research from your peers, your department peers, your university peers, and also of course you get input from your outside research peers. And so, it is a big deal. So, I would say that would probably be the big sort of single moment there because, yeah, as an academic researcher, you built really towards that in many ways for a long time. And it is a validation from your peers, from your research peers. So, it's good. (associate professor, psychology, research university)

These two radically different perspectives indicate that views vary widely, based upon experiences and assumptions or values. For the sociology professor, the process was flawed, based upon a system of personal preferences, and her responses were decidedly in the form of a negative emotion. She judged the process based upon experiential merits. For the psychology professor, the tenure process conforms to the values of the academic profession—peer review—and, thus, it is by definition "good." He judges the process by its assumed qualities, not its experiential ones.

If these are conditions and situations that affect, reinforce, or repudiate identity—standard university processes of evaluation of faculty work—then the overlay of an externally imposed, market-oriented ideology that is applied and controlled by a managerial class (Gaffikin & Perry, 2009) constitutes an add-on to the traditional customary demands and stresses of the university. This add-on means that university structures and processes are no longer arranged solely or primarily for knowledge production and dissemination (Gaffikin & Perry, 2009). Thus, given the variation in faculty experiences and assumptions, the application of managerialism will have different effects upon individual faculty based upon their identities and the extent to which managerialism verifies or negates the identity of academic professionals. This may explain why entrepreneurialism has become a component of academic work and identity in the past three decades (Clark, 1998; Etzkowitz, 2001; Marginson & Considine, 2000; Wang, 2018).

As the profession moves toward values and behaviors aligned with market liberalism, the personal and the professional are seen to come into conflict (Gonzales et al., 2014). Within a neoliberal context, inner life becomes detached from occupational and professional roles (Davies, 2005; Sennett, 2006), and full-time tenure track faculty in universities are subject to the conflict between professional values and organizational demands. In Canadian universities, faculty indicate increased experiences of stress and anxiety, "feelings of being colonized and compelled into compliance" (Butterwork & Dawson, 2005, p. 59). The contemporary university promotes economic entrepreneurial activities accompanied by performance measures and fabricated actions by faculty to meet these measures (Butterwork & Dawson, 2005). That is one strategy—enact behaviors and create products that conform to expectations. Yet, deceptive compliance is not the only strategy. Responses to neoliberal and managerial pressures can also result in faculty development of positions or movements to oppose these pressures, with one prominent example provided by Canadian and U.S. scholars, referred to as "slow scholarship" (Mountz et al., 2015). Such positions are efforts to reattach the personal and the professional and, as well, to provide stability to an insecure professional position where organizational demands do not match professional role standards. They are actions that resist negative identity demands.

A more typical response from faculty to both the encroachment of neoliberalism into academic life and the threat to academic professional identity may be avoidance, a defensive posture to ignore demands that affect academic professional identity and which run counter to academics' idealized perception of their university's identity. In order to maintain self-esteem and the integrity of an academic professional identity, individuals view their university as legitimate; what nullifies the legitimacy of the university as an academic institution and reinforces it as another kind of institution (e.g., business) is ignored or rationalized as faulty (Humphreys & Brown, 2002). Elite narratives of universities—those promulgated by executive administrators and reinforced by mid-level administrators and subsequently by faculty—can counter the assumptions of academic professionals. The business model of the university at a comprehensive university in a Western state is one such narrative. A modern languages faculty member holds this narrative at bay by avoidance. Yet, this response does little to relieve anxiety.

> I remember that we had one provost, two deans. And now we have like four different provosts . . . a lot of specialization. . . . [We have] really fancy names that are empty meaning in my opinion. . . . [T]he business model that we are getting into . . . I prefer not to think about it. . . . Because I like to sleep; I need to sleep. . . . I don't even want to think about that. . . . I mean all of us (faculty), we have a lot of anxiety, but . . . I learned how to deal with that. (associate professor, modern languages, comprehensive university)

Although this faculty member notes that this condition of the university as a business is ever-present ("this can affect you on a daily basis"), she rationalizes her avoidance and her improvement in coping with the demands. As well, she gives herself an escape route. "I see myself dealing with this much better than six months ago . . . I'm not going to be here forever. . . . So, I am here doing my job and my duty."

The Ambiguity of the Academic Professional Identity of Full-Time Tenure Track Faculty

Whereas U.S. scholarly literature has focused upon full-time tenure track faculty in large part as a homogeneous professional group, affected in their work and identities by their institutional type (e.g., research university, teaching university, community college) and by their disciplinary affiliation, the institutionalization of neoliberal values and practices marks this conceptualization as out-of-date and not accurate. Western, including the UK, Canadian, Australian, and New Zealand, literature that addresses academic professionals offers a conceptualization of both management of the academic profession and the work and identity of faculty in a more critical, complex, and nuanced way. This body of literature does so by connecting academic professional identity to organizational identity, or university identity, within a neoliberal framework. Although there are various external pressures upon academics that could lead to identity alteration, most of these pressures in the United States (e.g., accountability) flow through the university.

The U.S. university's identity as a corporate body (Donoghue, 2008; Gould, 2003; Tuchman, 2009), in competition with other universities for students, resources, faculty, and status, in pursuit of nongovernmental resources (e.g., foundation grants, donations), and even its efforts to gain legitimacy in the public eye, has placed excessive demands upon full-time tenure track faculty. These demands include measurable performance in areas of teaching, research, and service, the adoption of new technologies in teaching, participation in university initiatives, the accommodation of more students, the pursuit of research grants, and reliance upon an authority structure where managerial interests are central and faculty authority is limited (usually and at best to a recommending role). Once full-time faculty in large numbers begin to accept such demands and accede to an authority structure dominated or regulated by a managerial class, then the faculty as a whole have been compromised, enmeshed in a system that has no excuses.

In the university managerial system, faculty monitor faculty, either through academic senate structures or department or school or college structures, and by means of department chairs, associate deans, deans, and senior faculty within a department. In that the U.S. university operates within the mythos of collegiality (Haviland, Alleman, & Allen, 2017), the assumption of faculty autonomy and the necessity for peer review, those who claim a faculty identity—senior faculty, department chairs, associate deans, deans—have a pass in their management of other academics. They claim they are faculty or researchers, and attach themselves to the identity that reveres or respects collegiality, autonomy, and peer review. Yet, in their managerial actions they do not possess an authentic academic professional identity, rather an administrative or managerial identity, couched in the rhetoric of academic professionalism.

In the claim that academic managers are faculty or researchers, the U.S. university is not seen to operate through new managerialism (Deem, 1998; Deem & Brehony, 2005), or with a dominant audit culture (Shore, 2008). It may also be a reason why critiques of the university's governance and management use the lens of academic capitalism (Cantwell & Kauppinen, 2014; Gonzales et al., 2014; Slaughter & Leslie, 1997; Slaughter & Rhoades, 2004; Walker, 2009), in order to elevate behaviors through attachment to knowledge. Steven Ward (2012) is among the few U.S. scholars to assert that managerialism in the United States is the same as in other countries and the same as in all industrial settings. Managerialism is a set of practices and ideas that "arrange[s] a group's activities in particular efficiency . . . and production-minded ways and as a broadly societal-level doxa that legitimates and expands the need for this particular type of control in practically all settings" (Ward, 2012, p. 48). In this way, the managed become the managers and the governed become self-governing who abide by the *doxa,* or self-evident truth, or belief, of the particular system of control. This is a form of embedded neoliberalism (Levin & Aliyeva, 2015) in the faculty ranks in U.S. higher education.

We have argued in this chapter that neoliberal logic has entered the U.S. university and led to at least a form of managerialism, not necessarily identical to Deem's *new managerialism,* but similar, and with full-time tenure track faculty akin to Ball's "new performance professional" (Ball, 2012b, p. 19). Thus, we offer a short response to our initial questions: "Are full-time tenure track faculty part of an integrated community of scholars?" Faculty are part of a community of scholars, but this community is disintegrating and losing cohesiveness. "Are they members of a fragmented professional culture?" Full-time faculty are members of an ambiguous or divided culture. With the adoption of neoliberal logic by the university, faculty encounter polarized value systems that direct the profession toward fragmentation. "Do they embrace nonacademic values of the marketplace or do they reject and oppose them?" Full-time tenure track faculty are becoming used to those nonacademic values that support academic endeavors, but they continue to perceive these as an external demand, primarily, one that is an addition rather than a substitute for academic values. "Are they independent actors or are they neoliberal subjects; or, are there variations and gradations in academic professional identity for full-time university faculty?" Full-time tenure track faculty have become players in, reproducers, and adaptors of neoliberalism and corporate culture in the U.S. university. They are managed (by deans, department chairs, other faculty, and themselves) and they manage other faculty (e.g., non-tenure track faculty) and themselves in a form of self-surveillance. Finally, does neoliberal ideology in the form of new managerialism disturb or distort academic professional identity? Full-time tenure track faculty have little ability to oppose the values of neoliberalism as practiced in their university; those who do oppose or resist, including their repudiation of their colleagues or their administrators, are those who endeavor to verify their academic professional identity and differentiate themselves from those who have accepted the neoliberal or corporate university. What both parties—non-opposers and resisters of neoliberal ideology—do share is coexistence or collaboration with two institutional logics: neoliberal logic and academic logic. For some, neoliberal logic exists in a separate sphere in the university organization, to be ignored if possible; to be resisted if a threat to academic professional identity. For others, neoliberal logic is integrated with academic logic in a collaborative effort to both sustain academic professional identity and to verify that identity.

Faculty responses to neoliberal logic (e.g., nonopposition, opposition, resistance) vary for members of another faculty population: non-tenure track (NTT) faculty. In the following chapter, we continue to analyze the views of both full-time and part-time NTT faculty. We argue that NTT faculty have less ability than tenure track faculty to oppose neoliberalism and that they experience management and micromanagement not only from academic managers but also from tenure track faculty. NTT faculty are protected from exploitation by their tenure line colleagues who do not demand their participation in decision making and institutional service. However, this protection functions as a form of exclusion that marginalizes NTT faculty. This marginalization has different effects on full-time and part-time NTT faculty. NTT faculty perceive tenure track faculty as their superiors and department chairs as their supervisors. Thus, their ways to understand their role in their university (and their organizational and professional identity) and their ways to cope with management differ from those of tenure track faculty. These understandings and coping mechanisms as well as their relationships with those who manage them are the subject of the following chapter.

Chapter 2

Non-Tenure Track Faculty

Professionals with Commitment and Self-Worth in an Exploitative Environment

As argued previously, neoliberal logic, through its arm of managerialism, touches all members of the academic profession and affects their workplace context. We focus here on the notorious managerial treatment of non-tenure track (NTT) faculty. NTT faculty are managed more overtly than tenure track faculty; and, they are not treated as equals by their tenure track colleagues. Generally, their academic professional identity is put into question, ignored, or dismissed by university members. NTT faculty accept, at least tacitly, that they occupy managed positions within the university. Nonetheless, they conceptualize themselves as professionals, and they seek to carry out their work accordingly—with autonomy and personal responsibility. Their reactions in the face of managerial behaviors differ depending upon their employment status, as full-time or part-time NTT faculty. The focus of this chapter, then, is upon the management of NTT faculty and their reactions to managerialism, including the different reactions dependent upon NTT full-time or part-time status.

Non-tenure track faculty have become a constant in the higher education landscape (Gappa, 2000; Schuster & Finkelstein, 2006). The increase of these positions is the result primarily of economic measures rather than academic strategies that universities have undertaken to respond to external neoliberal pressures (Levin, Shaker, & Wagoner, 2011). Conditions such as the decline in government support, loss of public confidence, the rise of new technologies, changes in retirement policies, competition among institutions to attract students, and a general restructuring of workplaces to increase nontraditional workers have pushed colleges and universities toward the normalization of faculty positions off the tenure track (Baldwin & Chronister, 2001). In addition, external demands for higher education institutions to reduce costs, control tuition and fees, increase undergraduate education, and increase faculty accountability have favored the increase of non-tenure track faculty positions in all higher education institutions in the United States (Baldwin & Chronister, 2001; Levin et al., 2011). As a consequence, faculty in non-tenure track positions are considered as a solution to an economic problem for universities rather than as providers of professional expertise for their organization (Kezar & Sam, 2011; López Damián, 2017).

In this state of affairs, the argument of this chapter is twofold. First, the characteristics of contingent positions at universities have negative consequences for the treatment of this faculty group (Levin et al., 2011): Non-tenure track faculty defray part of the cost of education. They use their own personal resources to overcome organizational barriers and carry out their work at universities despite their treatment as labor. By doing this, they become the ideal worker in the (market-oriented, cost-effective) neoliberal university. They cope with managerialism, and through their actions they reinforce, albeit inadvertently, neoliberal logic.

Second, managerial practices for non-tenure track faculty are guided by a complex scholarly and practitioner understanding of them as both part of a professional group who has specific knowledge and skills as well as a labor force that needs to be controlled tightly and bound loosely. Management of full-time non-tenure track faculty and micromanagement of part-time non-tenure track faculty have become normalized. Non-tenure track faculty do not share the same status, respect, and legitimacy in the organization as their tenure track counterparts. However, they are expected to perform their work by subscribing to professional values. Their professional identity suffers as a result of this dualism of their treatment and what is expected from them. Their identity is ambiguous, fragmented, and insecure (Levin et al., 2011; Levin & Montero Hernandez, 2014); it is not anchored (Sennett, 2006) in their university organization. Yet, and regardless of organizational obstacles, non-tenure track faculty adhere to professional values of academics and educators (López Damián, 2017). There are, however, some distinctions between the behaviors of part-time and full-time NTT faculty; for example, part-timers' coping strategies protect them better than those of full-time NTT faculty.

In this chapter, we do not analyze the workforce restructuring practices of universities and their replacement of tenure track faculty positions with non-tenure track (part-time and full-time) faculty positions: These practices have been studied and documented by other scholars elsewhere (for example, Rhoades [1998] identified six different strategies for the substitution of full-time tenure track positions with part-time positions that ranged from layoffs to the restructuring of curriculum). Rather, the purpose of this chapter is to explain the actual practices employed for the management of non-tenure track faculty on the job, the role of their colleagues as organizational members who manage non-tenure track faculty, and the role of non-tenure track faculty as professionals who manage themselves. That is, we ask, "What does managerialism look like for non-tenure track faculty?" and "What is non-tenure track faculty's role in the corporate or neoliberal university?" We answer these questions through the integration of literature on the conditions of non-tenure track faculty work, interviews carried out with more than one hundred (part-time and full-time) non-tenure track faculty and department chairs at research and comprehensive public universities in seven states in the United States (for more information about the data, refer to the Appendix), and data from national surveys and reports.

The Context

The organization of labor in the United States is guided by principles that weaken the relationship between individuals and institutions and reduce the value of work (Sennett, 2006). Sennett identifies three current challenges that individuals face due to the *culture of the new capitalism* and the organization of labor. First, institutions have decreased the time of employment for various groups. Short-term work relationships with an organization—in contrast to career-like relationships—have changed the life-narrative of individuals, who may see their sense of self altered without a clear organizational anchor. Second, the definitions and demands of talent necessary in institutions have changed. The ideal of craftsmanship (the specialization of performing one task or function well for long periods of time) has been replaced by an idea of meritocracy that values individuals' ability to perform many tasks for short periods of time. Third, the place of individuals in an organization is unclear. The ideal woman or man in the culture of new capitalism is the one who is self-oriented to short-term relationships with organizations in which her or his voice is not heard and in which commitment to the organizations is not valued. As a consequence, individuals have short-term relationships with organizations that do not value specialization (craftsmanship) and that do not promote organizational loyalty. Sennett's description of the culture of new capitalism applies to higher education institutions (Levin et al., 2011).

Traditionally, universities have been conceptualized as organizations in which intentions (e.g., planning, rules, hard structures) are not a strong guide for action. Loose coupling (Weick, 1976) in universities was considered to foster and reinforce the traditional values of academic work (e.g., autonomy, collaboration, and collective governance [Deem, 2004]). However, more recent views of the university—based on current organization of work and economic trends—have highlighted the need to make universities more "tightly organized" (Deem, 2004, p. 120). This new organization of work has as a major purpose to increase universities' efficiency and goal achievement (such as those enunciated in strategic plans and accreditation self-reports). Thus, recent policies, with embedded managerial ideologies for university goals, have sought to increase the control of administrators over organizational members and over academic work (Ball, 2012a, 2012b; Ward, 2012).

A managerial view of faculty includes measurement of productivity, guidelines, and regulations for accountability, and the shift in control of academic work from academics to managers (Deem, 2004; Tuchman, 2009). Organizational actions of managers are neither haphazard nor without connection to strategy; they are rationalized as efficient and transparent. Labor practices have implications for the work of all faculty—both non-tenured and tenured: short-term productivity pressures for faculty work have increased and additional administrative duties for full-time tenure track faculty are expected (Cannizzo, 2018). Academics have become managed professionals with limited self-government for full-time faculty and marginal support for part-time non-tenure track faculty within their organization (Levin et al., 2011; Rhoades, 1998; Ward, 2012).

The growth of faculty in non-tenure track positions is considered one of the most important indicators that the values of higher education institutions and academic work have been shaped through the adoption of principles of hypercapitalism, neoliberalism, and managerialism (Levin et al., 2011; Slaughter & Rhoades, 2004). Rhoades (1998) argues that the increase of these positions signals that the prestige of the academic profession has decreased at state public universities and that faculty have become managed professionals with less control over their work than in previous decades. More recently, Finkelstein, Martin Conley, and Schuster (2016) have termed this growth of non-tenure track faculty and the diminution of tenure track faculty as *the radical redistribution of academic appointments.*

Within this reshaped or redistributed profession, non-tenure track faculty are members of the academic profession who face the three challenges identified by Sennett (2006) and, as a consequence, are at the bottom rung of the faculty status ladder. They are treated qualitatively differently than tenure track and tenured faculty. However, in spite of their diminutive position, inadequate treatment by their organizations, and the exploitative organizational environment, non-tenure track faculty express high levels of commitment to their job (López Damián, 2017). Yet, it is precisely because of these circumstances that they separate their self-worth from their organizational self as they seek anchors for the usefulness* of their work.

Characteristics and Types of Non-tenure Track Faculty

Part-time faculty, adjunct faculty, full-time non-tenure track faculty, lecturers, visiting scholars, and teaching assistants are all part of the non-tenure track faculty group (Baldwin & Chronister, 2001; Thedwall, 2008). This faculty body includes individuals whose main relationship with the university is their professional contract (i.e., part-time faculty, adjunct faculty, full-time non-tenure track faculty, lecturers) as well as individuals who study and teach on a part-time basis in their campus (i.e., teaching assistants, graduate employees). Although increasing numbers of graduate students (teaching assistants) have been responsible for the teaching of undergraduate courses, formally, they are not considered part of the faculty (JBL Associates Inc., 2008). Furthermore, graduate employees have characteristics that are not comparable to other groups of non-tenure track faculty, such as their average age, their academic background, and their professional experience. To avoid a faulty or unequal comparison, we have excluded them from the analysis of non-tenure track faculty, even though we recognize their role as academic professionals. Instead, we focus on the analysis of two subgroups of non-tenure track faculty: part-time and full-time non-tenure track faculty.

The number of individuals in the non-tenure track faculty group is growing to the degree that NTT faculty comprise almost half the faculty

---

*We use Sennett's (2006) definition of usefulness as the individual's view that their work contributes to what matters, and, thus, what has value.

population at universities in the United States, and on some campuses they have become the majority of faculty—for example, figures of the California State University indicate that in 2017, 62 percent of the faculty in the system were off the tenure track (The California State University, 2019). The increasing number of non-tenure track positions has been documented widely. According to figures of the National Center of Education Statistics [NCES], non-tenure track faculty numbers increased 93 percent from 1975 to 1995, and part-time faculty increased 103 percent in the same period of time (Benjamin, 2003; Lechuga, 2006). Between 1993 and 2003, the majority of new full-time faculty were hired as non-tenure (Shaker, 2008). In the decades from Fall 1995 to Fall 2015, the number of part-time faculty at degree-granting postsecondary institutions increased by 95 percent, while the number of full-time faculty increased by 47 percent (NCES, 2016). In 2015, 48 percent of the 1.6 million faculty in postsecondary institutions were hired on a part-time basis. That is, the trend for new hirings have favored non-tenure track positions over tenured and tenure track positions as well as part-time over full-time positions (American Federation of Teachers, 2009).

Non-tenure track faculty are not only numerous but also complex in their employment contracts, professional backgrounds, and organizational functions. The heterogeneity of non-tenure track faculty suggests that the faculty in this group are more complex professionally than tenure track faculty, who are themselves a diverse group (Gappa, Leslie & Trice, 2007; Schuster & Finkelstein, 2006). Individuals in non-tenure track positions are heterogeneous in their academic background, professional background, type of contract, and motivations for seeking the position, as well as in their ethnicity and race (Antony & Hayden, 2011; Baldwin & Chronister, 2001; Gappa & Leslie, 1993; Thedwall, 2008). However, faculty in non-tenure track positions share two characteristics based upon their employment contracts: They are hired on a short-term basis (term by term, year by year, or a maximum of three-year appointments) and they have fewer organizational rights and less support than tenured and tenure track faculty (Gappa & Leslie, 1993; Gappa et al., 2007; Kezar, 2012; Kezar & Sam, 2011). Scholars recognize that, clearly, a two-class faculty system has emerged in the United States: non-tenure track faculty largely occupy an instructionally centered position and always are accorded lower status in comparison to tenured and tenure track faculty (Baldwin & Chronister, 2001; Gappa, 2000; Kezar & Sam, 2011; Levin et al., 2011; Ochoa, 2011; Shaker, 2008).

Non-tenure track faculty are defined by their universities by their economic worth: that is, how much money the institution saves with their appointment (Bousquet, 2008; Cross & Goldenberg, 2009). Arguably, the increased reliance on these positions is a measure made consistent with market-oriented and managerial practices. The use of non-tenure track faculty has been characterized as a budget solver (Umbach, 2007) and a cost-effective measure (Cross & Goldenberg, 2009; Lefebvre, 2008). Rationalized by their universities as economic entities, non-tenure track faculty have no job security, have few or no job benefits (e.g., health insurance), depend on measures for their reappointment that resemble customer satisfaction, have little institutional support for the performance of their work, and have limited access to physical spaces, institutional activities, and departmental decision making (Dobbie & Ian, 2008; Gappa & Leslie, 1993; Levin et al., 2011). That is, full-time and part-time non-tenure track faculty have inferior working conditions and rights compared to their tenure track counterparts.

Notwithstanding the similarities among non-tenure track faculty groups, there are essential differences between part-time and full-time non-tenure track faculty. On the one hand, the number of full-time non-tenure track faculty is considerably lower than the number of part-time faculty, which is the largest single category in the academic workforce (American Association of University Professors [AAUP], 2017). On the other hand, each group faces unique challenges and opportunities (Levin et al., 2011; Thedwall, 2008). For example, full-timers receive significantly more benefits and support from departments than part-timers (Townsend, 2003). The most important difference between non-tenure track faculty subgroups relates to universities' work expectations. Full-time non-tenure track faculty are hired, in the main, on an annual basis, with limited renewable appointments (between one and three years), and are expected to perform research and/or teaching and little or no service (Thedwall, 2008). Full-time non-tenure track faculty are expected to decrease the overall workload of tenure track faculty and enable them to participate in research, service, and campus life (Gappa et al., 2007). Finally, full-time non-tenure track faculty receive compensation that, although lower than that of tenure track faculty, is higher proportionally than that of part-time faculty (Kezar & Sam, 2011).

In contrast to these expectations for and characteristics of full-time non-tenure track faculty, part-time non-tenure track faculty are hired on a term by term basis, primarily to teach. However, part-timers are more likely to have consecutive appointments at a single university for longer periods of time than full-time non-tenure track faculty. The American Federation of Teachers of Higher Education in its 2010 survey of part-time faculty found that the majority of respondents (73%) worked for more than six years in one institution and that more than one-third (41%) worked eleven years or more at the same campus. This figure, however, is not to be confused with part-timers' job security, given that their contracts can be discontinued at any time. Usually, part-time faculty are not expected to participate in research, service, or departmental activities; their primary activity is teaching (Kezar, 2012), and only in a few cases are office hours and training indicated as part of their responsibilities (Levin et al., 2011). Overall, compensation, work expectations, and participation expectations have different consequences for these two groups of contingent faculty. Accordingly, in the following sections we discuss, separately, the consequences of market-oriented and managerial practices in higher education for both of these groups.

Part-time Faculty as Neoliberal Workers: Exploited and Engaged

It seems counterintuitive that organizations that seek the generation and distribution of knowledge, that traditionally have valued collegiality, and that are considered at the center of social mobility, are also responsible for exploitation. However, universities in the United States can be accused of the use of exploitative practices against part-time faculty (Bousquet, 2008; Cross & Goldenberg, 2009). Universities model business corporations in the way they treat non-tenure track faculty (Bousquet, 2008), and these practices are connected in the scholarly literature to the adoption of neoliberal practices (Levin et al., 2011; Ward, 2012). Although tied generally to economic rationales, neoliberal practices are also imbued with ethical issues (Ball, 2012), and one of these is the treatment by institutions of vulnerable populations.

The exploitation of part-time faculty in public universities in the United States has been well documented by national surveys (e.g., AFT Higher Education, 2010; The Coalition on the Academic Workforce [CAW], 2012), empirical research (e.g., Benjamin, 2002), and scholarly articles (e.g., Goldstene, 2012). For example, these sources indicate that part-time faculty members' income per hour is 64 percent less than that of full-time faculty (Monks, 2007), and that "the average pay from a single institution for part-time faculty teaching on a per section basis [$7,066 in 2016, according to the same AAUP report] is well below the federal poverty line of $16,240 for a family of two" (AAUP, 2017, p. 9). Given that approximately 45 percent of faculty are hired on a part-time basis in public comprehensive universities in the United States, the magnitude of this problem is a significant one for U.S. higher education.

The inferior compensation of part-time faculty relative to that of full-time faculty is justified in that the latter perform only teaching, while full-time faculty are also responsible for research and service (Benjamin, 2002). The rationale of this argument is that part-time faculty are paid less because they work less than full-time faculty. However, part-time faculty do not receive salaries that cover the full extent of their formal responsibilities. For example, part-time faculty, regularly paid by the hour (Monks, 2007), are not paid to conduct office hours, grade student work, prepare syllabi, meet with other faculty who teach similar classes, or respond to e-mails or texts from students (CAW, 2012). However, universities do expect them to carry out these activities. One prominent argument is that because part-time faculty are not paid to perform these activities, they neglect to perform them (Benjamin, 2002) and that the quality of teaching and learning in universities decreases as a result of increases in part-timers (Baldwin & Wawrzynski, 2011). However, there is no evidence that this is the case.

Research based on U.S. data sources found that part-time faculty express passion, love, and appreciation for their work (AFT Higher Education, 2010; López Damián, 2017; Meixner, Kruck, & Madden, 2010; Thirolf, 2013). Such research contradicts numerous assumptions about part-time faculty, and extends rationales for the treatment of part-time faculty in universities beyond economics. For the majority of part-time faculty, teaching is their primary professional role (Antony & Valadez, 2002; Gappa, 2000) to which they dedicate their time and effort, and to which they express a long-term commitment (CAW, 2012; López Damián, 2017). That is, the claim that there is a direct relationship between poor job circumstances and part-time faculty members' underperformance and lack of work engagement does not hold up in all or even a majority of cases (López Damián, 2017). A part-time faculty member in a public comprehensive university pointed to the incongruity between her work and the payment she receives for it, which does not prevent her from efforts to undertake meaningful work.

> Adjunct faculty do not do this job for the money. It is horribly paid. If you would look at the number of hours I put into class preparation and teaching, and break that down by salary and hourly weight, I make less than minimum wage in the amount of time that I put in. And I do that on my own; nobody's telling

> me to do that. I do it because I care. (part-time faculty, health sciences, comprehensive university)

This faculty member's explanation voices a common concern among her colleagues, who not only perform the activities they are expected to perform but also are conscious of the limitations of their remuneration. Yet, they perform their activities due to a personal interest in undertaking this particular job.

> This is quite a luxury to be able to do this work. . . . But, I also get to work at a state university, which I love: the environment [and] the students. I get to do what I love; I get to do what I am passionate about. . . . I basically do it for free. It is a lot of volunteer work. . . . And the compensation is terrible, just terrible. My annual salary [here] was like my bonus in my last job. Yes . . . it is terrible. (part-time faculty, nursing, comprehensive university)

Part-time faculty express positive emotions about their work. However, personal satisfaction with their work is what they receive instead of a fair payment, not in addition to fair payment (Donoghue, 2008).

The salary scheme used to pay part-time faculty work does not match the actual time that they use for this activity. Universities in the United States have started to change this scheme. For example, in California, public comprehensive universities' compensation includes part-time faculty's office hours. But the mismatch between part-time faculty's work and salary continues as a problem nationally that has yet to be addressed. In other words, strategies for an equitable salary are limited, informal, and, at most universities, part-time faculty are underpaid. Furthermore, studies and surveys of part-time faculty members' perceptions of their work have found that although the majority of part-time faculty express high levels of satisfaction with their work (between 60% and 80%, depending on the study), they express low levels of satisfaction with their work circumstances (Antony & Hayden, 2011; Antony & Valadez, 2002; Hoyt, 2011).

Low compensation is only part of the problem: less than ideal work circumstances are a constant in part-time faculty members' experiences. Part-time faculty members lack the resources they need to carry out their work; they face limited support from their colleagues and staff; and, they receive limited or no recognition for the quality of their work (Meixner et al., 2010). In the view of the majority of higher education scholars, these circumstances limit part-time faculty performance and hinder their ability to serve students (Benjamin, 2003; Bettinger & Long, 2004; Ehrenberg & Zhang, 2005; Umbach, 2007).

Regardless of the negative work circumstances that part-time faculty face on a daily basis, they perform their formal and informal expected work activities. Part-time faculty are highly skilled professionals—a large number of them (up to 87%) have graduate or professional degrees (CAW, 2012)—with training in their discipline and motivation to perform their job. That is, they act following principles of a professional work ethic and values associated with faculty work (López Damián, 2017). These characteristics do not play in their favor when they face austere work circumstances. Quite the opposite: engagement with their work, professional ethics, and appreciation for their professional activities make part-time faculty more vulnerable to the exploitative practices of a managerial, corporate university.

Part-time faculty use their own resources (and sometimes family resources) to solve problems in the university or to provide materials that the campus does not have or provide to them. Limited state funds have pushed public universities in the United States to reduce budgets (Archibald & Feldman, 2011) and become more cost-efficient. Indeed, for universities, the bulk of their funding is used to pay salaries and wages (Goldstein, 2005), while other aspects such as furniture, equipment, and office supplies are secondary and deferred expenditures. As a consequence, from computers to furniture and to printer paper, part-time faculty contribute to the higher education enterprise with much more than their work, according to their narratives of work experience.

> You do a lot of things at home: You use your own cartridges for the ink in your printer; you use your own office resources, and that gets can get expensive. (part-time faculty, human development, comprehensive university)

> My computer, that they gave me, is from two thousand eight and it doesn't have software that is up to date, like my students with their computers. . . . In Spring twenty fifteen, I was promised a new laptop. . . . Finally, in September, it was like, "No, you are not getting any [computer]". . . . Eventually, my father-in-law was nice enough to buy me a new computer. (part-time faculty, English, comprehensive university)

Congruent with neoliberal values, individuals are left on their own (Ball, 2012a, 2012b). Universities as organizations do not support part-time faculty's work; individuals are expected to be responsible for their own labor and its costs. Repeatedly, part-time faculty are in the situation in which they need to use their own resources to perform their job.

Although part-time faculty indicate that their universities do not provide them with the basic materials for them to perform their work, this circumstance (limited support, lack of resources for them) has been normalized to the extent that it is accepted by part-time faculty themselves. Moreover, part-time faculty perceive that their lack of dependence upon the university to solve their basic work needs is a positive personal trait and shows their commitment and professionalism. "I need access to a computer which I just use my personal laptop. . . . I don't need a whole lot actually. . . . Textbooks, I typically will contact the publisher and ask for a desk copy. . . . I am pretty self-sufficient" (part-time faculty, psychology, comprehensive university). Although there is a sense of pride for part-time faculty who are able to be self-sufficient and not depend on the university in their job performance, there is a main and underlying feature that plays a role in part-time faculty's problem-solving attitude: their lack of job security.

With term-by-term appointments, part-time faculty have little or no job security. Fewer than 10 percent of the part-time faculty at universities who responded to the CAW survey (2012) indicated they had some degree of job security or seniority rights. Although there are part-time faculty who may have three-year contracts within a given university (for example, those who have three consecutive yearly contracts in a California State University system are offered a three-year contract), once these contracts end, universities are not obliged to rehire the faculty member. The lack of job security places part-time faculty in a position of disadvantage and forces them to perform activities that are necessary for them to carry out their work but that are beyond their job description. The tenuous nature of their employment sets up this population for further exploitation. A part-time faculty member articulated a prominent example of how his attempt to make himself valuable to his department resulted in a benefit for all but not as much for him.

> For years after the person who basically showed to me how to do these labs left, I started doing the lab setup. . . . I come in and I set up the rock for trace and I set up the labs for each given week whatever lab is being taught. And I was basically doing it for free because, initially, when I was going quarter to

quarter and even on the annual basis [contract], I could have been replaced at any time. So, I wanted to make myself valuable. So, I started doing that. . . . [T]here is no lab technician for our department. So [the department chair] said: "We'll see if we can get you paid for this," [and] the union rep didn't like it. But then, when the department chair said, "Hey, we'd like to pay [Rick] for setting up the labs," she was told that everybody gets paid for lab set up and take down. If you're teaching a lab that's incorporated into the pay scale for being a lab instructor. So, I'm saying, "Does that mean that since I've been doing all the labs set up that everybody else is being overpaid?" (part-time faculty, geology, comprehensive university)

This part-time faculty member's experience is a representative example of a situation common to numerous part-time faculty: They do as much as they can for their department in order to make themselves valuable, needed, and competitive, thus, less disposable. This pressure to keep their job is perceived by part-time faculty as a reducer of collegiality: "The entire university system is not set up for team work; it's [set up for] individual accomplishment. . . . It's not how are we going to work together, because people don't care what other people are doing" (part-time faculty, communications, comprehensive university). Individuality becomes a value that guides their work, and part-time faculty see themselves competing with one another. They become "neo-liberal professionals" (Ball, 2003), emblematic employees in a neoliberal regime. They experience professional life as an enterprise of the self and are pushed to "embrace self-care and maximization of self-interest" (Layton, 2014, p. 172) in their professional life.

Limited job security, austere organizational resources, a high degree of work engagement (López Damián, 2017), and a higher than deserved degree of organizational loyalty constitute the ideal recipe for the exploitation of part-time faculty. The confluence of these circumstances is a near-perfect situation for part-time faculty to become neoliberal subjects (Ball, 2003). Part-time faculty's work engagement, that is, their appreciation for their job, positive attitudes toward their professional activities, and their own perception of significance of their work at a given university, motivates them to perform their job regardless of organizational limitations and obstacles (López Damián, 2017). This occurs in conjunction with the possibility of them losing their connection with the job they love (López Damián, 2017).

The institutional treatment in higher education of part-time faculty reflects a labor force that is abused both in remuneration and working conditions (Anderson, 2007). This situation is common internationally, as well. In Australia, the UK, and Canada, the refrain is the same: Part-time faculty are aligned with marketplace needs and demands (Levin et al., 2011). They are instruments of economic efficiency and neoliberal subjects par excellence (Ball, 2003). However, economic efficiency means that the financing of higher education has changed from reliance upon public sources to private sources. These private sources are, to some degree, part-time faculty themselves. Efficiency as a value associated with higher education has another consequence for part-time faculty: universities have developed strategies to control their work and make them accountable for students' learning. In addition to limited support for and exploitation of part-time faculty, higher education institutions' structures are organized to try to control and regulate (manage) part-time faculty's work.

The Normalization of Micromanagement of Part-Time Faculty

Part-time faculty positions are hybrids that combine a profession and an occupation. Although as argued in the Introduction and chapter 1, all university faculty are in one way or another *managed professionals* (Rhoades, 1998), faculty have specialized knowledge and abide by self-regulations such as peer review and professional codes of ethics and standards of practice. Yet, scholars in the United States have noted the decline over the past two decades of faculty self-governance (Finkelstein et al., 2016; Kezar & Sam, 2011; Schuster & Finkelstein, 2006), with diminution in control over their profession. This loss is attributed to a rise in managerial influence and control (Scharff, 2015, Ward, 2012). In advanced states of managerialism, everyone is expected to manage and to be managed (Kok, Douglas, McClelland, & Bryde, 2010; Locke & Bennion, 2011; Winter, 2009). Because part-time faculty are at the bottom of the faculty ladder, the pressures of managerialism are potentially more deleterious to their employment status than for other faculty members (Kezar & Sam, 2011).

Part-time faculty members' work, their use of resources, the content of their classes, and the judgment of their work are not determined by themselves, as is expected from professionals. Part-timers are not accountable to their peers, as are professionals, but rather to managers, as their employers

(Deem, 2004; Rhoades 1998). Although part-time faculty have some degree of control (autonomy) over their work in courses (e.g., teaching approaches), other elements of their work (e.g., scheduling) are determined by policy, rules, and institutional requirements of their universities, without their participation in these. Compounding and indeed reinforcing their lack of a professional identity as academics, the absence of job security for part-timers endangers their limited autonomy and academic freedom (Bradley, 2004; Ehrenberg & Zhang, 2005; Rhoades, 2008).

Changes in the value of craftsmanship (Sennett, 2006) for the academic profession take a specific form. Part-time faculty are pushed to serve a variety of teaching needs rather than rely upon their expertise for specialized courses. Faculty as professionals have specialized knowledge that corresponds to a discipline or field. In addition, within that field, there are subfields of specialization that may become a given faculty member's expertise. For part-timers, specialization is not just not valued but even counterproductive. New part-time faculty are better positioned in a university if they avoid overspecialization so that they can leave the door open to teach whatever course that is offered to them. "They [universities] offer whatever is available" (part-time faculty, psychology, comprehensive university). Thus, part-timers need to be flexible labor.

Reduction in the value of craftsmanship means that part-time faculty must adapt to the acceptance of assigned courses and the organization and preparation of curriculum on short notice. Over time, if part-time faculty survive the standards of teaching evaluations, their limited inclusion in the departmental business, and constant shifting of the scheduling of classes, they may obtain some regularity in their teaching. "Psych 110, it's Reasoning and Problem Solving, and Psych 331, it's Psychology of Personality. And I always teach those two classes" (part-time faculty, psychology, comprehensive university). However, even those part-time faculty who have an entitlement (i.e., the right to be hired the following year based upon their credits for teaching) and have a condition of regularity in their course assignments, or even the probability of reappointment, nonetheless have little control over the structure of their work.

> That never changed. I'd always had six units, but how those six units took shape, I did not know. I didn't know if it was three years of classes, three years of supervision, six units of classes, or five classes and one supervision. . . . I didn't know which class it was at . . . or where I would supervise that I didn't know. (part-time faculty, education, comprehensive university)

Part-time faculty have little control over their workload and what comprises their teaching. Even in cases where job security is not a problem, that is, when they know that their work relationship with their university will continue, their work within the university is uncertain. Ultimately, they are insecure.

The management of part-time faculty is in the hands of the administrators, primarily the academic managers—department chairs, department heads, and program coordinators. In organizations, "[t]he role of managers is to determine ways to take parts of the skilled labor and develop automated processes to do similar or related work more cost-effectively" (Kezar & Sam, 2011, p. 27). Academic managers are no different with respect to part-time faculty than are managers of business or industry: They are determiners of whether a particular part-time faculty member is performing their job effectively and if they are to be retained.

Department chairs, or heads, are the primary source of communications with part-timers. In public universities, department chairs can decide whether or not to hire and rehire part-timers, and they are responsible for part-time faculty members' evaluation.

> Officially, I am empowered to offer them work. . . . I mean, right now, there is money to fulfill our obligations to the union contracts, and to fulfill our obligation to the individual part-time faculty members, but, if there wasn't [money], for some reason, then . . . there would be less work to be offered, So, I am kind of bound by the budget and, then, by the contract. (department chair, comparative literature, comprehensive university)

Accordingly, part-time faculty indicate that their primary personal relationship in the department is with the department chair, and department chairs perceive that non-tenure track faculty treat them as if they were "the boss." Indeed, one part-time faculty remarked that department chairs have too much power over non-tenure track faculty.

> They have so much authority; it's unbelievable. There was somebody with thirty-five years in [this university]. He was a really nice man, and they just fired him. I think he got into some friction with the chair but that wasn't an excuse. (part-time faculty, history, comprehensive university)

Department chairs or heads' values and the cultural practices of the department are the critical elements for the inclusion or exclusion of contingent faculty in departmental activities, the academic community, and campus life (Gappa, 2000; Waltman, Bergom, Hollenshead, Miller, & August, 2012).

> We do have monthly part-time faculty meetings. Not every department on campus has these regular meetings for part-time faculty. So, within our department that kind of keeps us in the loop as to policy changes at the university or if something is coming up that we should be aware of. Or, [if] they're interviewing a new faculty member or a dean, they'll share that information to try to get us to provide input and feedback on that process. (part-time faculty, biology, comprehensive university)

Part-timers who are included in their department's activities are conscious that the way in which they are involved is not the norm of the university and that participation depends on their department chair's personal interest in treating part-timers as members of the department.

> I have to say that our department chair is very . . . good about keeping the lecturers, the part-timers, informed. . . . He said, "When I came here, I was a lecturer, I understand." . . . [This is] his personal attempt; [it] is something that is important to him, and he is making the move on his own. He is not getting a course release for it. Nobody is telling him to do it; [it] is just something that he feels is important to do. (part-time faculty, English, comprehensive university)

Department chairs' managerial discretion means that the experiences of part-time faculty vary not only across universities but also within one university, with some part-timers attaining almost full membership in their departments, while in other departments part-time faculty are kept to the margins. Department chairs or heads are not the only department members who manage part-timers.

There is a complex hierarchy in departments, primarily in those departments in which there is a large number of part-time faculty in charge of similar or consecutive courses (e.g., general education courses, introductory courses). Part-time faculty themselves indicate that tenure track faculty are managerial figures for part-timers. In class-laboratory courses, in the California State University system campuses, tenured faculty members (referred to as lead faculty) are responsible for the coordination of a course, and several part-time faculty teach its associated laboratory sections. "You have a lead faculty that kind of coordinates the syllabi, how the program is going to go, and, then, communicates with any adjunct faculty or part-time faculty" (part-time faculty, nursing, comprehensive university). In the sciences, from which the organization of classes into laboratories and lectures originates, the "laboratory" section of the class involves actual laboratory work. In other courses, such as communications, laboratory means a "hands on" section of the course. In these class-laboratory courses, lead faculty are compensated for more credits (1.7) for teaching the class section in comparison to part-time faculty's compensation (1.3 credits) for teaching the laboratory. This compensation does not match the amount of time they use to teach, plan, or evaluate their section. The organization and compensation structure of these class-laboratories signal that part-time faculty are seen as subaltern to tenure track faculty and that their work is secondary to that of lead faculty. Another central element of this course-laboratory structure is that the lead faculty member has periodical meetings with part-time faculty.

> It [the meeting] was "a few of us get together," those of us who are part-time with the professor whose class that is and the department chair. It was not a dialogue in that respect, but it was, "How is this going?" And, then they started looking at the numbers and then the large numbers of classes, and [asked us], "How do you do it?" We talked about that. (part-time faculty, communications, comprehensive university)

Meetings for these courses inform and direct part-time faculty's work and ensure that part-timers teach the same content in the same order. "We all teach the earthquake lab the same week. We all teach the igneous rocks lab the same week. . . . [E]verybody does the same lab worksheet" (part-time faculty, geology, comprehensive university). This organization of work seeks efficiency through the reinforcement of a division of faculty labor and a hierarchical structure of the profession.

Although part-timers are responsible for the planning, teaching, and evaluating of their laboratory section of the class, they report to a tenured faculty member who controls the course. "They [the professor and the department chair] wanted to make sure we were in the same track, and we are" (part-time faculty, communications, comprehensive university). This course-laboratory organization conflicts with part-time faculty members' autonomy and positions them more as teaching assistants than as professors: Thus, their status is reduced from professionals to apprentices. Nonetheless, although this course-laboratory structure is a managerial strategy designed to regulate part-timers' work, part-time faculty do take advantage of this interaction and employ it as an opportunity to enact their professional values.

For part-timers, this course-laboratory structure of work provides them a space for interaction with their peers, and through these interactions they seek to exchange views and experiences of their classes and their students with others, in an effort to influence their department's curriculum and teaching goals. However, this influence is contingent upon the attitudes and receptivity of tenure track faculty.

> We actually had a meeting also about updates and corrections to our lab manual, and, so, the [tenured] professor who is involved with that is very interested in knowing what's on our minds because we're the ones teaching the lab and we see issues that come up. Then we'll bring them up to her [the lead faculty].
> (part-time faculty, geology, comprehensive university)

Part-time faculty acknowledge that their influence in their department is limited. "I mean, what was the point? If the point was to follow through there was follow through, [but] there was no dialogue" (part-time faculty, communications, comprehensive university). That is, although part-time faculty align their everyday practices with professional values, this does not guarantee that the department or the university will see their views as valuable.

Part-time faculty members' work is controlled and monitored. However, given that management of this faculty group is general, applicable to all, and not compartmentalized for each part-time faculty, the claim of both part-time faculty and department chairs is that the work of part-timers is not "micromanaged." "So, we're not micromanaged [to the extent] that you must use this power point slides, [or] you must talk about this first, second, third, fourth, fifth" (part-time faculty, geology, comprehensive university). "So, I don't really want to micromanage people, tell people what we have to do and how they want to do; it's up to them" (department chair, sociology, comprehensive university). This absence of "micromanagement" is then perceived by part-timers as respect for their professional capacity, skills, knowledge, and abilities. Yet, this perception ignores the actual level of management of part-time faculty, which includes control over their workload, scheduling, class content, salary, and their participation in non-teaching departmental activities.

The pressures on public universities, including self-imposed pressures, to demonstrate efficiency have resulted in the management of part-time faculty work to the extent that management of their work has become normalized. For example, part-time faculty in public universities are not managed in the specificities of how they evaluate their students. However, their work is managed so that their work achieves the indicators that universities need in order to demonstrate that they are efficient, productive, and legitimate places of learning. The grades given to students is one of these indicators.

> We have to tell them what is our grade compared to the other classes, because if you work hard and your students enjoy your class, and get good grades, and at the end your students' average grade is higher than others, that's not good. That's not good for you because then [they think], "Maybe it is too easy." You have to be tough. (part-time faculty, history, comprehensive university)

Although part-time faculty explain that they have some degree of control over both what they teach in their class and the level of depth they chose for a topic, if they want to maintain their job, they must comply with organizational rules that are based on a culture of mistrust. That is, these rules assume that part-time faculty need to be monitored in order to behave professionally (e.g., teaching with quality, grading fairly) in their everyday work.

In the United States, in the past two decades, the work of non-tenure track faculty has become managed more tightly with the increase of accountability demands in higher education institutions (Levin et al., 2011). Part-time non-tenure track faculty in universities have little control over their work, and, thus, their professional identity within universities resembles that of employees in a corporation. However, given that management is discrete and part-time faculty have a degree of autonomy in their work and a sense of a professional self, they find themselves anchoring their professional identity to their work (what they do), rather than to their career in a university (where they do it). This new anchoring is explored in the last section of the chapter.

Full-Time Non-Tenure Track Faculty:
Second-Guessed but Committed

In comparison to part-timers, full-time NTT faculty suffer less exploitation: They have better employment conditions. In addition, full-time NTT faculty are expected to participate more in university life than part-time faculty. Because of these conditions and expectations, they are likely to have more available resources to carry out their work than part-timers (Kezar & Sam, 2011). Due to their employment conditions, full-time NTT faculty appear to have closer ties with universities than do part-time faculty (Levin et al., 2011). However, higher education institutions' use of full-time NTT faculty, consistent with institutional priorities such as economic efficiency, organizational flexibility, and maximization of labor potential (e.g., teaching large numbers of students), limits the integration of full-time NTT faculty, fully, into university life.

Full-time NTT faculty's work circumstances are less than ideal. They receive significantly more benefits and support from departments than part-time faculty. For example, 75 percent of full-time NTT faculty in English receive health and retirement benefits (Shaker, 2008). However, salary, benefits, and support for full-time NTT faculty are less generous than for tenure track faculty (Levin et al., 2011; Shaker, 2008), and this is a problematical condition. A full-time NTT faculty member at a state university details their predicament in relation to personal benefits.

> "I've gotten some good experience in this job, but the lack of benefits—particularly insurance and pension—has been a problem. If I planned to stay here, my actual years of service would be low as far as the retirement system is concerned." (Feldman & Turnley, 2001, p. 8)

Nonpecuniary benefits are a consolation prize rather than an additional advantage for NTT faculty. However, salary differentials change according to institutional type. Research and doctoral institutions tend to pay lower salaries to full-time NTT faculty than master's and baccalaureate institutions (Rhoades & Maitland, 2008). Full-time NTT faculty cost the university between 20 and 50 percent less annually than tenure track faculty (Rhoades & Maitland, 2008) depending on their primary focus or work (research, teaching, or administration).

Full-time NTT positions have an emphasis that may or may not be congruent with an individual's preferences. Baldwin and Chronister (2001) identify four types of full-time NTT faculty according to their primary functions: teachers, researchers, administrators, and other academic professionals (e.g., clinical service). Individuals in full-time NTT positions perform research, teaching, administrative work, and participate in committees in different degrees (Baldwin & Chronister, 2001). That is, full-time NTT faculty have a variety of roles but usually they specialize in one activity (Thedwall, 2008). Moreover, the majority of full-time NTT faculty (two-thirds) focus primarily on teaching; and all full-time NTT faculty teach at least one course more per term than their tenured and tenure-eligible counterparts (Baldwin & Chronister, 2001). Thus, the involvement of full-time NTT faculty in non-instructional work (e.g., committees, student advising) is more limited than that of tenure track faculty.

Full-time NTT faculty are hired primarily to decrease the overall workload of tenure track faculty so that tenure track faculty have time to participate in research, service, and campus life (Gappa et al., 2007). This view of full-time NTT faculty as workload releasers is the basis of the perception of this faculty group as illegitimate academics—thus, their academic professional identity is not verified. A full-time NTT faculty member with a research focus at a state university describes how his work was not legitimate academic work in the view of their colleagues.

> "I do all the data collection for my group, but others take the data, write [these] up, and do not include me as an author. . . . However, they want me to include them on my publications (since they need the publications for tenure review whereas I don't), but they don't want to include me on their publications. I'm not considered a real part of the research team (despite twenty publications as a senior author), and I'm considered a second-class citizen, since I am not on the tenure track." (Feldman & Turnley, 2001, p. 8)

There is an implicit perception that only lesser-quality individuals are willing to accept positions off the tenure track (Baldwin & Chronister, 2001). Indeed, scholars have argued consistently that full-time NTT faculty are considered nonelite (Levin et al., 2011), worker bees (Deem, 1998; Levin, 2006; Welch, 2000), academic proletariat (Kupiec Clayton, 1991), second-class citizens (Baldwin & Chronister, 2001; Benjamin, 2002), bullpen faculty, workhorse faculty, and subfaculty (Baldwin & Chronister, 2001). That is, distinct from tenure track faculty, who have freedom to set their research and teaching agendas (or at least have a say in their teaching schedules), full-time NTT faculty have work that is conditioned and determined by others (i.e., by the university or the department).

In addition to their teaching or research focus, full-time NTT faculty may carry a supplementary assignment, such as special projects, student advising, or other administrative duties (Thedwall, 2008). Yet, when full-time NTT faculty carry out these assignments, the primary institutional intention is not for them to participate in university life, but to allow "tenure-eligible faculty some additional release time to use for research or other responsibilities" (Thedwall, 2008, p. 16). That is, their participation in committees is instrumental, and they are included more in administrative time-consuming tasks than in important decision-making committees (Levin et al., 2011).

> "There was someone who used to work here before, and she was very vocal in the faculty meetings and she was actually resented for it. The attitude was basically, 'You're a [nontenure track faculty member] why are you making so much noise?' . . . [In] the faculty meetings it's kind of like you're sort of in the background. You can be seen but not heard, or be heard quietly. Ok, but I don't know if it's really disrespect, but because we're nontenured, that gives us an odd place in the department, and they don't know how to take us." (NTT faculty, English, research university, in Shaker, 2008, pp. 165–166)

Full-time NTT faculty's attempts to participate in decision making or other nonteaching activities are hindered by the status of their position as "less-than." This perception devalues their efforts, which are seen as peripheral to university life. Mary Kupiec Clayton describes her experiences off the tenure track and explains a change in her self-perception due to organizational behaviors toward NTT faculty. "I became for them what they saw me do, and what they saw me do was what was left over after the regular faculty chose their own teaching assignments" (Kupiec Clayton, 1991, p. 649). Kupiec Clayton's experiences exemplify how the utilitarian view of faculty in NTT positions takes a toll on these faculty members' self-perception—their self-categorization as academic professionals is not only not verified but also negated. Repeated treatment as "academic proletariat" situates NTT faculty in marginalized and outsider status in relation to tenure track faculty and to the institution itself (Kupiec Clayton, 1991).

Although faculty in NTT positions are an abused workforce that lacks employment stability, they develop a deep attachment to their workplace and their organization (Levin et al., 2011). NTT full-timers take on additional responsibilities to those stipulated in their formal contracts such as advising students, directing programs, conducting research, and engaging in service, as well as acquiring institutional grants and taking advantage of professional development opportunities as they are made available (Shaker, 2008). " 'I'm putting in 80 hours instead of 60 for my pathetic little $28,000' " (Sara, English, comprehensive university, in Shaker, 2008). Participation in activities that go beyond their formal role activities—which are named extra-role activities in work engagement theory—are both a consequence and evidence of their commitment to their organization (López Damián, 2017). Attachment and commitment to their university are not developed by members of this faculty group due to a naive view of their work or their position. But, for full-time NTT faculty, universities are places in which they can develop intellectual and creative work. " 'The work itself is extremely satisfying. It suits my creative needs.' " (Full-time NTT faculty, comprehensive university, in Feldman & Turnley, 2001, p. 11).

Full-time NTT faculty tend to be highly motivated to perform their work due to the intrinsic satisfaction they develop from their work, and this motivation drives them to be productive at teaching and service—arguably as much as or more so than their tenure track counterparts (Shaker, 2008). However, full-time NTT faculty express a decrease in their job satisfaction over time, while simultaneously there is an increase in job-related stress (Feldman & Turnley, 2001; Gappa et al., 2007). Gappa, Austin, and Trice (2007) hypothesize that the causes of NTT's negative emotions are the result of the conflicting demands and high expectations in organizations for full-time NTT faculty. Feldman and Turnley's (2001, p. 14) data suggest that negative emotions are associated with a perception of unfair treatment: " 'I dislike being treated unfairly by administrators when new positions become available. . . . The idea that loyalty will be rewarded is a naive dream that is reserved for the truly delusional' " (NTT faculty, comprehensive university). That is, over time, full-time NTT faculty's sense of marginalization and exploitation increases and affects their relationship with their university as well as their self-perception. This point on the effects on self-perception as a professional, or one's professional identity, is developed in a subsequent section.

In Limbo Between Freedom and Control

Full-time NTT faculty occupy roles situated between their tenure track colleagues and part-time non-tenure track faculty. Similar to tenure track faculty, they are managed by a bureaucratic structure for full-time employees, and they are managed as professional academics who are subject to neoliberal policies and managerial regimes. They have lost or never attained the full status of a professional with autonomy, who self-regulates their work and participates in collegial decision making (Tight, 2014). Their lack of full status as members of the profession and the absence of verification of an academic professional identity position full-time NTT as dependent on their colleagues to determine their working conditions. Purcell (2003) describes his experience as an NTT full-time faculty member, an "Acting Assistant Professor, Temporary," who viewed full-time tenure track faculty as "embedded in a system of oppression" (p. 132).

> Many on the faculty were clearly not sure how much interpersonal investment to make in me, since they assumed I would not be around forever. . . . [O]ne faculty member . . . didn't approach me until near the end of my first year in the department. She was not interested in meeting me, however, but in discovering if I would be available to teach the large introductory lecture course, a course she was scheduled to teach but did not want to. (Purcell, 2007, p. 133)

Purcell's experience suggests that the work of non-tenure track faculty is seen as a temporal resource that accommodates the work of authentic academics. Dissimilar to tenure track faculty, full-time NTT faculty lack permanent job security, status, and an acknowledged role in governance (Levin & Shaker, 2011). This separation reflects a stratified faculty system in universities, even for those non-tenure track faculty who are full-time.

The stratified faculty system brings problems to universities and departments: The concentration of full-time NTT faculty in teaching-oriented tasks has as a consequence a disconnection between tenured and NTT faculty (Baldwin & Chronister, 2001; Shaker, 2008).

> My colleagues were entirely uninterested in my pedagogy. On the one hand, this lack of interest was good. It gave me the freedom to pursue innovative and even experimental pedagogies. . . . On

the other hand . . . I was unable to contribute ideas, or learn from the ideas of others, because few were interested in talking to me about pedagogy. (Purcell, 2007, p. 136)

Besides this professional disconnection between tenure track and full-time NTT faculty, Baldwin and Chronister (2001) identify that, due to their concentration in teaching-oriented tasks, full-time NTT faculty view the needs of the department as focused on teaching, while tenured and tenure track faculty are more likely to view research as central and as a priority, particularly in research universities.

At the larger university level, a similar divide occurs in which a focus of tenure track faculty is on larger university structures, such as governance, whereas this is not the case for full-time NTT faculty (Shaker, 2008). Yet, although full-time NTT faculty may recognize that their status as non-tenure track is an important issue, this status is not central in their assessment of their university's primary shortcomings. For them, issues such as quality of instruction are more salient.

"At one point [the university president] said, 'We all know [full-time NTT] numbers on this campus are a real problem' and everybody started nodding so vigorously, I thought their heads would roll off, you know? A large group of bobble-heads essentially agreeing that that's the main problem on campus. . . . I was pretty disgusted. The biggest problem isn't sagging academic standards, or the fact that every time we raise academic standards our enrollment seems to go down so then we quietly change them behind the scenes so that we can keep our jobs? . . . It's us, really?" (NTT faculty, English, in Shaker, 2008, p. 173)

NTT faculty do not perceive that their environment enables or facilitates them to participate fully. They have limited participation in a core activity of the academic professional identity: shared governance. Over time, full-time NTT faculty's ability to contribute to their department decreases: " 'My role at the meetings mostly is to sit and listen; I almost never do anything else. I get to vote once in a while. But, as far as my contribution—almost nothing'" (NTT faculty, English, Shaker, 2008, p. 166).

From the perspective of the faculty profession as a whole, full-time NTT faculty are "a force in the diminution of the power, influence, and dominance of tenure track faculty" (Levin et al., 2011, p. 206). That is, with the inclusion of full-time NTT faculty as part of the faculty body, as well as the proliferation of part-time NTT faculty, power in universities moves toward administration. Full-time NTT faculty are hired so that the administration has more opportunity to regulate faculty members' work assignment and time distribution (Baldwin & Chronister, 2001). The cost of managerial treatment of faculty as a commodity comes in the form of a fractured professional identity (Levin et al., 2011).

Ambiguous and Divided Identity

Non-tenure track faculty negotiate their identity as employees of a higher education institution, as members of a disciplinary field, and as constituents of the academic profession. Indeed, values of these domains shape the ways in which faculty understand their position and work (Austin, 1990), and these values have different meanings for the two subgroups of non-tenure track faculty. Due to their work circumstances, full-time non-tenure track faculty are closer professionally and personally to the organization, including its practices and values, than are part-time faculty. In Kezar and Sam's (2011) view, organizational structures position full-time NTT faculty more as traditional professionals than as employees and part-timers more as labor than as professionals. The distance, professionally and personally, between part-time faculty and their organization is a condition that pushes part-time faculty to find a different anchor for their professional identity. For full-time NTT faculty, distance is between academic professionals with low status and those with high status. The low status of full-time NTT faculty denies them what is possessed by full-time tenure track faculty: an academic professional identity and a professional identity that is sanctioned by their university. Whereas full-time NTT's professional identity is ambiguous, divided, or fractured, part-time faculty's identity is fluid and flexible, not anchored at the university, but potentially elsewhere.

The work circumstances of part-time faculty are associated with a professional identity that is divided between self-perception as professionals (primarily in the classroom) and a self-perception as nonprofessionals (in their department [Levin & Montero-Hernandez, 2014]). However, this identity division becomes a source of strength for part-time faculty, a defense to counteract the depersonalization originated by neoliberal and managerial practices. Part-time faculty may move fluidly between their self-perception as specialized and effective instructors or educators, as members of a higher education unit or department (Levin & Montero-Hernandez, 2014), and as practitioners of specialized knowledge (López Damián, 2017). A part-time NTT faculty in the field of education acknowledges the negotiation of her identity as a professional.

> When I'm working with the business council, I'm part-time faculty because it's about association with the university. When I'm working with the Department of Education, I'm an education consultant. So, it just depends. . . . The part-time faculty [job] . . . tends to be what the lay person sees [as] more impressive than a consultant. (part-time faculty, education, comprehensive university)

Part-time faculty have the potential to construct a narrative (Levin et al., 2011; Sennett, 2006) that is not anchored in their role in one organization. Thus, their professional narrative, the one they use to construct their professional identity, is not controlled by the organization, but is a narrative that is anchored in what is essential to their work, rooted not in a specific organization but in themselves (López Damián, 2017).

This narrative, however, is a double-edged sword. With part-time faculty focused on their intrinsic motivations to teach (e.g., appreciation for the activity, enjoyment of relationship with students and colleagues, interest in currency in their field) and the nonpecuniary benefits of teaching (e.g., a flexible schedule, access to future colleagues, that is, students), problems with wages and working conditions are likely to remain overlooked. This creates a situation where both wages and working conditions remain unjust for the overall population of non-tenure track faculty (Kezar & Sam, 2011), and, thus, exploitation of this faculty group will continue in the managerial, neoliberal university.

For full-time NTT faculty, the effects of managerial treatment come in the form of a fractured rather than flexible professional identity (Levin et al., 2011). Specifically, their academic professional identity is limited by managerialism. NTT full-timers have arrested identities, hybrid identities, and blended identities (Baldwin & Chronister, 2001; Levin & Shaker, 2011; Levin et al., 2011); they are anchored in their relationship with a university. The effects of a faculty hierarchy are considerable for full-time NTT faculty.

> From years of living with the professional understanding that I was not an equal participant in the life of the profession, my

> university, or my department, I internalized the notion that I
> did not yet know enough to be able to speak with any authority
> about any subject. (Kupiec Clayton, 1991, p. 650)

Mary Kupiec Clayton found herself writing from the periphery, trying to be part of a community that marginalizes non-tenure track faculty and conceives of her as an outsider, a nonacademic. Full-time NTT faculty professional identity is anchored in an organization that devalues this population, manages them, and sees them as economic entities. They are more limited in their options than part-timers to create new narratives of their professional selves.

For non-tenure track faculty, if they anchor their professional identity in their relationship with their university, they will view themselves as workers, as temporal labor that needs to be controlled, regulated, and guided by administrators, academic managers, and colleagues. However, not all non-tenure track faculty do anchor their identity with their university; instead, they anchor their professional identity in their discipline and consider the value of their job attached to their community, or society, or their country—maintaining the saliency of their academic professional identity. That is, although, as Sennett (2006) notes, individuals no longer have organizations as anchors for their career, this does not mean as a consequence that they lose all sense of a professional self.

Management of non-tenure track faculty, both full-time and part-time, reflects the advancement of neoliberal ideology in the university. In part, as universities continue to face resource demands, primarily the need to finance their expanding activities and budgets, and in part as universities seek legitimacy and prestige, they resort to practices associated with neoliberalism. These practices include tighter controls over organizational behaviors by a managerial class through such measures as Responsibility Centered Management (Birnbaum, 2000), rewards for measurable productivity and punishments for lack of the same, and monitoring, including self-monitoring by academics. If neoliberalism operates through the logic of the market, then competition is central (Saunders, 2014), and full-time and part-time non-tenure track faculty are at risk for the maintenance of their employment and compelled to satisfy their students and their tenure track faculty colleagues if they want to continue in their positions. With increases in non-tenure track positions, the majority of university faculty face insecurity in employment in large part because of the ways in which they are managed.

In this chapter, we have explained the ways in which NTT faculty are managed and the ways in which they respond to management. Their behaviors thus differ considerably from full-time tenure track faculty discussed in chapter 1. Yet, these two groups of faculty share commonalities. For both, tenure track and NTT faculty, managerialism has negative effects on their professional identity. Moreover, in the academic hierarchy sharpened by managerialism, both groups describe department chairs as either the managerial class, or representatives of that class, for their department. In chapter 3, we continue our analysis of managerialism in the U.S. university. We explain department chairs as dual members of the academic profession and the managerial class, who have formal or explicit demands derived from the two logics that coexist in universities. Thus, we analyze department chairs as faculty with an academic professional identity and a (self-denied) managerial identity.

Chapter 3

Department Chairs

Dual Roles, Dual Identities

In this chapter, we describe the role and behaviors of department chairs and department heads in a university context. As the majority of chairs and heads begin their academic roles as faculty, most face the experiences of full-time tenure track faculty discussed in chapter 1: their academic professional identity is weakened by neoliberal logic, and they adapt not only their behaviors but also their self-conceptions (e.g., professional identity) to this logic. The argument here is that, in some distinction from tenure track faculty, department chairs have a formal role as manager that affects their identity standards as academic professionals. Thus, they have potential to develop a managerial identity while their academic professional identity can serve as a vehicle for them to defend academic values (Clegg & McAuley, 2005). Although the academic professional identity may not be verified by their faculty colleagues, department chairs do not reduce the saliency of this academic professional identity. Department chairs seek to protect both tenure track and non-tenure track faculty from neoliberal logic and managerial practices. In order to do so, they either oppose neoliberal logic or blend neoliberal logic with academic logic. Yet, the possibilities to resist both neoliberalism and managerialism are limited, and department chairs' efforts are not recognized by their faculty colleagues.

The position and role of university department chairs or department heads (terms that we use interchangeably) are of considerable significance to the management of the academic profession. However, the scholarly literature on department chairs in the United States is limited in both quantity and scope. Of the scarce number of journal articles, books, and monographs on department chairs, the majority of the publications on this population are restricted to descriptive and prescriptive texts (e.g., Gmelch & Mishkin, 1995; Knight & Trowler, 2001; Leaming, 2007; Roach, 1991; Tucker, 1984). Of the few research-based publications on department chairs, the majority are quantitative in nature and provide little explanation of the behaviors of department chairs. Some have examined the relationship between department chair effectiveness and role ambiguity or job satisfaction (e.g., Carroll & Gmelch, 1992; Roach, 1991) as well as the stress and career ramifications service as a chair (Gmelch, 1991). Other works either enumerate a long list of tasks and outline the domains of the chair (such as curriculum, student issues, conflict and personnel, faculty and staff hiring, faculty development, budgets, spatial assignments, and research and teaching responsibilities [Hecht, Higgerson, Gmelch, & Tucker, 1999]), or provide a series of recommendations on how a chair should proceed with the execution of their role in the form of best practices for leadership and conflict management (e.g., Gmelch & Carroll 1991; Knight & Trowler, 2001; Quinn, 2007; Tucker, 1984).

The value of these texts for practitioners is questionable, and there is no follow-up research to examine these texts and their recommendations' efficacy. Scholarly descriptive and prescriptive texts are not only limited in their practical application but also, and pertinent to our purposes, they fail to capture data that reveal the role of department chairs as reinforcers or resistors of managerialism in a neoliberal higher education system characterized by scholars, such as Ball (2012b) and Levin (2017), as increasingly competitive, prestige driven, and market centered. Indeed, department chairs' understandings of the connections and tensions between academic logic and neoliberal logic remain unexamined in the literature. Furthermore, their own role in the behavioral interactions based upon these logics is, prior to our work here, unexplored.

The literature does provide some guidance about department chairs' roles and work contexts through its predominantly descriptive, informational offerings. Department chairs rotate, typically serve fixed terms (Quinn, 2007), and perceive this role as temporary (Gmelch, 1991, 2004; Moore, Newman, & Turnbull, 2003). Chairs are responsible to (and sometimes for) different constituents, which include the dean, faculty, staff, and students. In some cases, chairs are appointed by deans or elected by faculty and then serve at the dean's pleasure. In other instances, the dean selects from a list of candidates recommended by the faculty. Alternately, the faculty may select the chair directly and then a chair is not subject to a dean's dismissal (Hecht et al., 1999). Similar to most higher education administrative positions, the department chair rarely possesses any formal training in administration or management (Aziz et al., 2005; Gmelch, 2004). There is an expectation, however, that "the chair must be a good manager" (Jeffrey, 1985, p. 15). Department chairs are in temporal positions and trained limitedly, yet they are in the midst of administrative, bureaucratic, and managerial tasks. It is these characteristics of department chairs that beckon us to question their role in a neoliberal university.

For universities, the majority of decisions (80% according to Roach [1991]) are made at the departmental level (Wolverton, Ackerman, & Holt, 2005). Thus, department chairs are located at the center of decision-making activities. The literature suggests that department chairs do participate in management activities (Gmelch & Miskin, 1995; Hecht et al., 1999; Tucker, 1984; Roach, 1991); nevertheless, the emphasis in this body of literature is on leadership, specifically on the role of department chairs as "academic leaders" (Gmelch, 1991; Hecht et al., 1999; Knight & Trowler, 2001; Quinn, 2007). For the most part, the literature overemphasizes an idealized notion of department chairs as leaders of autonomous, powerful faculty who respect shared governance and model Mintzberg's (1979a) professional bureaucracy. Such a conception is not in accord with current scholarship on the university and its actors (Gould, 2003; Readings, 1997; Schuster & Finkelstein, 2006; Slaughter & Rhoades, 2000; Ward, 2012).

The managerial activities and the role of department chairs as managers, while noted in the literature, are underemphasized or accompanied by warnings and heeds for department chairs. Department chairs embody several roles or ideal types, which include manager, scholar, faculty developer, and leader (Carroll & Gmelch, 1992). While some chairs tend to lean toward one identity or emphasize one role, others are suggested to adopt several of these roles together (Carroll & Gmelch, 1992). Gmelch (1991) asserted that chairs who embrace the manager role should model a bottom-up approach: Deans serve the chairs; chairs serve the faculty; and, faculty serve the students. The literature warns department chairs against behaviors that are overtly managerial and suggests that "close supervision" of faculty may result in greater levels of tension (Gmelch & Carroll, 1991, p. 112); it asserts as well that employee-centered approaches that are consultative are preferred (Bare, 1986). The exhortation is that department chairs should aim at faculty involvement and avoid excessive exertions of power on their faculty who themselves "hold exceptional power due to their professionalism"

(Gmelch & Carroll, 1991, p. 113). The prescriptions from this literature are that the relationship between faculty and administrators should not be sacrificed for any reason and that open subordination of the chair to the faculty is an "appropriate strategy" (Gmelch & Carroll, 1991, p. 118).

We call into question the literature's rhetoric that characterizes department chairs as primarily academic leaders, and we assert that this population of academic administrators is both managed (by their deans and central administration) and are full-blown managers (of both tenure track and non-tenure track faculty) in denial of their role in the reinforcement of managerialism, academic capitalism, and neoliberal ideology. We use original data from department chairs from six public research and comprehensive universities in the United States (see Appendix) to argue that despite their professed allegiance to academic logic (academic values, missions, and behaviors), they are also enactors of neoliberal logic (market-driven behaviors and values). We show that they blend, as well as compartmentalize, these divergent logics in line with the views of Thornton, Ocasio, and Lounsbury (2012) on institutional logics. With a foot in both the faculty and administrative worlds, department chairs devote the bulk of their time to administration, and the roles and responsibilities of the chair impede department chairs' abilities to perform their scholarly duties (Gmelch, 1991). Although department chairs may claim and adhere to an academic professional identity, the responsibilities of the chair position make the pursuit of scholarly activity almost impossible (Carroll & Gmelch, 1992; Gmelch, 1991). Chairs perform "all functions from the menial to the managerial to the inspirational" (Hecht et al., 1999, p. xi). The longer a chair serves, the more likely they will adopt the leader/manager combination (Carroll & Gmelch, 1992). Chairs are managers, who not only assess the productivity of faculty with a weighted point system but also establish the productivity expectations for their faculty, hold regular performance counseling sessions (Tucker, 1984), and "convince the dean that the department is producing" (Hecht et al., 1999, p. 206). Thus, we perceive a paradox: If chairs are allegedly academic leaders, rather than overt managers, why is the majority of their time devoted to management activities and not to academic endeavors?

Department Chairs in the Context of Neoliberalism

Department chairs are members of a university characterized as neoliberal (Slaughter & Rhoades, 2000). In the neoliberal university, they are potential extensions of the academic capitalist regime (Slaughter & Rhoades, 2004), extensions of a neoliberal state (Ball, 2012a), and handmaidens to the restructuring of the university into a liberal market enterprise (Ward, 2012). In this context, each individual is "an entrepreneur" (Lorenz, 2012, p. 602); individuals' roles are directed toward buying and selling services (Lorenz, 2012); and, market values usurp the democratic values of personal freedom and equality (Giroux, 2002). Department chairs manage their departments and their faculty, and they do so within the accepted structures and values of a university as a corporate body (Gould, 2003). Department chairs or heads become members of a hierarchy that seeks to direct academic work toward the privatized, competitive marketplace. In the corporate university, they are incentivized to behave as entrepreneurs, and pushed to generate new strategies to increase the efficiency, efficacy, and revenue of their departments.

Department chairs are managed by their superiors (the dean and central administration) who perpetuate the logic and values of managerialism, despite department chairs' efforts to resist the practice and ideology. Although department chairs articulate the values and the identity of the academy, they are, nevertheless, cogs in and contributors to the managerial wheel. Department chairs occupy a dual role that overlaps the managerial core and the academic core—they exist "at the heart of the tension between the two systems" (Gmelch & Burns, 1993, p. 260). They play the role of mediators between faculty and administrators (Gmelch & Carroll, 1991). Whereas deans are more removed from the individuals who are affected by the decisions they make than chairs, chairs have direct contact with faculty and must deal with the ramifications of their decisions with their faculty colleagues on a daily basis (Hecht et al., 1999). Thus, whether they are willing to acknowledge this identity or not, department chairs embody the quintessential definition of a manager.

Department chairs' dual managerial and academic roles may both match and be at odds with their identity. Department chairs may conceptualize themselves as managers, as faculty, or as both managers and faculty; but these personal definitions do not necessarily match the institutional definitions of their role or their faculty's understandings of their role. As members of the university, they are endowed with identities that are based on their organizational position (institution-identities), their relationship with others (discourse-identities), and their membership in nonorganizational groups (affinity-identities) (Gee, 2000–01). These forms of identity are bestowed upon them regardless of individual department chairs' personal preferences and understandings of their core identity (Gee, 2000–01). If an individual's personal preference is recognized as meaningful by others, this identity is verified (Stets & Burke, 2000) and validated. Thus, department chairs' identities are both verified (Stets & Burke, 2000) and rejected (Gee, 2000–01) by members of groups in which they self-categorize—faculty and other academic administrators (department chairs, associate deans, deans, provosts).

The roles and identities of department chairs are simultaneous: They coexist (Gee, 2000–01) and are both salient (psychologically significant) in different situations (Stets & Burke, 2000). Department chairs have both their chair position or role and their faculty member position or role as institution-identities; that is, both identities are defined and sanctioned, officially, by their university and, in dialogue, by faculty. In universities, the category of faculty exists in contrast to the category of administration. These "contrasting categories" (Stets & Burke, 2000, p. 225) have varying degrees of power, prestige, and status. That is, in terms used by Gee (2000–01), department chairs are in-group members and out-group members of identity roles and professional roles that oppose each other. Department chairs, then, are simultaneously verified and rejected (Stets & Burke, 2000) as both faculty members and administrators or managers.

Department chairs are thus insiders and outsiders to faculty endeavors, and insiders and outsiders to administration endeavors. This continual verification and rejection of their social identities plays a role in their behaviors and in their understanding of their professional self. Their institutional position challenges department chairs' identity as academic professionals, demands from them managerial behaviors, normalizes neoliberal ideology, and asks them to become translators or blenders of this ideology. However, their professional identity as academics provides them the attitudes, beliefs and values, affective reactions, behavioral norms, and styles of speech (Stets & Burke, 2000) to oppose neoliberal demands.

Department Chairs as Managers-in-Denial

Department chairs' explanations of their work suggest that there are diverse roles that chairs fill—not just as department chair but as faculty members; yet, in the main, they identify with their academic role and reject association with the managerial role. A department chair's view of himself exemplifies this common self-identification among individuals in his position: "I view myself as a faculty member, not as an administrator. I view myself as a leader of a group of faculty" (communications, comprehensive university).

This adherence to the academic professional identity may be (1) a coping mechanism in the face of cognitive dissonance in their professional identity and role, (2) an approach to the reconciliation of neoliberal logic and values with academic logic and values, (3) a way of distancing themselves from the managerial realm perceived by their faculty colleagues as the "dark side," or (4) a combination of any these three. University department chairs teach, sometimes continue to conduct research, although more limited than in the past, supervise undergraduate as well as graduate students, and work for and on behalf of their department. Although they execute administrative and managerial tasks—such as budget planning, managing, reporting, fundraising, and the supervision of staff—department chairs do not often describe themselves as managers, deciders, or planners, but more often as handlers of sensitive matters—such as the promotion or advancement of faculty. In the neoliberal university, department chairs are managers-in-denial.

Although department chairs often describe the breadth of their work as teaching, research, supervision, and departmental service, they spend a considerable amount, even a majority, of their time on administration and administrative tasks. "[I give] less time to research. Yeah, no doubt about that . . . [and] I teach less than regular faculty" (modern languages, comprehensive university). Any involvement in teaching is secondary or disruptive, and research is usually of a supervisory, managerial nature—where work is delegated to post-docs or graduate students, or even undergraduate students or staff, and their supervisees are autonomous. To maintain her research agenda, a chair of linguistics negotiated a research assistantship position when asked to perform the chair position. Although this chair's research agenda continued, she was not the one who conducted the research.

> [The research assistant] runs the lab. So, now if something comes up with the lab, a computer breaks or someone can't find a password or somebody needs something, I say: "Ask him." . . . [H]e is also analyzing the ton of data that I had and I had not the chance to analyze, write up. (linguistics, research university)

Department chairs are burdened by administrative activities and are compelled to minimize or curtail research, teaching, and instructional-related curriculum. In order to cope with the managerial responsibilities of his role, a biomedical sciences chair explains the need to apply managerial approaches, including efficiency and control mechanisms in his research lab. This chair enacts managerial behaviors in his academic work.

> [I] have had to develop a new relationship with my lab and encouraged their independence but still have good oversight, so both giving them more rope but holding it tight at various points like, "No, we have to have mandatory meetings." . . . "You're going to have to meet with me. Sorry, it's going to be at five o'clock." (biomedical sciences, research university)

Chairs perform various managerial activities they were unaccustomed to carrying out as faculty: These are clearly managerial duties.

> Well, I vastly underestimated the amount of work being chair. I wasn't entirely naive. I understood a certain amount of it, but, as chair, you're involved in labor relations. You're involved with minor labor relations grievances, but you're also formal labor relations and formal grievances. There [are] budgetary issues, structural planning. In our unit, our campus, we have an out-standing thing going on, which is expansion: cluster hiring—a real opportunity, but we have a struggle because we have an aging infrastructure. . . . [Y]ou have . . . [to ensure] compli-ance. . . . [W]hat has changed is becoming aware of so many elements of the running of the unit that, frankly, you took for granted or you knew at a certain level. (biomedical sciences, research university)

A major component of the chair role includes personnel relations and evaluations. These activities require not only substantial time commitments but also individual judgment. Indeed, the review process for promotion, advancement, and general evaluation requires both academic logic and neoliberal logic, in the form of collegiality or "fairness" (academic logic) and surveillance (neoliberal logic). A chair of psychology expresses his commitment to fairness as self-justification for his own participation in the surveillance of professionals and the measurement of outcomes—both managerial behaviors indicative of a neoliberal logic.

> Every year that I've been chair, we've had between ten and fourteen advancement cases . . . in Fall [quarter]. That's extraordinarily time consuming because each of the faculty numbers has a file that's prepared that has everything they've accomplished over the evaluation period. All of their teaching evaluations . . . for

all of the courses, the papers that they've published, the service that they've done. . . . All of that needs to be evaluated. . . . [W]hen we have the faculty meeting on the cases, I need to have a good understanding of the strengths and weaknesses of the files, so that I can manage the meeting. Because it's incumbent upon me. My responsibility is to make sure that the process is fair. If it should be positive, I need to make sure that the faculty are focused on evaluating the right criteria, weighting them correctly. There's no bias involved in it. (psychology, research university)

Other activities of the job of chair, such as graduate student advising, grant writing, and research, are subordinate to their administrative work. These other job tasks are often relegated to spare time, such as during the summer period.

I try to get that (research) done over the summer because over the summer . . . there's not much to do as chair. . . . I can devote a lot of time over the summer to the big research projects that the students have, like writing the grant proposals, which become their qualifying exams or writing papers for publication which become their dissertations, but more importantly become the papers that they're the first authors of. Those take . . . a huge amount of time, but I can do that over the summer. It's very hard over the year. If it needs to be done over the year, it just gets done over the year. (psychology, research university)

Although department chairs serve in an administrative capacity, their positionality within the organizational structure, including the dual environment of the academy, and within the administration are contested in their self-reporting of what they do and where they situate themselves. Even though department chairs operate primarily in the administrative realm day-to-day and engage in neoliberal behaviors and activities such as the management of professionals, budgets, bureaucratic processes, and campus policies and often with a focus on measurable outcomes, they align themselves and their professional identity with the academic realm.

[T]he chair is between the shared governance of the faculty and the administration. So, I always joke and say that the chair gets squeezed by both sides. But, the chair is firmly located, in my mind, in the faculty side of the discussion. So, very pedantically, the chair is responsible for doing the merits and promotions, for doing the teaching assignments, for overseeing the quality of the teaching. You're there to be the budget oversight on the division for your graduate program, for whatever initiatives. So, you have to look at the whole budget for the whole unit. A little bit more on the intangibles, you have to realize that you're chair for the faculty, but that you're chair for everyone in the unit . . . from graduate students, staff, volunteers, and all of that. So, you got to decide how you're going to deal with that. Your job is to help facilitate the faculty meetings, facilitate committee appointments, [and] distribution of workload whether it be teaching [or] service: In general, foster good relations, provide mentorship. You don't always have to be the actual mentor, but you have to be responsible for ensuring mentorship of folks by proper individuals. (biomedical sciences, research university)

For many department chairs, chairing the department is often a second stage of their career, in large part either because their research productivity and research projects have plateaued or because retirement is looming. The role of the chair gives them the justification for their reduction in activities such as research productivity, or even teaching, and provides them with continued legitimacy as contributors to the department. "I'm not a young scholar. . . . In ten years, I'll be retired. . . . I'm filling the need for the department [that is, administrative work]. . . . I do the minimum of what I have to do for scholarship" (sociology, comprehensive university). For some, a decrease in their productivity does not affect their outlook on their career achievements. A psychology chair at a research university exemplifies this characteristic.

My research, honestly, had plateaued anyway. And so, in the early stage of my career, probably the first ten years or so that I was here, I was a pretty big name as a researcher. I'm very honest about self-evaluation. And in the last seven or eight years or so my productivity has been at an adequate level, but it's not been astounding. And the impact of the work has not been as astounding as it used to be. I used to be like in newspapers and stuff like that, kind of—which is not a very good measure, but it was high impact work . . . I got press attention. And so now, it's been more like I'm doing work, or the lab is doing work, that's relatively important, but it's not like important. (psychology, research university)

In spite of his acknowledgment of his decreased research productivity, this psychology chair expressed his hesitancy to join the administration and described his initial perception of the administrative side of the university negatively. His description of, and reflection on, his perceptions of the administration are a tool in his own self-discourse to position himself as separate from the administration and management: an outsider who is not one of them. Through this rhetoric, he is able to affirm his academic professional identity and cast off any assumptions that he might be inclined toward a managerial identity. He frames himself as a casual acquieser to the pressure to lead, and separates himself from both the responsibility to manage effectively as well as the negative connotations of membership in the administration—a position that isolates him from his academic peers.

> I almost had a disrespect for administrative service, and really the kind of service that I valued most was off campus service: things like being on a grant review committee . . . service that was directly related to research. . . . [If] someone that said to me they enjoyed being chair of a department, I would think that there was something wrong with them. And basically—and I'm not even exaggerating—that's basically the way I felt about it. So, when I was asked to be chair of psychology, I thought I would be terrible at it for a huge variety of reasons, and really didn't want to do it, but they were kind of insistent. So, I thought, "Okay, fine. I'll try it for a year, and then you guys will discover it was a mistake, and 'Thank-you very much. Go back to doing research. We'll find someone else.' " (psychology, research university)

Although this chair of psychology had been in this position for four years and indicated that he would carry on for at least one more, he acknowledged that the outcomes of the job are neither energizing nor self-renewing. "[I]t is a burnout kind of a job. It just sucks the life out of you." Yet, he projected himself as an academic who enjoys chairing his department but not for an extended period of time. In an attempt to quell his negative emotions about his professional obligation and the misalignment of his managerial role with his academic passion, purpose, and identity, he provided a justification for why he has remained the chair.

> I've enjoyed doing it. It's been fun. It's a terrific department. The faculty treat me very well. The dean is phenomenal. . . . He's a tremendous decision maker; makes very quick decisions. He doesn't make you wait. . . . And so, that's been a hugely important for me is having both. I'm sort of between the department at one end and the dean at the other; and, the staff here's phenomenal as well. (psychology, research university)

In most cases, the chair intends to return to the faculty after the completion of their service as chair. "Right now, we are working on a succession plan. I don't plan [on] doing another term" (sociology, comprehensive university). Indeed, research of the 1990s and early 2000s indicates that this intent is the norm (Gmelch, 1991, 2004). In those cases where there is intention to return to a faculty role, chairs can remain more connected during their chair tenure, at least attitudinally, to their teaching and research and their academic professional identity. "I'm not building that [research] . . . I am focusing on teaching, which is why I came here. . . . I teach one class, but I do a lot of mentoring . . . so I have a lot of student contact" (sociology, comprehensive university). A chair of biomedical sciences at a research university spent a majority of her time in an administrative capacity; she viewed the chair role as temporary and expressed concern with maintaining alignment with the academic realm.

> [The role of chair,] it's very much a rejuvenating activity. . . . I think if you're going to be chair and doing something administrative and you're not dedicated going to a pure full-time administrative route, if you want to make sure the chair really is staying on the faculty side of shared governance, staying really aligned, you have to do something that keeps you fully aligned. And, that's wh[at] I find the [research] center does, and it keeps me aligned for things. (biomedical sciences, research university)

The duration of the role of chair and alignment with a managerial orientation are likely influenced by the disciplinary context (this argument was advanced originally in the 1990s by Carroll's [1991] work). In specific fields, such as the field of medicine, chairs serve for long periods as a result of the necessity to develop long-term relationships with external or corporate partners. These relationships serve a market purpose—to advance the reputation of the department, increase revenue generation, and build connections for the purposes of student job placement. A chair of psychiatry at a research university, who had been chair for sixteen years at his previous institution and had now served as chair at another university for five years, embraced neoliberal logic and a managerial identity. The nature of his responsibilities corresponded to his self-perception as a CEO of a business, not as an academic department head. Although he was adamant that chairs, such as himself, should not serve for a long-term period, he explained that in some cases extended terms for chairs were beneficial for the business of the department.

> Medical school chairs usually have longer tenures and some flunk out after a year or two. But, that's never the plan and if they stay on beyond that, sometimes they stay on for twenty plus years. . . . I mean we're basically [a] business. I mean we do have medical students, so a certain amount of time we can probably run the medical student teaching here with a handful of faculty, two or three even. And then, we have residents who are housed staff in the hospital, who are supervising, but most of our business is being basically a service industry, medical practice. As the chairman of department of psychiatry, we avoid the term head. . . . [W]e should be called CEO of a practice organization here. Eighty to ninety percent of our budget is based on [income]. . . . [T]hat's why one-year tenure time [as department chair] wouldn't make much sense because you really build up business relationships over time, and you need more than that. (psychiatry, research university)

Regardless of department chairs' original rejection of the managerial role and identity, they find themselves carrying out surveillance of their colleagues and organization and management of departmental resources. In order to guarantee support for their department and their colleagues, chairs are compelled to respond to the demands of their university.

> We have a target number of full-time equivalent students that we are expected to enroll every semester. . . . Although, in practice, it's not quite the linear relationship that I'm going to make it

> sound, officially. Budgets are tied to the success of meeting targets, the success at enrolling the correct number of FTES (full-time equivalency students). So, there is an incentive. . . . [We] have an incentive system in place to make sure that you are scheduling responsibly and efficiently, and all that good stuff. (English, comprehensive university)

While, as faculty, they were able to escape from some of these pressures, as department chairs, they become part of the managerial function of the university. They need to operate by these management rules and norms, regardless of their own personal values.

> I think now that it's easy to have some kind of cognitive dissonance. You know, wanting to think of [yourself] as still a professor. . . . But, if it's true that the duties that make a successful chair overlap, slightly, if at all, with the duties that make a successful professor, and if I'm physically not even in the same place [as faculty], then who am I kidding? You know, it's just easier to say, "Well, this is this thing that I'm doing now. I now have a slightly different job, and that's okay." (English, comprehensive university)

Faculty is their academic professional identity, their identity or affinity group, and manager is their role as well as their institutional identity, which has standards for their behaviors and actions. Who they are and what they do intertwine in a complex duality.

Dual Identities

Department chairs embody dual identities: as academics and as managers. Most of chairs' time and energy are devoted to administrative work, yet their academic professional identity, or at least the professional identity (scientist, psychiatrist, or educator), is maintained and asserted as the primary identity.

> I still very strongly identify as a faculty member. . . . When somebody asks me what I do for a living, I say "I'm a professor." But then, when they ask me, "What do you teach?" which is always the very next question, I say, "Well, I'm in the child development department, but I'm actually not teaching now

because I'm department chair." Department chair is definitely very strong in terms of my professional identity but faculty still comes first. (child and adolescent development, comprehensive university)

This primary identification or self-categorization as academic professionals is a way to deny participation as managers in the neoliberal regime and to cope with negative emotions associated with identity or role incongruence. Such a condition can lead to dissonance or identity confusion, or it can be a mechanism for identity equilibrium. That is, by reliance upon an academic rather than a managerial identity, chairs play to their primary audience, the faculty, and can receive identity validation (Burke & Stets, 2009). For a chair of psychology, there is evident confusion and tension over professional identity. This chair describes himself in accordance with his discipline and academic identity, and in the next moment admits to engagement in a behavior consistent with neoliberalism—bragging and self or group promotion. In the neoliberal university, where a chair holds an academic identity with managerial responsibilities, the term *brag* is instrumental, that is, a rhetorical term that can be used to sell the department and its accomplishments. By bragging—selling or marketing the department—the chair hopes and even expects to gain resources and prestige. Thus, by upholding an academic professional identity and by marketing or selling his department, he blends or segregates (Thornton et al., 2012) neoliberal and academic logics.

> I still define myself as a scientist, oddly enough. . . . When people ask me . . . I say, "I'm a scientist," and then I go, "Oh, I'm a professor." It's almost an automatic. . . . And so that's how I think of myself, as odd as that may sound, spending ninety percent of my time the last four years as chair and thinking that's important and enjoying it. . . . I definitely define myself as chair now because I understand that I am a representative of the department, and I actually take that seriously. I do things to brag about the department even though it feels weird. It's like I wouldn't brag about myself, but I would brag about the department. I do that because it's part of the job. (psychology, research university)

Department chairs, perhaps a minority, speak of themselves in neoliberal, market-oriented terms. They describe their work as a business function; yet, their academic work is valued as primary, particularly at research universities.

Although administrative work requires the majority of his time, a chair of psychiatry framed his managerial work as of limited importance in the context of the mission or values of the department and university.

> I'm what you call a CEO, chief executive officer, and that takes up a lot of my time and a separate bill. . . . I see patients as a commission too. In fact, I see far more patients than a lot of faculty do here, and I have to divide that up. That does not overlap very well because my job as the chief here, as a chairman of the department, is a business function, much more than anything else. And, if you let that get in the way of being a clinician or teacher for that matter, I mean you're in bad shape, right? (psychiatry, research university)

Department chairs' identity as academics provides them with a justification to carry out what constitute market-driven behaviors. Although department chairs maintain and give priority to their academic identity over an administrative, or managerial, identity, their roles shift, and, along with their role, what they value alters from when they served full-time as faculty.

> [W]hen I was a tenured faculty member I didn't necessarily think about what the goals of the department were. I mean, we had a faculty retreat once a year where we'd talk about them, but . . . I never felt that much a part of the department in a sense. . . . I was here forever, but I was very much a part of the teaching community. But, my long-term goals were not necessarily intertwined with what the department's long-term goals were. They weren't necessarily opposed, but I didn't define myself by what was going on with the department. I do now. (planetary sciences, research university)

The department chair role enables those who were previously and solely faculty members to redefine academic work, including its values, behavioral norms, and significance.

In the context of role playing, from a dramaturgical perspective (Goffman, 1974), department chairs play the role of the administrator as if it is a stage performance and they are costumed characters. One chair described her initial views as a department chair as an outsider in administrative meetings and indicated that she changed her attire to blend in with the corporate and administrative culture of her new role as chair.

> [N]ow I go to these [administrative] meetings, and there are people
> with very nice clothes and nice makeup and nice haircuts, and
> all of those things, with a very corporate presentation. . . . I go
> to these meetings and look around and I notice who is wearing
> what and notice what the men are wearing and I notice what
> the women are wearing, and I notice what department they're
> from. . . . [I]f I am sitting next to the guy from the tree ring
> lab, or the guy from the agricultural outreach—he is probably
> dressed a little more like me—. . . . I didn't worry about that
> stuff [my apparel] before becoming head. And now if I go to
> broader meetings across many departments I notice the cloth-
> ing. . . . [O]n days I meet with the dean's office . . . it's still
> within the range of what I used to wear. I do have dress-up
> clothes and I did always wear dress-up clothes some days. (bio-
> medical sciences, research university)

She has acquiesced to the logic of her neoliberal environment and managerial role.

As well as dramaturgical performance, chairs engage in organizational combat. The chairs' authority and influence are contested. A chair
of linguistics at a research university expressed her exasperation over the
bureaucratic barriers and technological challenges that she faced in her
role as chair. Although she occupied a position where others expected her
to act, the complexity of the university prevented her from action. "I'm
supposed to have access . . . I don't even know to which things I don't
have access to that I am supposed to because how would I find a list of
which ones?" (linguistics, research university). A chair of mathematics and
statistics at a comprehensive university lamented over department chairs'
influence in significant budget matters, and referred to faculty salaries as
one example. "Department chairs don't have a whole lot of power in terms
of [faculty] salary increases." A chair of biomedical sciences at a research
university underplayed her power and influence and espoused the values
of shared governance and aligned herself with academic logic, particularly
collegiality and peer relationships. "I don't do this by myself: We do this
with our staff; we do this in conjunction with our faculty. Partly, again, my
job is to summate. But as chair, your job is finally to get it done." Here,
she implies that decision making, in the context of budgets, for example, is
a collective effort that involves the faculty and staff. Yet, she also indicates
that at times she receives directives that are outside her control. Thus, she is
required to adopt a more authoritarian position that aligns with neoliberal

logic. From a social identity perspective (Stets & Burke, 2000), department chairs embrace the norms and characteristics of the administrator role when their interactions with faculty demand that managerial role. This biomedical science chair and the linguistics chair noted above are examples of the ways in which chairs in the university are both managed and managers.

> [Y]ou are then the one saying, "Okay, this has been the sentence handed down and you have to deal with it." So, it's yours to try to navigate all of those things, and, ideally, you want to be one of the family. But, you have to also realize that there is a power dynamic, and I think this is a problem many folks don't realize. . . . Because of being chair, I negotiate their salaries. I do all these things: their merit promotions; all these kinds of stuff. There's an implied power dynamic. So, on one level, I don't feel any power. I feel like I'm the servant to everybody, but it doesn't matter what my perception is. It's the other. So, you cannot get offended when people are peeved at you. You can't let it go to your head when people love you either. (biomedical sciences, research university)

The power dynamics and tensions over power between chair and faculty arise because faculty possess their own identity as academic professionals, an identity perceived to be in "natural" contrast to administration.

Members of the faculty bestow upon their department chairs an identity as members of a group different from the faculty group, as members of administration. This othering placed upon department chairs is founded upon authority differentials: on department chairs' authority over faculty.

> I want to say for the most part it's [our relationship] collegial, but I am their boss so there's a little bit of an authoritarian element in it, but it's very limited because . . . we're all grounded in our professional identities. . . . And the psychiatrist is an independent practitioner, so they practice their skill set, according to professional standards and their own conscience. In terms of their monthly paycheck, I'm the one to make sure that comes out, and I check on their productivity to justify their salary. . . . So, there's an administrative reporting relationship. But most of our relationships are grounded in collegiality. (psychiatry, research university)

Indeed, the duality of the role of department chair as professional—faculty member and department chair—is compounded or made more complex by the considerable identity ambiguities of what James Gee (2000–01) refers to as the institutional identity, conferred upon them by their organizational position, and the discursive identity, which is constructed and maintained in their interactions with others, in this case, departmental faculty members.

These identity ambiguities include what department chairs understand as their role and expected performance both as a faculty member and as a department chair, in addition to their own views of their personal characteristics. Department chairs define themselves with personality traits that do not match the properties of managers and administration: "I'm shy," "I am not a leader-type," "not a political animal," and, "I don't deal with conflict really well." Due to his lack of customary managerial traits, a department chair in psychology, similar to other department chairs, is somewhat confounded by his enjoyment of the role of department chair.

> I actually am enjoying things I don't normally like doing. I don't understand it. I don't really understand it. It's a mystery to me because it's not me. I'm not a leader-type. I'm shy. I don't like being—this is rare for an academic person—I don't like being on stage. I've gotten used to being in front of a class. That's still not something I seek out. I'm very much a background person. (psychology, research university)

Although faculty tend to dismiss themselves as a proper or authentic chair, they indicate that the role does fit them due to their ability to carry out the work. "I'm very mission oriented, and the mission is very clear, and I believe the mission, and I believe I'm being productive in furthering the mission of the department" (psychology, research university). "They are very different roles, academic faculty versus academic administration. So, I think just that [the reason I was invited is because] I am efficient, that I am organized. I think I'm pretty easy to work with" (child and adolescent development, comprehensive university). Department chairs reconcile their lack of identification as administrators with their personal traits and abilities that made them effective department chairs.

Identity ambiguity is further fed by department chairs' distance from administration. Department chairs have more contact with upper administration than faculty; however, their relationship with other academic managers is limited and hierarchical. "As a chair, I don't have any meetings with the dean. It's the division chair who runs . . . the meetings with the deans" (modern languages, comprehensive university). This distance from other administrators may enable department chairs to separate themselves from the category of manager. For example, the psychology department chair noted above does not use the term *administrator* or *administration,* but *administrative* as an adjective: "I'd say I spend in Fall probably 80% or 90% of my time involved in administrative activities on behalf of the department" and "I actually don't enjoy analyzing data for administrative purposes" (psychology, research university). Department chairs use the term *manage* to indicate that they organize departmental internal situations (e.g., a personnel meeting for faculty advancement). They do not understand themselves as managers in the sense of Mintzberg's (1975) or Dunsire's (1973) views of managers or administrators who strategize, make decisions, lead a group of professionals, execute decisions, and implement policy. But, they do see themselves as buffers and defenders of faculty.

> Sometimes you have to go to the dean and say, "You know, my colleagues are really, really opposed to" whatever it is that the dean has suggested, and so "let's figure out another way that we can move forward on this." (Hispanic studies, research university)

Department chairs have to cope with their limited power to make decisions, the university's expectations that they manage their colleagues ("Deans who hire us, we report to the deans, don't want to deal with departmental issues . . . they just expect you to be a good administrator, to do that" [Hispanic studies, research university]), and their colleagues' resistance.

Department chairs' time is devoted to a role as head of the department, but they do not self-identify as a manager or administrator: They do not develop a managerial identity, and their self-reported actions do not signify that they behave or act as managers or administrators. Yet, their behaviors betray and negate this self-reported academic professional identity. We assert that this misalignment between the self-reported academic professional identity and role and behaviors can be explained through a chair's need to reconcile, in the self, divergent, incompatible neoliberal and academic logics. Chairs define themselves by what they want to be and by what their academic colleagues value and trust—other academics. Yet, chairs must perform their administrative and managerial roles and responsibilities. They are unsettled by their own acknowledgment of the work they do as chair. This work is perceived as lesser than the work of faculty in the eyes of their faculty; that is, it is work done by those no longer productive in research or teaching, or both. From the perspective of faculty peers, chairs have taken the step into the "dark side." Indeed, their state of denial and firm self-identification as academics may be a way to resolve their own discomfort or negative emotions and stigmas associated with the managerial role demanded of them in their university.

Department Chairs as Potential Shields in the Management of the Academic Profession

Department chairs cling to their academic professional identity as faculty—as scientists, as artists, as researchers, and as teachers. Nonetheless, they carry out duties and responsibilities that identify them with the university's administration and with the policies and practices of the administration. In that these policies and practices are characterized in the scholarly literature as neoliberal (Ball, 2012b; Levin, 2017; Ward, 2012), and that those who govern and manage the university are part of an academic capitalist knowledge regime (Slaughter & Rhoades, 2004), department chairs are among the purveyors of neoliberal policies within their departments. That is, as front line managers, department chairs subject their faculty to neoliberal policies even though, similar to their faculty, they too are neoliberal subjects (Ball, 2012b; Davies, 2005). Their identity is both a product and an agent of the systems and structures within which they work (Briggs, 2007). In the context of new managerialism (Deem & Brehony, 2005), the faculty member who is also a department chair and the department chair who claims to be faculty is one and the same person (Briggs, 2007). In identity theory, individuals have multiple identities, dependent upon the social structure in which they function, and they "act to protect and verify their conceptions of who they are" (Burke & Stets, 2009, p. 5).

Even though the department chair can be identified with a managerial regime, and indeed with neoliberal practices, the insistence of department chairs that they have identities as faculty, as academic professionals, as scientists, and as educators suggests that neoliberal logic has not necessarily replaced academic logic in the U.S. public university. Furthermore, although department chairs may perceive neoliberal logic as forced upon higher education generally, and their university specifically, they do not view themselves as responsible for, or as actors in, the replacement of academic logic by neoliberal logic.

Department chairs of public universities possess plural identities. They rely upon their academic professional identity as a source of meaning and an explanation of their experiences within the university (Castells, 1997). In this sense, then, department chairs are the bulwarks against managerial infringement upon the work of faculty. One department chair of ethnic studies at a research university claimed that the position allowed him to resist neoliberal trends, or at least not become complicit with the administrative side within his university.

> I did a little bit of the administrative work [before]. . . . [P]art of what I saw in [that] administrative [position] is these are administrators who don't know any faculty; they have minimum contact with students; they are never in a classroom, and . . . it's like if they are listening to a faculty member work it's more like: "Well, would this be a good story that I can put in a magazine?" Or, like, "Would a donor be interested?" So that profound disconnect between the administrative apparatus and the institution is part of why I wanted the department head [position], kind of a job to support the faculty and the teaching and the research that is happening. That feels much more appealing than working on the administrative side. (ethnic studies, research university)

Although department chairs comply with neoliberal logic in their managerial behaviors, they can defy neoliberal logic in their adherence to academic logic and their academic professional identities. Department chairs are in a position to oppose the erosion of academic values within a neoliberal institution.

Department chairs have agency to behave as academic leaders, rather than as overt managers. Although most department chairs devote the majority of their time to management activities and not to academic endeavors, this overload of managerial tasks protects other faculty from managerialism and neoliberalism. Department chairs pursue academic endeavors in their managerial role and blend academic logic and neoliberal logic. This blending ensures that neoliberal logic does not replace academic logic fully. However, the blending of these two logics further feeds the managerial monster in the university and limits department heads' actual ability to oppose neoliberalism, market behaviors, and managerialism.

In recent decades, alterations in public universities (e.g., demands for productivity and resources, technological change) have pushed faculty to participate more in department-level management. The department chair position, once a long-term appointment, is now a position filled for shorter periods of time.

> We had had a professor here who was chair for thirty-five years. . . . He was very influential on the students, and when he was ill . . . another professor stepped up to take over that position, but he had done it under very, very difficult circumstances because the transition was so chaotic. . . . So, when the person who stepped in took over. . . . We knew that it was going to be for the three-year term. He didn't want to do more than that. So, that started a new tradition, that everybody would do it for three years, and I felt it was kind of a duty to take that also. . . . It's nice to have this rule, but it's a lot of work. . . . So, it's nice to share it too, because it's a lot of work. (theatre, research university)

With limited-term appointments (which have a duration of between three and five years and with only one, or no, continuing reappointment), a larger number of faculty members are likely to participate in department chair positions.

> We decided that . . . we should just do it for three years, step aside, let somebody else take over, and it would basically rotate through all the full professors eventually, whether or not we thought they were going to be good chairs. (mathematics and statistics, comprehensive university)

Arguably, this increased participation will augment faculty's knowledge about the actual reach and limitations of the position, as well as the actual power held in the department chair role. We anticipate that as more faculty are likely to become department chairs, their understanding of the role and their acceptance of themselves in the role will become more normalized, but that their ability to resist neoliberalism will endure.

In this chapter, we argued that department chairs are members of the managerial class of their university. Although the faculty body is the group to which they identify themselves, management is an activity they carry out. Higher-level administrators are those with whom they have to negotiate their departments' needs and goals, and from whom they seek support. Yet, regardless of their self-asserted academic professional identity, department chairs resemble managers more than they resemble faculty. Their interactions with faculty, their work activities, and even their discourse places them in a role as manager, even though they eschew such an identity. Thus, the effects of neoliberal logic differ for academic managers and for academic faculty. To continue this argument, in the following chapter we focus on another academic manager group, academic deans.

In chapter 4, we explore a group whose role at the university involves neither instruction nor research. Their primary role is management. We argue, nonetheless, that, although the role of academic deans is primarily managerial, their professional identity is connected to academic values and goals, or academic logic. Academic deans' behaviors are aligned more closely with neoliberalism (and are thus more aligned with managerialism) than those of department chairs. Although academic deans have less direct contact with tenure track faculty, non-tenure track faculty, and students than do department chairs, their behaviors and actions have considerable effects upon all of these groups. We develop this argument in the following chapter and conclude with a comparison between department chairs and academic deans' responses to neoliberal logic and characteristics of their academic professional identity.

Chapter 4

Academic Deans

Double Agents of Two Institutional Logics and Two Institutional Domains

Chapters 1, 2, and 3 focused on faculty and department chairs. Given that the majority of academic deans have a faculty, and perhaps a department chair, background, those chapters help to explain the effects of neoliberal logic and managerialism on the higher level of academic management at universities: academic deans. While for faculty groups and department chairs, managerialism and neoliberalism are near-invisible abstract forces, for deans, these forces are visible and shape their decisions. We argue that in comparison to faculty and department chairs, deans play a conscious and active role in the promulgation of neoliberal logic, through perpetuation or opposition, or both. The enactment of their management role is a result of specific challenges and tasks that deans encounter and that are foreign to faculty. Similar to department chairs, academic deans maintain a professional identity that is both academic and managerial in which they adopt elements of academic logic and neoliberal logic. Thus, in this chapter we rely on social identity theory to explain academic deans. We close this chapter by pointing out the differences in the perspectives and understandings of faculty, department chairs, and deans.

The academic dean position sits on a delicate fulcrum between the academic and administrative realms within the public university. In almost all cases, individuals who become academic deans originate from the faculty body (Moore et al., 1983) and, particularly at research universities, hold faculty appointments in addition to their dean appointment. As espoused in the scholarly literature, deans are perceived of, traditionally, as members of the "dark side"—an unaffectionate term for members of the administrative body. Whether or not their behaviors and actions live up to this negative connotation is up for debate, and a matter we address in this chapter. The scholarship on academic deans and their role in the reinforcement of neoliberalism and managerialism is both insufficient and divided.

The argument here, an argument advanced originally by one of the authors in Martin (2018), is that, indeed, academic deans at public research and comprehensive universities enact neoliberal and managerial behaviors in response to an audit and performance-driven culture in U.S. higher education institutions; however, they also act as a line of defense against the infiltration and takeover of neoliberal and managerial values into universities (Martin, 2018). That is, deans also express, with firmness, an adherence to traditional academic values, and, in doing so, confound the position, enunciated in the literature, that they are managerial enemies of the faculty body (Martin, 2018). Academic deans, as members of both the administrative class and the faculty body, are positioned strategically within their organizations to resist external pressures and develop strategies to protect academic work (Martin, 2018). This phenomenon stems from both the largely temporal character of the dean's role (i.e., term appointments), the socialization deans receive as faculty, and the professional identity of deans as academics.

Although the main source of data used to justify the claims in this chapter comes from thirty-eight interviews collected from twenty academic deans from four University of California (UC) campuses in 2016 (for more information about the research project for this data set, review the Appendix), we utilize data pulled from other studies on deans, as well as deans' first-person accounts published as scholarly and newspaper pieces to demonstrate applicability across other public universities in the United States. We use as well data from interviews with department chairs of public comprehensive and research universities (see the Appendix) to illustrate the external perception of deans in U.S. universities. It should be noted, however, that data-driven studies on academic deans' behavior are limited, particularly in the United States. The prevailing orientation of the literature on deans omits connections to ideologies, and instead focuses upon the functional role of deans and university management. There is little contentiousness in the scholarship around what deans do, and we do not intend to suggest their actual day-to-day tasks differ from what is proposed by existing literature. Indeed, we agree with this scholarship, and our data support the notion that deans manage and participate in managerial activities. What is of more interest to us is the exploration of how, or in what ways, deans segregate, blend, or replace neoliberal logic with academic logic; and, moreover, how the exhibition of logics relates to the professional identity of deans and their demonstration of managerial behaviors. This latter topic has yet to be examined in the scholarship in the United States.

As a supplement to our data and the limited qualitative data on deans, we rely on Deem, Hillyard, and Reed's (2007) work on academic deans in the United Kingdom to support our assertions; and, although the context differs in some ways, the behaviors are similar and allow us to expand the reach of our findings to other institutions outside the UC system in the United States.

An Academic Dean, Yes; A Manager, No

Academic deans hold an administrative role that faces specific challenges, and encounter particular organizational structures not experienced by other administrators (i.e., department chairs, provost) or members of the faculty (Bright & Richards, 2001; Tucker & Bryan, 1991). In the view of a department chair, good deans and good faculty have different skills: "You could be horrible at being a professor and, yet, still be quite a good dean. And, I think that's actually not coincidental" (department chair, English, comprehensive university). The primary tasks of the dean include raising revenues for their unit, hiring and firing, managing the budget and making financial decisions with assistance from the chief financial officer of the unit (CFO) or assistant dean, developing strategic plans, ensuring compliance with institutional policy, mediating and resolving student issues such as grade appeals and conduct violations, and representing their schools, colleges, or divisions at institutional and public events and meetings. Deans may identify as both administrators and faculty. For example, 59 percent of the participants in Wolverton, Wolverton, and Gmelch's (1999) study identified as both. David Perlmutter (2018), a dean in communications from a Texas research university, explained, "When I ordered business cards, I made sure they read 'professor and dean'" (para. 5). However, although they embrace the dean position, the very nature of the deans' day-to-day tasks make them undeniable managers; yet, most deans do not identify with the manager label (Martin, 2018).

The rejection of the manager label may correspond to the temporal nature of the deanship in that deans' appointments are often impermanent and usually short term (Gmelch, 1999). The typical length of tenure for an academic dean is five years (Wolverton, Gmelch, Montez, & Nies, 2001); however, there is some variation by discipline. Business school deans serve an average of five years (*Financial Times*, 2015), pharmacy school deans for 5.7 years (Assemi, Yu, Liu, Corelli, & Hudmon, 2017), and law school deans in the United States serve for an average of three years (Goldberg, 2014). Furthermore, although deans' career paths vary (Moore et al., 1983; Wolverton & Gonzales, 2000), with 60 percent of deans serving as department chairs and 40 percent of deans serving as associate deans prior to their deanship, nearly all academic deans in research universities are hired from the faculty or have held a faculty position (Martin, 2018; Moore et al., 1983). Deans do not view themselves as long-term administrators. Approximately 22 percent of female deans and 26 percent of male deans plan to return to faculty after their term ends; and, only 23 percent of female deans and 28 percent of male deans view their deanship as a step toward a provost position (Wolverton & Gonzales, 2000). The remainder plan to either retire or stay as dean. Indeed, faculty who exemplify academic values and are perceived by the faculty as *primus inter pares*—first among equals (Brown, 2000)—may be more likely to be selected as deans.

The selection of deans from the faculty body is another characteristic that shapes the context in which deans identify themselves professionally. Faculty insist that deans should be one of their own (faculty) and would "resent their Dean being appointed by powers outside the faculty" (Lockwood & Davies, 1985, p. 122). As a result of the temporal nature of the academic deanship, deans may be influenced most by the socialization they received as faculty prior to their deanship; however, socialization does not cease when faculty enter a dean role. Faculty learn the values and norms of the academy through organizational socialization (Tierney & Rhoads, 1993). When a faculty member transitions to a deanship, they undergo continued socialization (Gmelch, 2000a, 2000b; Speck, 2003; Wolverton & Gmelch, 2002) and draw on past administrative experience and relationships with other administrators and faculty to learn their role; or, they resort to trial and error (Del Favero, 2006a) as a final option. Most deans lack formal training (Martin, 1993; Wolverton & Gmelch, 2002) and encounter challenges as they negotiate their administrative role and develop the skills necessary to thrive as a dean (Firmin, 2008; Foster, 2006; Griffith, 2006; Palm, 2006; Standifird, 2009). Clearly, then, academic deans, according to the scholarly literature, are not predisposed to managerial work: they do not gravitate to the dean's role because of their intent to shift their career projection. Paula

Allen-Meares (1997), a former social sciences dean at a research university in Illinois, explains in a self-revelatory piece that the deanship was not a career goal. "To be perfectly honest, I did not have a specific career plan to become a dean when the opportunity emerged. It just happened" (p. 84).

Yet, in spite of deans' proclivities, the position itself makes demands upon what they do and ultimately on their institutional identity (Gee, 2000–01). The socialization process is imperfect and can result in confusion, or cognitive dissonance, for deans. Deans lack clarity about their directions, role, and reporting structure (Martin, 1993). "The administrative arm of the academy functions under expectations biased by an unwritten code" (Wolverton & Gmelch, 2002, p. 103). This middle management role (Martin, 1993; Wolverton & Gmelch, 2002) is "Janus-like," or double-facing: deans are expected to respond to administration and faculty simultaneously (Gmelch & Burns, 1991, p. 18). As well as responsiveness to two primary parties, they are responsible to staff, students, external communities (Rhoades, 1990), and donors. Deans—and this is especially the case for women and minority deans—undergo role ambiguity, role conflict, and stress in the context of their own identity as well as their institutional type (Wolverton & Gmelch, 2002) despite their self-identification as credible and effective leaders. An example of stress that can stem from identity issues is described by Allen-Meares:

> I am an African American female. . . . I want to go on record that women in such leadership positions [deanship] have unique experiences and struggles. . . . Assumptions about women—their ability to lead, to make tough decisions, and to break through the male-dominated informal and formal networks to gain influence—still operate in the minds of some. (1997, p. 83)

Although Allen-Meares's example relates to gender identity, the ambiguities of the deans' position generate role conflict regardless of gender and ethnic background.

Role conflict may arise from both internal and external sources. As they "fulfill dual roles and have dual identities" (Lorenz, 2012, p. 628) and "seek to mitigate a tension between remaining true to their scholarship and performing properly as administrators" (Wolverton & Gmelch, 2002, p. 101), deans can face psychological or emotional tensions. External sources of conflict result, for example, from contradictory messages from their provost to reduce the budget and pressures from their faculty to invest more in their school or college (Wolverton & Gmelch, 2002). That is, deans must compromise and negotiate divergent sets of values, norms, and pressures, as well as adapt their professional identities to situations of compromise and negotiation. Indeed, the temporality of the deanship and the socialization deans receive both prior to and during their tenure contribute to deans' lack of identification with their administrative role and preferred adherence to an academic professional identity. These characteristics of the academy, coupled with the pressures and responsibilities of the deanship, and a highly competitive, defunded higher education environment over the past several decades, create circumstances that allow and perhaps require deans to behave as both enactors of managerial and neoliberal behaviors and resistors of managerial and neoliberal values (Martin, 2018).

Yet, some of these behaviors are muted or ignored in scholarly literature in the United States even though the rhetoric of deans is "filled with corporate discourse" (Isaac, 2007, p. 47). At best, the literature assumes that the university is a professional bureaucracy (Mintzberg, 1983), where deans coordinate functions in a meritocratic organization. The preponderance of literature is pre-2000s, and the literature on deans that exists both pre and post-2000 ignores neoliberal initiatives and practices that have entered the university, such as accountability measures (audit culture), academic capitalism, and new managerialism. These initiatives and practices have resulted in a changed environment for the management of the academic profession. A handful of UK, Australian, and other Western scholars do address this environment for management and by extension their work can be applied to deans in the United States (e.g., Deem & Brehony, 2005). In some distinction, in the UK, deans, as members of a larger administrative group, are identified as managers who enact behaviors associated with surveillance, control, and private-sector business practices; they value efficiency and effectiveness in the operations of their organization (Deem, 1998; 2004; Deem & Brehony, 2005; Deem & Hillyard, 2002; Deem, Hillyard, & Reed, 2007). Substantiation of these behaviors and values of deans within a U.S. context is limited. Discussions of new managerialism, referred to in the United States as new public management, center primarily around management fads such as Total Quality Management (TQM), Management by Objectives (MBO), Zero-Based Budgeting, and Business Process Reengineering (BPR) (Birnbaum, 2000). The few who have examined the managerial behaviors of academic deans focus on academic capitalist, or enterprising, behaviors more than managerial behaviors. In the face of declining financial stability in higher education and neoliberal changes in policy in the United States, deans become drivers of academic capitalism initiatives focused on innovation and entrepreneurship (McClure, 2016) and are pressured to utilize managerial approaches in their schools and colleges (McClure & Teitelbaum, 2016).

Yet, we do find, empirically, that academic deans in the United States embody neoliberal logic, such as an orientation toward the market, the view of students as customers, the commodification of knowledge, a return on investment, the pursuit of grants, and generation of revenue (Martin, 2018). The adoption of this logic is normalized and unquestioned by deans (Martin, 2018). Allen-Meares (1997, p. 85) described her initial tasks as dean as focused on "the added challenge of raising funds to build a new facility . . . how to increase effectiveness and which factors contribute to excellence in role performance" (social work, research university). Deans perceive these values and tasks as necessary for the survival of the institution and the unit in a highly competitive environment (Martin, 2018). Yet survival is only one goal; the pursuit of prestige and notoriety is also a motivation for their behaviors (Martin, 2018). In other words, deans not only acknowledge neoliberal logic but also perpetuate that logic.

As the transition from faculty member to dean is largely a role shift, deans must choose between allegiance to faculty values or to management values (Martin, 2018), that is, academic logic or neoliberal logic. Perlmutter (2018, para. 5) illustrates his own negotiation of his identification as faculty and dean: "I have tried hard to remain a member of the faculty in spirit even if I am a dean in appointment" (communications, research university). However, the expression and adoption of logics are more complex. Although neoliberal logic is present in the rhetoric and behaviors of academic deans, deans also cling to traditional values and priorities congruent with the academic profession (Martin, 2018). Neoliberal logic and academic logic are not characterized by the deans as mutually exclusive (Martin, 2018). On the contrary, deans rationalize the adoption of neoliberal logic and expressions of neoliberal behaviors as a necessary mechanism for the pursuit of traditional academic values and goals—such as faculty autonomy, knowledge creation, knowledge dissemination, student learning, graduate student mentorship, innovation, and original and unique contributions to the profession and society (Martin, 2018). For deans, to play by the rules of neoliberal logic becomes the means to maintain academic logic.

There are at least two types of deans in the context of a contemporary research university, positioned within a neoliberal educational environment defined by scholars such as Ball (2012b) and Ward (2012): (1) deans who dismiss all notions of a tension between academic values and neoliberal values, and (2) deans who acknowledge the tension between these different sets of values and reconcile those tensions by blending or segregating neoliberal logic with academic logic (Martin, 2018). Academic deans, specifically at research universities, operate in an academic mode as well as a managerial mode, but their academic background and their allegiance to faculty in their unit structure their behaviors and actions. In this way, deans can satisfy their largest and primary constituency, and rationalize their behaviors to their superiors (e.g., provost, president). Yet, some deans emphasize the managerial mode on a larger scale and suffer from disapproval by and ultimately detachment from their faculty colleagues, while they satisfy the demands of their superiors as long as they contain disruptive behaviors in their units. Contrary to research that indicates that disciplinary orientations influence administrative behaviors in faculty who become deans (Del Favero, 2006b), neoliberal behaviors are adopted by deans from all types of disciplinary backgrounds (Martin, 2018) and are not exclusive to disciplines perceived, traditionally, as revenue generating—such as those in the sciences and engineering.

Deans Embrace the Neoliberal Environment

Deans accept their neoliberal work environment as part of larger economic and sociopolitical context in which they function (Martin, 2018). Deans reference external factors such as national and local trends in state reduction of budget allocations to higher education as explanations for their work context. Although they speak of the reduction in state-issued resources and revenue with lamentations, they accept their situation and condition as unalterable and the context in which they must navigate and manage their schools and colleges (Martin, 2018). Some deans describe the constrained fiscal conditions as more disconcerting than others; nevertheless, deans resign themselves to accept the situation.

> We receive now just over eight percent of our budget from the state. We are one step away from being private universities, and anybody who's going to complain that Jerry Brown (governor of California) isn't providing for us, or, you know, that the system just isn't supporting us properly—we are a public university—just completely misunderstands the real world. (dean, liberal arts)

As exemplified by this dean of liberal arts, deans acknowledge the neoliberal context of their university. They accept that they do not have influence over the macrolevel, sociopolitical, and economic trends and that opposition to these trends would not help their universities. These taken-for-granted assumptions are at the basis of deans' rationalization that their role as dean is to help their colleges and schools to navigate this context effectively.

Deans indicate a level of comfort with neoliberal logic and behaviors such as revenue generation and reporting requirements because they perceive these activities as a matter of social responsibility (Martin, 2018).

> Federal dollars are tax dollars. So, I feel completely comfortable in justifying . . . I need to justify to my grandma how her tax dollars are being spent in my lab. I think that's part of our responsibility as scientists. . . . That's a part of our social responsibility. (dean, sciences)

The manner in which deans enact and justify neoliberal logic and its corresponding values and behaviors with academic logic and its corresponding values and behaviors may be dependent on both their circumstances as deans in highly academic and research-centric universities and their acceptance of their resource-constrained environment.

Deans Blend and Segregate Neoliberal and Academic Logics, Values, and Behaviors

Deans espouse neoliberal logic and enact neoliberal behaviors, and they blend these with academic logic and behaviors. They conceptualize students in neoliberal terms, as customers to be served. However, this conceptualization is not only perceived as compatible with the academic mission and academic values but also moderated by academic purposes (Martin, 2018). Deans mix and compartmentalize the two value sets simultaneously.

> We have customers. They have to be satisfied. We have to make a bottom line or we don't exist. But it just isn't a business; there have to be principles involved. If it were just satisfaction, we would just be a diploma mill. (dean, sciences)

Deans describe students as both customers and products (Martin, 2018). They do not perceive the neoliberal label for students as problematical to the academic mission of the university. A dean of science explains neoliberal activities associated with the values of performativity, such as the pursuit of prestigious, highly productive faculty and high performing staff, and blends these activities with academic logic.

> This is a university; our number one mission is to educate. . . . Those [students] are the number one products. We have a set of customers we have to serve: students and parents, faculty and staff, people who employ our students, agencies and companies who fund our research. If they are giving us money, I have to serve them. (dean, sciences)

The educational mission, including knowledge dissemination, is compatible with market and corporate values for this dean, who uses a commercial argument to support actions (Martin, 2018). Responsibility to the community, or a commitment to service to society, a value that is a bedrock of academe (Austin, 1990), mutates into responsibility to investors.

Academic deans articulate general consensus on what constitutes "products" of their universities, and these include faculty research. These products are understood as commercial or market goods. "You have to have a clear vision of the product, which is (a) the students we produce and (b) the research we produce" (dean, social sciences). Deans borrow terms from the economic marketplace associated with the neoliberal value of performativity (Martin, 2018). "We have to have good outcomes. We measure good outcomes in a variety of ways" (dean, sciences). Yet, in spite of these neoliberal discourses, deans do distinguish between business and university practices (Martin, 2018). They describe themselves as resource managers with academic goals and blend the neoliberal logic of quality, productivity, and measurable outcomes with the academic logic of education, including intellectual growth, merit, excellence, and innovation, as well as fairness for students.

> [T]he business of it is to take the resources you have. My job is to take the resources I have and give the best quality education, the most cutting-edge quality of education, and to make sure students are treated fairly. That means I have to know how to use our resources, when to invest to start new classes, start new approaches, do new things. That's what makes my output. My

output is a certain quality of education, a certain success rate of our students, a certain environment where people feel stimulated. Having our faculty stay instead of leave. The academics, we don't like to think of it as a business. If you think of a business, the goal is to make a profit. My goal isn't to make a profit; my goal isn't to spend as little money as possible. My goal is to take what I have and produce the best I can and not worry about profit. (dean, sciences)

Deans rationalize the invocation of neoliberal behaviors as a mechanism to pursue academic missions. They do not portray revenue generation activities, corporatization of higher education, and marketization of higher education as problematical or in conflict with academic logic. They engage in corporate partnerships and other neoliberal endeavors and view these partnerships as positive and beneficial.

There are resources and then, of course, when you bring industry into the mix; industry has resources of its own. And if it's willing to put those resources into collaborations, well great. . . . There's been a new vice chancellor for industry relations. And, he has totally changed the culture. And, as a result now, when I go talk to companies, they go, "Oh, yeah [we understand]." . . . In fact, companies are coming here going, "How can we interface with you?" You know. It's really different. (dean, sciences)

Deans express actions that emanate from neoliberal logic such as revenue generation and brand identity as a prerequisite for the attainment of the academic mission in a highly competitive, resource-scarce environment. Deans defend neoliberal behaviors and logic emphatically as the basis for institutional, financial survival.

The first thing you have to do is soundly run and soundly finance the institution—the rest is all bullshit if you don't have that. . . . It is a fool's errand to run any part of the university without thinking about grants these days. Fifty years ago . . . [i]t was relatively cheap. People built their career around inexpensive research. You have to piece together the money as best you can. . . . You have to define a brand identity to make the money. This notion that if it's corporate money, it's going to be a distortion to the mission is ridiculous. (dean, social sciences)

Academic deans do not perceive that corporate-like financial strategies necessarily damage academic endeavors.

Furthermore, deans portray revenue generation as a mechanism for the pursuit of research goals. "[This campus] is so big because there's huge amounts of resources from research. . . . There's benefits to being a research university to the state, to the nation, to the world" (dean, sciences). For deans, the generation of revenue allows for the achievement of the primary academic value and mission of the university—knowledge generation—as well as the attainment of local and global-scale social benefits. That is, academic values are the reason to carry out market-driven behaviors.

Academic deans espouse prestige, notoriety, and excellence as firmly held values. Neoliberal logic and market-based values, such as competition, rankings, product differentiation, and product superiority, are viewed by deans as neither troublesome nor incompatible with academic logic and values, such as intellectual freedom and merit, or social justice, such as racial, ethnic, and gender diversity, within the institution.

> You shouldn't have to sacrifice diversity for prestige. . . . If you care about quality and you're looking for the most interesting ideas, ranking and prestige will take care of itself. It's folklore that diversity is in competition with excellence. (dean, social sciences)

Deans perceive that it is both feasible and rational to blend neoliberal and academic logics.

Regardless of their conscious use of market and corporate values and organizational strategies to enact these values (which are at the core of neoliberal logic), deans, particularly at public, research universities, do not position themselves as managers. They insist that faculty autonomy and shared governance are of considerable importance to their university's culture. This insistence places them in the same stream of thought and values as full-time tenure track faculty. Indeed, deans indicate that academic logic takes precedence over managerial logic (Martin, 2018). Interference with faculty autonomy is met with opposition to and ultimate rejection of managerial behaviors. "I think the academy is very suspicious of professional managers because they don't have the academic interest of the institution at heart" (dean, social sciences). For deans, attempts to replace academic administrators with professional management experts would be resisted by faculty. The balance of power within the public research university is weighted toward academic logic, which include notions of shared governance and faculty autonomy.

> You realize very quickly that in a university and like a corporation, the dean presumably has a lot of power. But in fact, in the university, because faculty have tenure and faculty have a great deal of leeway in what they wish to do, the dean actually is not as powerful as people think him or her to be. (dean, social sciences)

Similar assertions were voiced by department chairs (see chapter 3) about the chair position and the dean position: power is perceived differently by those in academic manager positions and faculty who are not in these positions.

When power is exerted by deans, it is used to obtain resources through the maintenance of strategic relationships across the institution. This behavior was captured in Isaac's (2007) study of women deans at one research university in the southeastern United States. Isaac (2007) describes how one of her participants, Dean Dare (pseudonym), negotiated power in relationships for the purposes of resource acquisition.

> "I think a lot of power comes from your personal connections from other powerful people, and I've been impressed by that . . . [h]ow positive interpersonal relationships with say the president or provost or the vice president actually gets you stuff. And I guess that stuff is what you might call power." (p. 54)

Even though Isaac (2007) used the quotation as evidence of how power was used in leadership, the dean's observation serves as a useful example of neoliberal and managerial behaviors. Isaac's (2007) dean treats relationships with administrative colleagues as a resource and as a revenue generating activity. The relationship with the administration becomes a tool to maximize what Isaac (2007) terms the dean's "productive power" (p. 55). Isaac's dean describes herself as a middle-manager—" 'But you know I still believe deans are middle management in this environment' " (2007, p. 54)—thereby positioning herself as someone with power but not too much power, that is, not the kind of power that could be responsible for behaviors and decisions with which the faculty body might disagree. Deans' former faculty colleagues do not endorse the corporate ethos in the academy (Bright & Richards, 2001), as "the two worlds seem starkly antithetical to most faculty" (Bright & Richards, 2001, p. 9).

Deans utilize their managerial skills to rally the faculty around a decision or mediate conflicts or disagreements to direct action when decisions cannot be reached by faculty, such as in merit and promotion reviews. "The division of responsibilities is very clear. . . . But again, the faculty are not unanimous. Sometimes there's a divided body even amongst the faculty. So, then, the dean's input becomes very critical" (dean, social sciences). In such cases in which faculty are divided, deans perceive that it is legitimate for them to enact their institutional authority and make decisions.

Deans might not always adopt neoliberal logic and its corresponding managerial values consciously (Deem et al., 2007). However, when deans admit to managerial behaviors, the managerial and performative demands are placed on administrative support staff or other academic administrative subordinates, such as chairs and associate deans, not faculty—who are described by deans as unmanageable as a result of their professed values of shared governance and autonomy.

> UC [the University of California] as a whole and [this campus] with a vengeance is a place where faculty have a shared role in decision making. Shared governance is not a myth here. [The faculty and I] never had a major fight. I never felt as a dean that I was in that situation. There should never be a situation where you haven't largely gotten people on board. . . . I basically had to clean house on the administrative staff, who were hired ineptly. I have a huge respect for staff, but, as the people who work for me can attest, it is not a good idea not to perform. They [staff] make the deans look good—it's not the deans. A team does not mean it's a perfect democracy. (dean, social sciences)

Administrative staff are not protected by the same principles that apply to tenure track faculty. Thus, deans can, and do, evaluate and terminate staff on the basis of their performance and productivity, in a role that casts the dean firmly in the managerial camp.

Deans adhere to the cultural norms of their professional academic environment and are reverent to the values of shared governance and faculty autonomy; as a result, they express managerial values and behaviors with limitations. A science dean in a UK university reflects upon the influence of faculty on deans' behaviors and on deans' consideration of approaches to management of faculty. "'You can't drive academics and tell them what to do, like herding sheep to work really. . . . And the more you try pushing them in one direction, the more obstinate they become'" (Deem et al., 2007, p. 120). As a consequence of this academic context, deans both blend and segregate academic and neoliberal logics. They separate the logics when the professional and the managerial are not compatible, for example, in personnel matters such as disciplinary actions or in periods of financial exigency (Martin, 2018).

Management is clearly one of the primary organizational roles of deans. Deans are accountable for revenue generation activities such as fundraising, meeting with donors, encouraging their faculty to pursue grants, and seeking out corporate partnerships. "The provost and chancellor do have to worry about money. . . . Certainly, I get pressure to fundraise, which I wouldn't say I'm a natural at, but I try to do my best" (dean, sciences). Yet, deans attribute the pressure to participate in neoliberal activities to higher-level administrators such as provosts, vice chancellors, and chancellors: these senior administrators in the minds of deans are the parties responsible for the commercialization of the university (Martin, 2018).

> The structure that the chancellor set up, [the chancellor] is on top, then vice chancellors are underneath, academic deans are at the bottom. . . . We are still dealing with the main mission of campus—it is shifting from being academic to a nonacademic environment. (dean, sciences)

This perception that the senior administration is to blame for the adoption of neoliberalism in the university corresponds to the views of faculty members and department chairs. This shared perception enables deans to maintain an adherence to academic matters first and managerial tasks second.

A dean's power and influence vary based upon university, school, and department level structure. While some deans describe high levels of administrative decision-making control, others concede and delegate authority to their associate deans and chairs.

> [T]he power? The power is elsewhere. . . . I'd say it's either in the department chairs, probably most in the department chairs, occasionally in the dean, but more it's the department chairs . . . probably . . . where the power resides. I don't micromanage. I want people to be innovative and independent . . . within what limitations there are. (dean, sciences)

This perception of further diffusion of power in the university—for example, here, that the main locus of power resides with department chairs—protects the dean from charges of infringement on faculty autonomy or rights.

Deans portray themselves as powerless against a neoliberal regime driven by both upper and lower-level administrators. This cognitive strategy allows deans to separate or remove themselves from responsibility for the reinforcement of neoliberal logic and corresponding neoliberal values and behaviors and project themselves as academics and proponents of academic values rather than perpetrators of neoliberal ideals. Deans' behaviors can occur as a reaction to save face with one constituency or another and meet their conflicted notions of legitimacy. That is, they must meet both their administration's and the public's definition of legitimacy as a fiscally sound university and their faculty colleagues' definition of legitimacy as autonomous academics who pursue the university mission of the creation and dissemination of knowledge.

In this context, and in the role of the dean, conflict with legitimacy is tied closely to internal conflicts with professional and role identity for deans. Institutional theory (Scott, 2014) can explain these conflicts and the accompanying deans' behaviors. When deans view the adoption of neoliberal logic as serving the greater academic mission, they experience minimal or no tension. However, when they reflect on the undesirable effects of neoliberal logic on their own work (increased pressure to fundraise), they seek to reconcile neoliberal and academic logics by either blending or segregating these logics, or they attribute negative effects and pressures to other administrators and external stakeholders. These behaviors indicate an unwillingness to be associated with the "dark side" of administration in a neoliberal university, as well as a rejection of a managerial identity. Furthermore, in contemplation of the negative effects of neoliberal logic, such as violations of academic freedom or emphases upon quantity over quality, deans deny complicity in the perpetuation of neoliberal values and behaviors. At best, deans have either normalized, or, at worst, denied any notion of a neoliberal threat to the academic mission.

The Academic Professional Identity of Academic Deans as a Key to Deans' Behaviors

In that the professional identities of deans are constructed within the structure of their organization and within their need to verify their role both within an academic organization and as academics, deans' stories and sense-making (Degn, 2015) rationalize their adoption of both neoliberal and academic logics and behaviors (Martin, 2018). The scholarly literature proposes that there is a link between professional identity and values (Trede,

Macklin, & Bridges, 2012). Academic deans at research universities hold fast to their academic professional identity and self-categorize (Stets & Burke, 2000) as faculty (or professor) or in accordance with their discipline (i.e., anthropologist, chemist). This adherence to an academic professional identity may account for the ways in which deans blend academic logic with neoliberal logic and academic behaviors with managerial behaviors. Deans root themselves in their professional identity as academics in order to cope with neoliberal pressures (Martin, 2018). Whereas deans' administrative role prompts conformance to and adoption of neoliberal logic, their academic professional identity, irrespective of their dean role, may be the foundation for narratives that sustain academic logic. Their narratives express their self-ascribed identities; and, these identity constructions can affect their managerial behaviors (Degn, 2015).

Earlier literature takes issue with our position. This may be the result of the negative connotations of the academic administrative world as "the dark side" (Palm, 2006, p. 59). The assumption was that faculty who adopted administrative roles, such as decanal appointments, abandoned their identity as faculty and academics. Indeed, in his work on transitions of faculty to the deanship, Gmelch (2000b) described the initial stage of the transition as a period of disidentification. During this stage, deans struggle with the loss of self-identification and "the loss of the faculty role that prescribed their behavior and made them readily identifiable" (Wolverton & Gmelch, 2002, p. 22). This earlier body of scholarship noted that only 7 percent of deans at all four-year institutions identify with the faculty role (Wolverton & Gmelch, 2002). In considerable distinction, academic deans in 2016 at research universities identify themselves "first and foremost" with a faculty, or academic, identity (Martin, 2018). " 'I've been a faculty member. I'm still a faculty member. I have many things that are still faculty motivations' " (dean, liberal arts). Deem, Hillyard, and Reed (2007), in the UK, as well, note that academic deans at universities in that country self-identify as academics. One of Deem et al.'s (2007) dean participants from arts/humanities specifies the characteristics of their professional identity: " 'If I had to put a label on myself, I'm still an academic, I still do some teaching, I still do as much research as I can' " (p. 106). Group-related identity—deans as academics or deans as administrators—is based upon a number of elements, such as context and values, as well as institutional culture.

Social identity theory postulates that individuals identify with socially based in-groups, groups perceived positively, and strive to distance themselves from out-groups, groups perceived negatively (Stets & Burke, 2000).

As members of the academy, deans are drawn from the faculty body, associate themselves with the in-group (faculty) and attempt to distance themselves from association with the out-group (administrators). This us/them framework is reflected in the literature and academic community that labels administrators as members of the "dark side" (Palm, 2006, p. 59). The self-categorization of deans as "faculty" allows deans to accentuate the "attitudes, beliefs and values, affective reactions, behavioral norms, styles of speech, and other properties that are believed to be correlated with the relevant intergroup" (Stets & Burke, 2000, p. 225), that is, faculty. Yet, as academic deans enact both academic and administrative roles, and are actors in the two organizational cultures (Birnbaum, 1988; Del Favero, 2006a), they occupy a position where membership in an in-group is also membership in an out-group and membership in an out-group is simultaneously membership in an opposite in-group. They must satisfy their faculty, their provosts, chancellors, and the general public.

Deans manage identities in relation to the roles they play at various levels, or in various contexts, of the university. Based upon social identity theory, the deans' identities have different "saliency" at each of these levels or contexts. Thus, on one level or context, a role identity might be more salient (e.g., the role of a researcher or professor) and that role "will be activated in a situation" (Stets & Burke, 2000, p. 229). On another level or in another context, the role of administrator (e.g., manager of finances) will have more salience and thus that role will be activated.

Deans negotiate both social identities and role identities (see Introduction). Negotiation of these identities requires engagement in "proper role performance" (Stets & Burke, 2000, p. 227) and the management of multiple identities and their related logics, values, and behaviors. It is irrelevant to the individual dean who must reconcile and negotiate multiple logics whether neoliberal logic and academic logic (perceived of in the literature as divergent and irreconcilable) are indeed incompatible. Deans must blend and segregate logics and values in order to maintain legitimacy for their complex identities and roles (Martin, 2018). Because the academic professional identity is the coveted identity for legitimacy, deans reconcile their academic and managerial identities and the accompanying logics by blending or segregating logics (Martin, 2018).

Deans who present themselves as active researchers rely primarily on post-docs and graduate students in order to continue their research productivity. "Most of my projects are done by members of my lab. I would like to spend more time in the research lab but I can't. . . . It feels like a luxury to have even an hour, two hours, or an afternoon" (dean, social sciences). Although deans are managers who spend the majority of their time in the performance of administrative tasks and management of their colleges or schools, deans at research universities self-identify as faculty with remarkable consistency. In cases where deans acknowledge they are administrators, their academic professional identity, nevertheless, manifests through continued participation in research and the expression of their own inquisitiveness. "I love analyzing things. So, whatever I do, even now as an academic administrator, I'm very intellectual about it. Why do I do it, what works, what doesn't work, you know? I almost see it as an intellectual activity" (dean, sciences). Yet, this tendency toward the analytical can also be used to reinforce neoliberal and managerial ideologies. Lockwood and Davies describe the role of the dean in UK universities in deans' analyses of operations for the purposes of maximizing effectiveness and efficiency. "[E]very responsible manager . . . should be involved in evaluative activity" (Lockwood & Davies, 1985, p. 303). That is, although deans describe their adherence to their intellectual and academic professional identities, their role demands that these proclivities be used for neoliberal purposes. A research university social science dean in the United States illuminates his use of an analytical approach to evaluate faculty and make decisions about resource allocation.

> We have to have standards. We cannot distribute money evenly. So, for that we'll say "We are going to look at your research. By how much you published over the last four years, what quality did you publish?" We set up a kind of committee to evaluate . . . who evaluate our faculty based on productivity or quality. (dean, social sciences)

This social sciences dean acknowledges and accepts managerial approaches to the evaluation of professionals and the allocation of resources. Although he notes that he has the role of dean at his university, when asked how he identifies himself professionally he says he "has not fixed himself to belong to one category or another." That is, he has not adopted his dean's role accompanied by a change to his professional identity, and likely clings to his professional identity as an academic and a faculty member.

Deans attribute their faculty, or academic, identity to several factors: The dean role is temporary; not a position that they consider to be valuable in their academic environment; and, not a position they sought out deliberately.

> A lot of people see themselves eventually either stepping down from a dean [role] and doing professorial type, research type things, or retiring, in which case they might continue some academic life as an emeritus faculty member. Even those who have further administrative aspirations, I think they recognize that to be competitive in the administrative job market being a very strong academic is very important. (dean, social sciences)

The academic community categorizes the deanship as a "lesser" role than the faculty position. One common perception among faculty and some deans is that the dean's role is filled by individuals who are no longer productive in research, and this perception may account for deans' reticence to identify themselves as administrators or managers (Martin, 2018)—to accept this is to accept the decay or demise of their academic professional identity. Deans also report that they reject the dean identity because they want to avoid perceptions of elitism (Martin, 2018). "It [role of dean] feels a little braggy. I think it puts people off a little bit" (dean, sciences). Deans alter their self-introductions and identity labels in response to different situations (Martin, 2018)—that is, identity activation is conditional upon its saliency (Burke & Stets, 2009). Outside the university, they identify as professors and teachers; within the university, they identify as researchers and experts (e.g., chemist, psychologist). In contexts with other administrators, they do identify as deans (Martin, 2018). A science dean rejects the dean, manager, and administrator identity because of its association with inefficient bureaucracy and paper-pushing behaviors. "When you have a managerial or bureaucratic system in place, it is very difficult to change. I didn't create paperwork for others either. Managing means you have to create paperwork" (dean, sciences). This dean disassociates himself from the manager label by distancing himself from the bureaucracy associated with managerialism.

In those instances when deans embrace their identity as dean, their dean identity is secondary to their primary identity as faculty. It is rare for a dean to embrace the dean identity unequivocally as a primary identity. The self-association with the dean and faculty identity has no direct relationship with deans' limited participation in teaching and research, as reductions in research and teaching are reported by deans who identify as faculty as well as those who embrace their dean identity. Whatever their official role and institutional identity (Gee, 2000–01), which is an ascribed identity, deans at research universities self-identify as academics, as researchers, as scientists, and most notably as faculty who occupy the role of dean. Academic logic, including a predominant role for faculty in governance of the university, is a critical foundation for academic deans; neoliberal logic, including the regulation of social behaviors through market principles (Gane, 2012), although acknowledged and indeed implemented, inhabits a parallel but separate domain to academic logic in deans' behaviors and behavioral rationalizations.

The silver lining in the management of the academic profession in higher education is that an academic professional identity is deeply embedded within deans and thus prevents domination of neoliberal logic within this influential group of administrative leaders. That is, deans must reconcile or balance these two logics and determine how to act, or manage, without abandoning either logic. Academic logic, with its corresponding academic values, staves off the takeover of neoliberal logic (Ward, 2012) and resultant new managerialism (Deem, 1998; Deem & Brehony, 2005) into the university. Deans represent the management within their universities but they are defenders of an academic ethos (Martin, 2018). It is in the interplay of identities and the negotiation of deans' values, logics, and roles that the institutional legitimacy (Thornton & Ocasio, 2008) of the university experiences both organizational stability and instability (Levin, 2017; Martin, 2018). Academic deans, then, are double agents (Martin, 2018), but not undercover agents. They manage out in the open, and their behaviors are transparent. If and how deans can maintain this sensitive balance as double agents will rely primarily upon the continuation of an academic culture and the preservation of academic logic within the university. The balance within academic management may also be conditional on the appointment of academics and scholars to fill the position of dean.

Similar to chairs and full-time tenure track faculty, deans manage others, self-manage, and are managed. However, distinct from tenure track faculty, non-tenure track faculty members, and department chairs, deans are not managed as academics but as members of the university managerial class. This distinction is clear for other members of the university.

> To be fair to her [the dean], I think this is a really hard to be an administrator. The president and the provost set the tone, and they get pressures from the government, and, so, there's lots of un-academic, there's lots of student affairs-y sounding stuff. There's lots of nonacademic stuff that masquerades as academic stuff. (department chair, English, comprehensive university)

Deans' achievements are measured with nonacademic indicators: the number of successful programs for which they are responsible, the quantity of dollars saved or dollars raised, the number of new students attracted to colleges and schools, and national reports and rankings. Thus, deans experience neoliberalism more openly and directly than their colleagues.

Distinct from department chairs, deans are allowed, although not expected, to participate in research or teaching, with some institutional exceptions.

> Like many full-time academic leaders at the rank of dean or above, I teach no classes. I have chaired only one dissertation in five years. I go weeks at a time without holding a single conversation that would pass as "intellectual." (Perlmutter, 2018)

This reduced participation in academic activities creates identity dissonance.

> It was a world I formally left almost 10 years ago, when I decided to pursue a career in academic administration. . . . My colleague [a history professor], too, had committee meetings, but his day's agenda included teaching two classes and meeting with three graduate students to discuss their dissertations. His shelves were lined with hundreds of scholarly books; mine are stuffed with reports. (communications, research university, Perlmutter, 2018, para. 2)

Arguably, for deans, identity dissonance is stronger than for other members of the academy. For deans, the academic career is a background element of their role, and their institutional identity, as middle-managers who are valuable if they prove to be efficient, takes the central position in the eyes of their faculty and administrative peers. Nevertheless, they self-ascribe a firm academic professional identity. They have traveled from managed academics to academics who manage.

In this chapter, we explained that given the background of academic deans as faculty members and likely department chairs, they share similar views of neoliberal logic with members of those groups, which are largely negative ones in contrast to their embrace of academic logic. Although deans align themselves with academic logic, similar to faculty and department chairs, they rationalize the adoption of neoliberal logic and its affiliated practices as a way to preserve academic logic and its affiliated values. Deans are academic and managerial professionals who identify both with senior administration (chancellors, presidents, vice chancellors, vice presidents) at their university and midlevel administration (i.e., deans and department chairs). Faculty and department chairs see neoliberalism and market-like behaviors as often reprehensible, and thus they distance themselves from the administrative community that is aligned with managerialism. Deans align themselves not only with senior administrators and midlevel administrators but also with faculty. Thus, they are double agents of two institutional domains and agents for both academic logic and neoliberal logic (Martin, 2018).

In the next chapter, we take a general view on managerialism in the university compared to our explanations in chapters 1 to 4. We explain the ways in which ideas, values, and behaviors are managed in the U.S. university. Additionally, we provide a comparison among the diverse forms of interaction (i.e., embrace, oppose, mediate) with neoliberal logic in the university.

Chapter 5

Higher Education Management
in the U.S. University

In previous chapters, we examined the roles of members of each subgroup of the academic profession as well as their responses to neoliberal logic and managerialism in the U.S. university, specifically in the context of what has been referred to for two decades as the neoliberal university (Slaughter & Rhoades, 2000). In this chapter, we explain the connections among these populations' roles in the management of the academic profession. In doing so, we advance our argument: members of the academic profession are managed, manage others, and manage themselves; and they adopt and enact neoliberal logic. However, they are not neoliberal subjects entirely: they are guided by academic logic as well. They defend academic work and the values that underlie academic work; they maintain an academic professional identity as university employees. Thus, we conclude that the U.S. university is not a neoliberal university, entirely.

Historical perspectives of modern management in the West address European military structures, the chain of command (Morgan, 2006), and the views of Fayol (1949), Taylor (1911), and others on mechanistic structures and processes (Morgan, 2006). Although the bureaucratic structure enumerated by Weber became in the twentieth century a central feature of organizational life (Morgan, 2006), management was not only conceived of as control but also reflected the agendas of those in power (Casey, 2002). The emphasis on owner, or manager, or commander control continues into the present in business and industry in advanced world economies. Mintzberg has demonstrated variations of structure with his concept of structure in fives (Mintzberg, 1992), and his power configurations (Mintzberg, 1983) locates sources of power that shape structure. For example, his management configuration of adhocracy comes close to an explanation of the structure and functioning of postmodern organizations such as start-up tech companies. Yet, more pertinent to universities is his concept of the professional bureaucracy (Mintzberg, 1979b)

For scholars, the professional bureaucracy as a model of the university in the United States (Mintzberg, 1979b) gave way to the corporate university (Bok, 2003; Gould, 2003; Kirp, 2003; Marginson, & Considine, 2000; Slaughter & Rhoades, 2004) as a more apt model. The collegial model of governance (Corson, 1960), once embedded in the professional bureaucracy, especially for decision making, gave way to managerialism (Deem, 1998; Rhoades, 1998). Yet, the concept of the professional bureaucracy as applicable to universities has endured, continuing to the present day. In the professional bureaucracy, the roles of academic professionals (i.e., faculty) and administrators, as primary actors in the professional bureaucracy, are rationalized and in line with earlier and traditional conceptions of universities in the 1960s and 1970s (Baldridge, Curtis, Ecker, & Riley, 2000; Corson, 1960), as well as with later scholarly views (Birnbaum, 1988). These conceptions and views presented two distinct domains in the university: the academic and the administrative. The core operators—the faculty—possessed authority over academic matters and the coordinators and executives, as well as those at the strategic apex of universities (i.e., presidents and board members or trustees), possessed authority over financial, legal, and human resources matters. Even in more contemporary critiques of the functioning of the university (Pusser, Kempner, Marginson, & Ordorika, 2011; Readings, 1997), Mintzberg's professional bureaucracy serves as an implied standard of the ideal type of university.

Institutional theorists (Scott, 2014) would indicate that the professional bureaucracy satisfies the three pillars of institutions: the regulative, the normative, and the cultural-cognitive. On the one hand, the professional bureaucracy provides a behavioral rule and regulations structure that enables academics to function in a stable, rational environment with both rewards and sanctions. This frees academics from individual administrative responsibility and situates rules and standards within roles. On the other hand, the professional bureaucracy enables professional norms and values as well as social ideals and verification to guide, support, and reinforce the legitimacy of actions. Thus, academics can behave within the rubric of an institutional logic (Thornton, Ocasio, & Lounsbury, 2012) that combines taken-for-granted assumptions about their actions (e.g., the activities of teaching and research) and give and take between institutional values, social values, and professional values. Academics as a group can and do, collectively, possess both institutional and social power, and individually they have agency to moderate or interpret institutional norms and regulations. The professional bureaucracy permits both group conformity and individual discretion. Academics can rely upon the rules and regulations of their university, or they can resort to the norms of their profession, their discipline, or their scholarly field.

However, Mintzberg's type is grounded on assumptions for the conditions and context of this structure: stable environment, primacy of the operating core, two separate but parallel administrative hierarchies, and administrative power granted by the professionals themselves. That is, faculty as the operating core have the central role in both the operations of the university and the authority structure of the university. Administrators have legitimacy through the willingness of the faculty to accede authority to this group. Such conditions and context in 2020 universities are questionable, and the professional bureaucracy may be a more ideal type or relic of an earlier age than an empirical phenomenon.

Indeed, both academic work and identity and the management of academic professionals are problematical states or conditions to the extent that these are fluid, unfixed, and dynamic activities and concepts. In the United States, the academic professional is a multirole and employment status category: full-time tenure track, full-time tenured, full-time non-tenure track, part-time tenure track, part-time non-tenure track (in various guises); lecturer, researcher, researcher-teacher, teacher, teacher-administrator, and a variety of service roles (e.g., committee member or chair of committee), as well as hybrid faculty-administrator roles such as department chair and associate dean. Although teaching assistants, graduate research assistants, and post-doctoral fellows can be lumped into the category of academic professional, for the purposes of this book, we did not include these groups. The scholarly research on these groups is nascent, and the populations are vast and diverse, which would mean a data collection activity of considerable proportions. There is also the problem of this population's subordination to tenure track faculty who are in the role of supervisors, which thus compromises the professional autonomy of this population. Academic administrators, such as deans, associate and assistant deans, provosts, and presidents/chancellors, can in several university types be viewed as academic professionals, particularly if they teach or conduct research. Yet, the scholarly literature is not consistent on this matter. If we consider their community of interest and their role responsibilities, which are primarily managerial, we would not include them as academic professionals. However, if we consider their professional identities and the professional norms and values they can, and in many cases do, adhere to, then we would categorize them as academic professionals. Department chairs or heads, in most cases, are aligned, in the literature especially, with faculty, generally share their community of interest with faculty, and have appointments primarily as faculty, even though in numerous activities (e.g., budget management) they are synonymous with management. We thus consider them to be academic professionals, although their sometimes divided roles and responsibilities provide them opportunity to adopt either an academic professional identity or a managerial identity, or both. Deans are not as aligned clearly with faculty, and there is considerable differentiation among this population with respect to professional identity or whether or not they are primarily faculty or administration. Furthermore, university type—research or comprehensive university—may differentiate dean populations.

What is evident over time, since the rise of the corporate (Donoghue, 2008; Gould, 2003) or entrepreneurial university (Clark, 1998), is that academic administrators, from department chairs to provosts, have become more focused upon neoliberal logic. In neoliberalism, market principles are reinforced by the state through the state's apparatus, and this applies as well to universities (Ball, 2012b). The state defines and regulates "social life through principles that come from the market" (Gane, 2012, p. 613). Indeed, neoliberalism departs from liberalism on the role of the state, and the state's accepted role in institutions.

> Whereas classical liberalism represents a negative conception of state power in that the individual was taken as an object to be freed from the interventions of the state, neoliberalism has come to represent a positive conception of the state's role in creating the appropriate market by providing the condition, laws, and institutions necessary for its operating. (Olssen & Peters, 2005, p. 315)

The contemporary university, with its origins in liberalism (Donoghue, 2008; Gould, 2003), is now understood as a neoliberal institution, with neoliberal values on the ascendant (Ward, 2012). These neoliberal values include, for universities, the acquisition of financial resources as well as material and measurable outcomes, from student graduation rates to publication numbers and grant funding (Levin & Aliyeva, 2015). The neoliberal university is in competition for outcomes with all other universities (and for research universities that can extend internationally), agencies, businesses, and public organizations and is a competitor of charities for financial resources. Indeed, as a nonprofit, charitable entity, the university holds up its goals as worthy of financial support (donations) in comparison to altruistic, humanitarian causes such as relief organizations.

Contemporary Management of the U.S. University

The shift from the professional bureaucracy to what the literature refers to as the corporate university in the United States can be traced back to Keller's *Academic strategy* (Keller, 1983), which enunciated the rationale for colleges and universities to operate as corporate business entities in order to improve efficiencies and effectiveness, especially in the management of resources and people. Keller was prescient about the withdrawal of both state funding and public support for the subsidization of higher education's rising costs. Slaughter and Leslie (1997) identify the 1980s as "the turning point, when faculty and universities were incorporated into the market to the point where professional work began to be patterned differently" and "undercut the tacit contract between professors and society because the market put as much emphasis on the bottom line as on client welfare" (p. 5). This alteration coincided with or was the result of faculty and university needs for increased funding (Slaughter & Leslie, 1997). The competition for external resources, whether private or public, manifested in competitive behaviors not only by institutions but also by faculty; Slaughter and Leslie (1997) called this phenomenon academic capitalism. Production in this light is not simply development of knowledge, such as that found in publications, but economic market behaviors that yield financial profits, such as research or training grants, patents, royalties, licenses, university-industry partnerships, contracted services (e.g., consulting), and spinoff companies. In order to produce and support academic capitalists and an environment of academic capitalism, universities not only reorganize but also transform management, which has been referred to as reengineering organizations (Casey, 2002). The practice for universities is promoted in William Massy's (2016) *Reengineering the university: How to be mission centered, market smart, and margin conscious.* Management of the university alters and adds to its goals (e.g., profit or resource acquisition), and management of the university alters its practices (e.g., efficiency, centralized authority, monitoring), as well as its structures (e.g., new or expanded units such as marketing, compliance, knowledge transfer). This is a departure from Mintzberg's professional bureaucracy. Faculty faced with such changes that threaten to overwhelm the traditional values of a university are unlikely prepared to resist. Indeed, they may be ignorant of or naive about the power of the global economy and international concentrations of wealth and power that both initiate and foster reengineering (Donoghue, 2008).

Yet, money alone is not responsible for alterations to the management of higher education. Institutional legitimacy and the drive for some form of prestige (e.g., rise in national and international rankings, unique organizational identity) gained through measurable and visible evidence have both influenced and shaped management practices in universities (Pusser & Marginson, 2013; Ward, 2012). In the UK, for example, research publications at individual universities are monitored nationally; the United States relies upon national and international university ranking systems to judge individual universities' production in publications (Pusser & Marginson, 2013), as well as other markers of imposed and socially constructed quality (e.g., membership in illustrious societies, grant money generated by individual universities). It is the prestige or acknowledgment of value that legitimizes the university as a reputable or decent or excellent university (Scott, 2014). Again, to develop and maintain this reputation, the university cannot be an accidental domain or what Baldridge et al. (2000) and Cohen and March (1974) in the 1970s called an "organized anarchy." The professional bureaucracy, as well, could not cope with the demands for both resources and prestige and thus had to give way, in practice at least, to what Marginson and Considine (2000) call the enterprise university and what Burton Clark (1998) calls the entrepreneurial university. Both of these universities need neither collegial governance and management nor even the rational approach of a professional bureaucracy but rather a corporate style of management. This then calls for new understandings and indeed for a new theory of the management of higher education, or at least explanations of the management of the various types of higher education institutions based upon institutional characteristics. That is, explanations can pertain to the management of the research university, the comprehensive or teaching university, and the community college, among other institutional types, given that in large part previous explanations have an implied assumption that the professional bureaucracy is the organizational form of these institutions.

The Management of Values

The institutional logic of the university pertains to an institutional field: that is, values, norms, and behavioral patterns in common across universities (whether internationally or nationally). Generally, this logic results in isomorphism within organizations that occupy the same field (DiMaggio & Powell, 1983; Scott, 2014). In universities, then, research, teaching, and service combine as the three functions expected of faculty (applied primarily to full-time tenure track faculty); promotion and tenure processes are embedded within individual universities' practices; and, the pursuit and dissemination of knowledge are taken-for-granted assumptions for the academic profession's mission. It is arguable that for research universities, a form of entrepreneurialism has become or is becoming an additional mission (Etzkowitz, 2001). Furthermore, this logic assumes a prominent role of faculty (usually tenure track faculty) in organizational decision making, most certainly on academic matters such as curriculum and instruction. Embedded within both the decision-making function and in determination of quality of academic behaviors (such as research and teaching) is peer review (Blackmore, 2005; Levin, 2017).

However, at the organizational level, at individual universities (or for systems of universities that fall under a common governance and management structure, such as The University of Texas or The University of California), other goals and values can be enacted, including the efforts to establish new logics. This phenomenon is evident in the presence of academic capitalist behaviors (Slaughter & Leslie, 1997), in quality initiatives (Birnbaum, 2000), in administrative practices of control (Gaffikin & Perry, 2009; Slaughter & Rhoades, 2004), and in what Shore (2008) in the international context, Tuchman (2009) in the U.S. context, and Levin (2017) in the U.S. and Canadian context refer to as an audit culture. Both Ward (2012) and Levin (2017) connect audit practices with neoliberal ideology and logic. Thus, within individual universities, the management of the academic profession operates within two domains: the domain of academic logic of the university and the domain of neoliberal logic, imposed by the political economy. Indeed, it has been argued within the UK context that neoliberal logic has become institutionalized within the university (Ball, 2012b), and a permanent condition. For the United States, Ward (2012) makes a similar claim, yet other contemporary U.S. scholars (Finkelstein, Ju, & Cummings, 2011; Finkelstein, Martin Conley, & Schuster, 2016) are not as definitive.

This presence of two major logics within the university suggests that management is not unitary in its behaviors if it is to foster organizational survival or at least to stave off frequent tumult and dysfunctionality. This also suggests that embedded in the management of the university, if the university is deemed a modern organization, or even a postmodern organization (Casey, 2002), is a dual set of values: those of the academic profession and those of the neoliberal state. Thus, managerial behaviors can be viewed as dualistic, or at least the product of a dualistic system of values. On the one hand, the department chair or dean, socialized within an academic discipline and a faculty culture of a university, acts, and indeed rationalizes action, in accord with academic values, such as professional authority and autonomy of faculty. On the other hand, that same department chair or dean acts, and rationalizes action, in accord with corporate values, such as maximization of economic outcomes and standardization of practices (e.g., increases in revenue generation, use of a specific technology such on online campus surveys and standardized evaluations, and corporate partnerships). At a comprehensive university, two department chairs, one in a professional school and the other in a natural science discipline, articulate this dual role of academic administrators. Not only does the department chair have a dual identity as faculty and administrator but also that role encompasses academic and managerial values. This department chair rationalizes her position by indicating that there are two parts to the role: management and leadership. When she performs managerial tasks, she is a manager; when she performs leadership tasks, she is an academic. But, as a department chair, she is not a faculty member.

> When I'm doing things like hiring people and doing evaluations of people, or planning a schedule, it seems . . . managerial. . . . I'm doing the leadership stuff, I think that['s] pretty, still in the academic realm. So, when I'm trying to help us decide what we want our curriculum to look like or how we can promote student success, or how we can improve our program so that students are reaching learning outcomes in a more effective way; that's very academic still, because I'm not just managing in any place; I'm not just administrating in any place. I'm administrating for an academic unit. So, when I'm involved in those efforts, it's still academic, but it's approached from a different perspective than if I was a faculty member, you know? But there's certain aspect of the job for sure that are just that of a manager. (department chair, professional school, comprehensive university)

At the same university, a natural science department chair suggests dual roles as an academic administrator are present, but the managerial role dominates, even though on his campus he is designated faculty.

> The role of the department chair is to . . . keep the wheels on everything. So, make sure the scheduling works; keep the students happy; keep the faculty happy; keep the dean happy. . . . [T]he short version is keep everybody happy. The long version is much more complicated than that. . . . I have to try and work on budgets for equipment and research supplies. I have to manage the schedules for faculty and for the part-time faculty. I have to manage the infrastructure projects that we have because we have lots of equipment and things like that. And I have to do all of the personnel evaluations for the staff and for the faculty. . . . [I]t's very different from being a faculty member and . . . you're now not anyone's friend anymore. . . . [W]hat you have to do are very different than what other faculty have to do. . . . [O]n our campus, we are still faculty; the chairs are not considered administrators and, so, it's difficult because you have responsibility; you're the person given responsibilities about making sure things work the right way, and . . . sometimes that means you have to tell people that they can't do something that they really want to do. That's not fun. (department chair, natural sciences, comprehensive university)

Yet, dual roles aside, this department chair, as well as other academic administrators, faces conditions of rapid change, such as expectations and requirements from external actors, including accrediting agencies and the state legislature, which this department chair claims controls his university ("We are directly under their thumb").

Organizational action and thus change involve and indeed emanate not only from new leadership (chancellor, president, provost) but also in response to demands from external bodies and requirements from organizational and system authority figures to follow their agendas and meet their objectives.

> I think that there's been sort of steady change, and then when President X changed, we saw . . . lots of changes, some of them were necessitated by WASC [Western Association of Schools and Colleges' Accrediting Commission for Schools], we got only a seven-year re-accreditation on our last visit, and, so, you know,

> [the president has] been working with the campus, and with everyone to try and up . . . our performance and what WASC wants us to do. And, there's also been a lot of work on graduation rates, mandated by the Chancellor's office. . . . [T]here's been lots of pushes with advising, with making sure people can get what they need, the courses, all that sort of stuff. . . . Then [the president's] also pushed high-impact practices, which we don't mind that. That's what we want; we want to work with students in our labs. And so, it's going fast; it's going faster now than it used to. I don't know if that's going to be sort of the fact of life or if it will ever slow down. Part of me hopes it does, because it seems sort of like at breakneck speed and difficult to keep up with everything. (department chair, natural sciences, comprehensive university)

These demands do result in conflict between faculty and administrators. The conflict that this department chair notices between faculty and managers is one of "quality versus quantity."

Academic deans at research universities are no strangers to the tensions inherent in their roles—they too contend with dual identities (Martin, 2018) and dual cultures. On the one hand, they assert themselves as scholars who serve their faculty under the thumb of upper administrative pressures and managerial structures. On the other hand, they speak the language and rhetoric of managerialism and the neoliberal state, and they accept and normalize neoliberal behaviors and perspectives as if these are necessary components of the pursuit of the academic mission (Martin, 2018). A former dean of engineering indicated that he devoted 25 percent of his time to research, and when asked about his identity indicated he was "faculty," and touted his academic achievements. "I have these accomplishments." He noted the expectation for academic excellence for those who serve in dean roles, and he espoused and invoked academic logic.

> This is a university; our number one mission is to educate. . . . If you come from these institutions, academically, you have to be good. . . . Many of these successful deans and chairs, they are academically successful. These are the kind of academic values people do not put in job descriptions but they look at it. . . . Faculty let administration do their things as long as they don't cross the line, or go over them. . . . The position of dean is not dictatorial, if you don't have the respect in your own

field, you can't expect faculty to respect you. (dean, engineering, research university)

Yet, this dean's articulation of academic logic also came hand in hand with neoliberal logic as the dean framed the university and his school as a producer and customer-oriented entity that is money driven.

> To get money, you have to have the best ideas. . . . Money will not buy you quality but it will buy you resources with which [faculty] can do their research. . . . Those students are the number one products. We have a set of customers we have to serve: students and parents, faculty and staff, people who employ our students, agencies and companies who fund our research. If they are giving us money, I have to serve them—and of course, the public citizens who pay our salaries. . . . We live in a competitive world—you have to distinguish yourself. (dean, engineering, research university)

Despite their role in the management of the academic profession, academic deans self-present a dual identity as both neoliberal decision makers and democratic or collegial leaders (Martin, 2018). Subtle managerial behaviors and tendencies are embedded in this former dean's self-presentation of a democratic leader identity.

> As dean, you make the decision and communicate why you made the decision you made. You let them present their views, have them share with everyone their views, and try to reach a consensus. If consensus isn't possible then the dean makes the decision and communicates that decision to the group. . . . I didn't create paperwork for others either. Managing means you have to create paperwork. . . . I authorized [my chairs]: "Make decisions! Don't bring everything to me." With my chairs, I did not have one on one meetings. "If you need to see me, schedule it . . ." If you don't let your chairs make decisions, you can't tell them "shame on you." You have to incentivize people, whatever you are doing. . . . I got the faculty together, got them on board, got them on one page. At first, my job was to understand the landscape—my job was learning about capabilities, strengths, and all those things. We started investing in areas. I counted on my people. (dean, engineering, research university)

Deans acknowledge the neoliberal and managerial activities of the larger organization in which they lead, yet they concede the responsibility for that logic and its accompanying values to the level of administration beyond the dean's position (Martin, 2018). By positioning himself as faculty, and "othering" (Brons, 2015; Davies, 2002) administration and managers from his own identity, the engineering dean absolved himself cognitively of any responsibility for the perpetuation of managerial behaviors and neoliberal logic.

> As an administrator, you have to fill up your activity report. . . . They invented a system at [institution name] that is very difficult to change. When you have a managerial or bureaucratic system in place, it is very difficult to change. The structure that [the top-level administrator] set up, his royal majesty is on top, then vice chancellors are underneath, academic deans are on the bottom—deans have been pushed to the third and fourth level—this is damaging to the academic institutions. . . . We are still dealing with the main mission of campus—it is shifting from being academic to a nonacademic environment. . . . When administration has head-on collisions with faculty, the administration say, "Faculty have tenure and I can't get them to do what I want them to do." Instead they should say, "I haven't been able to convince them of it." (dean, engineering, research university)

In justifying his actions, this engineering dean separated himself from administration, noting that this group is responsible for the move of the university to a "nonacademic environment." He chastises administrators for their lack of collegiality with faculty. In this sense, he separates himself from other managers.

> Othering is the simultaneous construction of the self or in-group and the other or out-group in mutual and unequal opposition through identification of some desirable characteristic that the self/in-group has and the other/out-group lacks and/or some undesirable characteristic that the other/out-group has and the self/in-group lacks. Othering thus sets up a superior self/in-group in contrast to an inferior other/out-group, but this superiority/inferiority is nearly always left implicit. (Brons, 2015, p. 70)

In Brons's terms, this engineering dean, then, positions himself in the group of a superior type of manager, a manager who defends academe and maintains academic values.

The tensions between dual roles, value systems, and identities are not limited to deans from science and applied science disciplines; they are also experienced by deans in the social sciences, humanities, and professional schools (Martin, 2018). A dean of humanities identified himself as a faculty member and a professor (he invoked the dean title only when he met with donors or other administrators). Yet, he accounted for 5–10 percent of his time in research activities, and had not taught recently. This dean described an institutional environment with deeply embedded academic values and pushback from faculty at any overstepping from the administration.

> You can get a lovely appointment as chair or dean or whatever, but the real hierarchy is how many books you have. . . . You find the person who's a great scholar and you put that person in a position where that turns into great administrative work partly bolstered by the respect that these quirky cantankerous other scholars have for this person. . . . [T]here's a lot of criticisms from the public about higher education and our effectiveness and efficiency, as in those sorts of things, but . . . I think that maybe we bring in leaders . . . who are really researchers and teachers and . . . I think faculty maybe are looking for a sort of validation and reinforcement of the existing culture. . . . [T]here's a sort of fear that if we, if you shift towards a more managerial business type of model, that this is somehow a threat to what is deeply ingrained in terms of tradition of the university. . . . [I]f it were proposed that the next dean of humanities be a very well-trained manager who knows everything about academia but has never held an academic appointment, I would dig in my heels against that. . . . There is inertia here, and it's not all bad. I mean, sometimes I hate it. But it is protecting an institution that still is the place where knowledge can be produced and critiqued and debated without the direct influence of capital. And that's precious. (dean, humanities, research university)

In this way, the dean asserts himself as one who values academic logic. However, within the same discussion his statement is decidedly more neoliberal in tone and logic.

[W]e've got to get those widgets and turn them into new and improved widgets, but for me . . . what we need to do in that context is make sure that we can continue to justify our research enterprise ever more closely in connection with the undergraduate teaching enterprise, because what the legislature sees when it looks at [the institution] or what the governor sees when he looks at [the institution] is the hundreds of thousands of undergraduates who come through. . . . And that's reasonable, that they're about educating the state, making sure we have an educated . . . workforce. (dean, humanities, research university)

In addition to the conflicting logics portrayed by the deans at the organizational level, the tension between logics also rests at the individual level. The humanities dean spoke in market terms about selling humanities to students, espoused the values of innovation and effective course design, and expressed his intent to implement outcomes assessments.

It's harder to attract people to the study of [a research specialization] or something traditional like that. So, my vision is to begin to change how we present those . . . preserving the things that have been good about that form of education while also giving students a better sense of how they can derive maximum value from them. If I had my druthers, our numbers of majors would proportionally track the size of the undergraduate student body and we'd see increases everywhere. Now the other way is to slice it up, if you look at our student credit hours. . . . It's about enabling certain kinds of innovation. . . . I got five million [dollars] . . . to make sure that even very senior faculty are getting up to date information about how to teach writing most effectively, how to teach languages most effectively, how to do course design, how to do evaluation, how to teach to diverse classrooms. (dean, humanities, research university)

In addition to embodying neoliberal logic and managerial practices as these pertained to enrollment and instructional quality, the dean lamented a faculty member's response to his request to move offices. "[O]ne faculty member delivered an impassioned defense of traditional academic values and stomped out." He stated that the "status and power of the faculty is based on their research engagement . . . [and this] gives them a voice in administrative decisions." However, this dean chose hierarchical authority rather than the authority of expertise or collegiality as the ultimate source of legitimacy, even though he acknowledged the presence and effects of both systems.

> We have hierarchy and . . . we have strongly anti-hierarchical tendencies all at the same time. And I think that influences relationships between administration and staff and public universit[ies]. [I]t is hierarchical, because finally the budget decisions will be made at the division level. (dean, humanities, research university)

Yet, the same humanities dean rejected the term *manager* as applicable to himself, and cited perspectives from [his research area], his academic specialization, and he thus separated himself, in his academic and philosophical articulation, from the identity of the manager. He concluded this rejection of a managerial identity with both expressions of distaste for management practice and an assertion of his academic professional identity. "I'm allergic to a lot of professional management type stuff and that probably reflects my own blinkered insularity as a humanities faculty member."

Thus, the academic administrator faces divided value systems, and, writ large, these systems stem from the two domains: academic logic of the university and neoliberal logic, promulgated by the political economy. Even in jurisdictions such as the UK, where there are claims that the domain of the neoliberal political economy, in the form of neoliberal logic, has either replaced academic logic (Ball, 2012a) or at least diminished its prominence in the university (Deem & Brehony, 2005; Shore, 2008; Tight, 2014; Winter, 2009), dual values underscore contemporary management of the university. Actions that reflect opposition to the domain of neoliberal logic not only highlight academic logic within the university but also reinforce the power of neoliberal logic (e.g., Donoghue, 2008; Mountz et al., 2015). Even scholarship that promotes the domain of neoliberal logic as a preferred state for the contemporary university (Massy, 2016) reflects in contrast the prevalence of academic logic within the university. Those who promote the use of managerialism or new managerialism to rescue the university in contemporary society consider the university a business or corporation, with flaws that emanate from its principal qualities and characteristics, such as its emphasis upon scholarship and research, organization by and authority of disciplines, and absence of outcome metrics. "[T]he academic business model as currently exercised by traditional universities harbors some fundamental flaws and indeed is no longer sustainable (Massy, 2016, p. 41). Yet, academic logic (Levin, 2017) persists, and it is either integrated with neoliberal logic or the two sit separately within the university.

Faculty in Academic Management

Faculty can be viewed as the objects of management (Deem, 1998; Finkelstein et al., 2016; Ward, 2012), and for non-tenure track faculty this is particularly the case. This does not apply entirely to full-time tenure track faculty, who are both managed by administrators as well as managers of other tenure track faculty and non-tenure track faculty. Generally, in the scholarly literature, full-time faculty and part-time faculty, tenure track and non-tenure track, share the same domain as "managed professionals" (Rhoades, 1998), managed by administrators, including department chairs, deans, and provosts, and officially by presidents and chancellors. However, full-time tenure track faculty function as managers of part-time faculty, lesser ranked full-time faculty (through voting rights, peer review, and seniority), and other full-time faculty including those with similar or higher ranks as a result of their work on committees. As faculty or senate committee chairs, faculty set agendas, organize and direct committee meetings, and can have substantial authority to speak and act on behalf of committees. As members of a committee, faculty, collectively, make decisions that other faculty in the university are required to act upon. This can include curricular and instructional matters (e.g., policies such as grading, course content, and student behaviors), faculty behaviors and conduct (e.g., with respect to students and to other faculty), and indeed governance (e.g., voting eligibility).

The roles of full-time tenure track faculty in the management of the institution and of other faculty are historical; in the scholarly tradition, this form of management is equated with governance (Corson, 1960; Hines, 2000). However, within the context of a neoliberal state (Ball, 2012a) and with the infiltration of market forces within the university (Slaughter & Leslie, 1997; Slaughter & Rhoades, 2004) and emphases upon entrepreneurialism and commercialization (Bok, 2003; Kirp, 2003), faculty behaviors, and indeed at times in their preferences, exhibit neoliberal tendencies (Levin & Aliyeva, 2015). Thus, in their governance capacity, whether as reviewers of their peers for evaluation (e.g., tenure and promotion, merit), as members of committees, or as chairs of committees, faculty can function as accomplices in a managerial regime that is shaped and reinforced by neoliberal logic.

First and rather obviously, full-time faculty self-manage and self-monitor, and adopt strategies to align their work with the reward structure and to accommodate personal interests. A professor of chemistry at a research university equates his competency with competitiveness.

> My major interest is in research, and then in teaching, and then in service related things. And, whereas sometimes people's careers evolve. They tend to shift. Maybe their research program sort of shrinks a bit, and they're not quite as interested in trying to compete for grants and all that kind of stuff, whereas I'd say I've maintained things pretty much about the same throughout. (professor, chemistry, research university)

In the tenure, promotion, and merit process, shorter times to production, increasing number of publications, publications in high-status (more visible) journals, and shorter times to apply for tenure are preferred. "You know instead of going up [for full-professorship] in three years, you want to go up in two years, or whatever: it's all about numbers and papers" (professor, chemistry, research university). This self-managing professional's behavior contributes to the norms for all tenure track faculty and reinforces the competitive nature of the profession for newer faculty who face challenges to achieve employment security and who are forced to adhere to an agenda signaled for others' interests and not their own interests. In line with neoliberal critics such as Gane (2012), and particularly education critics Ball (2012a) and Ward (2012), faculty, specifically full-time tenure track faculty, not only monitor and thus manage colleagues but also self-monitor. They promote neoliberal logic and corresponding values such as "excellence" (Saunders & Blanco Ramirez, 2017), a euphemism for a standardized category in monitoring performance through quantification that has commandeered traditional academic notions of quality. The performance of faculty, both tenure and non-tenure track, is measured (e.g., impact factors for publications, student evaluations for teaching) by faculty themselves.

Non-tenure track faculty members' participation in management is less overt than that of tenure track faculty; yet, non-tenure track faculty engagement in management is prevalent in U.S. universities. Similar to tenure track faculty, non-tenure track faculty self-manage, participate in evaluation, and push themselves to comply with increasing work demands and institutional productivity measures.

> [In] this institution . . . I turn in a notebook with the work I've done and then what this institution seems to be focus[ed] on [is that] I give too many students A's and B's. So, their recommendation was I drop a rubric and make my class harder. . . . It was odd to me to be told to make my class harder so students aren't successful. And I've talked to a couple of other instructors who also work at the other institution and here and they've been told the same thing, so it's something consistent. (part-time faculty, kinesiology, comprehensive university)

Non-tenure track faculty do not participate in the management of other faculty; however, they do participate in competition with one another, are instrumental in cost-effective strategies (they use their own resources to cover supplies their universities do not provide to them), and they have become the ideal neoliberal workers in the U.S. university: exploited, committed, and productive (Levin, Shaker, & Wagoner, 2011; López Damián, 2017). This has consequences for their personal life, noted by a part-time faculty in sociology at a comprehensive university. "I already have an issue with work life balance with teaching." Yet, non-tenure track faculty (particularly those in part-time positions) maintain a strong academic professional identity despite the challenges they face, including structural and managerial impediments imposed upon them. Their role as managed, rather than managers, distances them from the potential cognitive dissonance experienced by other academic groups such as tenure track faculty and chairs and deans.

Academic deans, department chairs or heads, and faculty in the U.S. university are all in interaction with managerial structures and behaviors. For faculty, their participation, whether willing or not, in management of other faculty and in self-management connects them to neoliberal policies and practices, including new managerialism (Deem & Brehony, 2005). Deans and department chairs or heads, in their managerial strategies and behaviors, sustain both academic logic and neoliberal logic, and blend academic values with neoliberal and managerial values. Proximity to the managerial role entails increased levels of engagement in neoliberal values and managerial behaviors for each academic group. Thus, deans exhibit more pronounced neoliberal and managerial behaviors and contend with greater tension between conflicting sets of values than department chairs, and they experience greater tension within their own dual and conflicted identities. A similar comparison exists for department chairs and full-time tenure track faculty. However, close proximity to the managerial role provides academic administrators with the institutional and organizational knowledge needed to circumvent and resist neoliberal ideologies. This phenomenon is a consequence of their career security as tenured faculty members and their individual willingness to avoid survival mode approaches and affirm their professional identity as academics.

Conclusions:
The Conundrum of Academic Management

It is in this perhaps uneasy or in some cases antagonistic relationship between academic logic and neoliberal logic where academic management is located in the U.S. university. The documented pervasiveness of new managerialism or managerialism in countries other than the United States, which includes an "audit culture" (Shore, 2008), may suggest that the phenomenon is not present, at least to an extent that poses a threat, in U.S. universities. However, this is not the case. In the United States, the manifestation of managerialism differs to the extent that it is often masked by, or conflated with, other behaviors, such as academic capitalism (Slaughter & Leslie, 1997; Slaughter & Rhoades, 2004; Cantwell & Kauppinen, 2014), entrepreneurialism (Lee & Rhoads, 2004; Mars & Rios-Aguilar, 2010), and commercialization (Owen-Smith & Powell, 2003). Yet, in large part, these behaviors are extensions and indeed consequences of a neoliberal political economy (Ward, 2012) and the logic of neoliberalism, or what social science and humanities scholars call the projects of neoliberalism, with a principal aim found in "*a programme of the methodological destruction of collectives*" (Bourdieu, 1998, para 4; italics in original). Thus, the professional identity of academics is a suitable target of this program, within the larger goal of the transformation of institutions into extensions of neoliberalism.

Although the principal tenet of neoliberalism is economic (Campbell & Pedersen, 2001; Crouch, 2011; Davies, 2014a), its characteristics and values have been attached to and associated with other domains such as social policy, law, government, and social institutions (Flew, 2014). Within the university, neoliberalism thrives because the contemporary U.S. university is resource dependent, competitive among its members and with other universities, and in pursuit of or striving for legitimacy, recognition, and prestige. One way or another, neoliberalism has become synonymous with U.S. university goals and actions (Gould, 2003; Ward, 2012). Moreover, the emphases upon neoliberal values undermine the U.S. university as a public sphere (Pusser, Kempner, Marginson, & Ordorika, 2011) of free inquiry and unfettered dissemination as well as of liberal education for students, which might include emancipatory pedagogies (Saunders, & Blanco Ramirez, 2017), or pedagogies that seek to balance power among social classes and suppress oppression and inequity in society. This results from neoliberalism's privileging of private interests and the advantaged who fit the criteria of merit, denial of social community and social welfare, standardization and homogenization of outcomes for measurement, and rejection of cultural value differences, including diversity of thought and feelings (Harvey, 2005).

Resistance to and countering of neoliberal logic, and indeed to the neoliberal project itself, are not singularly focused activities. They do not rest on saying "No," or on the critique of parts or aspects of neoliberalism, such as self-interest or economic motives. Resistance may necessitate the elimination of the order of neoliberalism, which is an all-encompassing and pervasive form of governance (Hamann, 2009).

> Specifically, in relation to neoliberal forms of governmentality, this [action] would involve resisting, avoiding, countering or opposing not only the ways in which we've been encouraged to be little more than self-interested subjects . . . but also the ways in which our social environments, institutions, communities, work places and forms of political engagement have been reshaped in order to foster the production of *Homo economicus*. (Hamann, 2009, p. 58)

Thus, self-critique of one's self-interests and critique of social and political environments by both individuals and groups are required in order to address the government of the self and the government of others. This suggests that those in the academic profession respond for the self and respond for the profession. In this way, according to Bourdieu (1998), academics can produce a new order.

> [F]orces still exist, both in state institutions and in the orientations of social actors (notably individuals and groups most attached to these institutions) . . . that . . . will be able to resist

the challenge only by working to invent and construct a new social order. . . . [Such an order] will not have as its only law the pursuit of egoistic interests and the individual passion for profit and . . . will make room for collectives oriented toward the *rational pursuit of ends collectively arrived at and collectively ratified*. (Bourdieu, 1998, para 17; italics in original)

It is clear that neither academics—full-time, part-time, tenure track, and non-tenure track faculty—nor academic managers—department chairs and deans—are entirely neoliberal subjects, in spite of the assertions of several scholars (Ball, 2012b). They do not match Hamann's (2009) definition of neoliberal subjects. "The neoliberal subject is an individual who is morally responsible for navigating the social realm using rational choice and cost-benefit calculations grounded on market-based principles to the exclusion of all other ethical values and social interests" (Hamann, 2009, p. 37). Indeed, as we have discussed and demonstrated, academics and academic managers express values and articulate behaviors that are grounded in academic logic, specifically the values of the university: academic freedom, which includes the unfettered pursuit and dissemination of knowledge, shared or bicameral governance, peer review as a standard of evaluation by experts, and education as intrinsically worthy. Not only faculty but also department chairs and deans espouse these values and note behaviors consistent with this logic. However, in the management of the profession, this logic can be compromised, overlooked, or rejected. Based upon our discussion, the conundrum of academic management pertains to the reconciliation of neoliberal logic with academic logic including the actions that follow from this reconciliation.

The management of the academic profession incorporates, of course, the interactions between those who manage and those who are managed. That is, the described, documented, and observed behaviors that occur between managers and managed. This would include the behaviors between and among deans, associate and assistant deans, department chairs, and faculty. At the more pedestrian level, it pertains to evaluation, assignment of classes and committee work, governance directives (e.g., a university committee's directives and policies, such as syllabus requirements and instructional policies), and budget and expenditure approvals or rejections. At the more legal and intense levels, it pertains to employment disputes, personal threats, and retaliative actions, which can be construed as illegitimate (such as fabrication of charges or allegations against a party). Indeed, one professor of psychology who served for several years in a senior administrative role responsible for campus faculty and administration disputes noted in 2017 that academic management included the sordid, illegitimate, unprofessional, and sociopathic actions of faculty and the university administrators' responses to and sorting out of these actions (Levin, 2018c). In such cases, academic management became more policing and disciplining than managing the academic profession, although a common practice under these circumstances is to find an appropriate body (e.g., senate grievance committee) to investigate and bring resolution and cessation to these actions. Except for disciplinary action by a supervisor (i.e., dean's disciplinary action against a faculty member), there is little that a single academic manager can do alone in the face of actions that emanate from a faculty member. In the case of a non-tenure track faculty member, the supervisor (e.g., department chair) can ensure that the individual is not offered another employment contract, either through an evaluation process or by the authority of their position as an at-will hire.

Yet, the purpose of our project and this book was to explain academic management and the academic profession, particularly the professional identity of academic faculty and academic managers. It was not to detail the behaviors and actions of faculty and administrators and their interactions; nor was the purpose to analyze these actions and behaviors and draw from this analysis a theory of behaviors and actions. Our purpose included the explanations of structures and values that both shape and influence behaviors of academic faculty and academic managers. In large part, we relied upon the self-reflections of members of these two groups to guide our explanations.

Our analysis of academic professional identity and the professional work of faculty and administrators can lead to understandings of the interactions between academic professionals and academic managers. Generally, these interactions are guided, shaped, and regulated by the social structure of the institution of the university. More broadly, they are part and parcel of the regulative, normative, and cultural-cognitive domains of the institution (Scott, 2014). In the present context—that is, the past several decades—neoliberal ideology figures as a major influencer of university behaviors, through the three domains of the institution. It is evident that external policies, such as neoliberal policies, have found their way into universities globally (Seddon, Ozga, & Levin, 2013) through both national and transnational politics and the movement of values across nations. Furthermore, in the United States, where there is a prominent role of the economic market in universities and in their development (Labaree, 2017), it is not surprising that U.S. universities have not only ties to the private sector but also practices that model the private sector. Indeed, such a connection is not new, but goes back more than a hundred years in the United Statees, as suggested by Veblen's (1918) description of universities' behaviors at the beginning of the past century.

Yet, if inertia is a major characteristic of institutions, and universities have been described as traditional institutions without substantial change over decades and with the transmission of values over centuries, then academic logic in the face of neoliberal logic is unlikely to disappear quickly. As noted by a dean of humanities at a research university, "inertia here . . . is protecting an institution that still is the place where knowledge can be produced and critiqued and debated without the direct influence of capital." Indeed, there is considerable evidence, and we contribute here to this evidence, to show that academic logic not only guides academics' behaviors but also influences those of academic managers.

Management of the academic profession in the U.S. university, then, is perhaps a conspiratorial endeavor: a union of academic or university values and neoliberal or market values. This conspiracy occurs within individual managers (including full-time tenure track faculty who manage other faculty) and between academic administrators and faculty. Professional identity as academics—as members of a shared organization and profession—is central, and the role of manager with attention to practice, to results, and to organizational priorities functions either in tandem or sequentially. Teaching is valued, but teaching is evaluated by some form of measurement, from student numbers for productivity to instructor popularity by students for evidence of performance (Saunders & Blanco Ramirez, 2017). Service is valued in formal evaluation systems (Gu & Levin, 2016), but faculty are socialized to downplay its importance due to its lack of priority or prominence in evaluations, even though service is emblematic of full-time faculty's participation in governance (Martin, Levin, & López Damián, 2014). Research is an essential philosophical justification for a university's operations, yet organizational value is placed upon the faculty's generation of research funding, awards, and quantity of publications in prestigious journals (Ball, 2012b; Ward, 2012). Teaching, research, and service continue as the core of academic endeavors, but their form and the expectations for these are shaped by neoliberal logic. Both academic logic and neoliberal logic are simultaneous, intertwined, and blended; as such, they play central roles in the U.S. university, in faculty members' values, behaviors, and identities, and in the management of academics.

Appendix

Data Sets

The arguments in this book were developed using theory, academic literature, and original data. Six different research projects that share a common thematic line, the academic profession in the United States and in the UK in a context of change, inform this book. In each of these research projects, one or more of the book authors participated. Each project focused on a different sub-population of the academic profession, and these collectively were conducted over an eight-year time span (between 2010–17). Each chapter and The Introduction in this book rely on data from one or more of these research projects.

In order to provide more information to our readers about our empirical data, we have constructed the following summaries and table. The table includes general details of each project. This, we trust, will help the reader to identify what data were used in each chapter. The descriptions provide additional information on each research project and their sub-population. Furthermore, results from these research projects are available in the form of conference papers, books chapters, research papers, and doctoral dissertations. We invite the reader to look for and read these scholarly pieces.

Project: Faculty Members' Professional Identity

This research was carried out by Professor John S. Levin, at the time responsible for the California Community College Collaborative (C4), at the University of California, Riverside. The objective of this project was to compare and explain the differences among faculty work and identity at different institutional types in the United States. The data included interviews from fifty faculty members at a community college, a master's comprehensive university, and a research university in southern California. Faculty from different ranks and disciplines, including both males and females, were included in order to account for the heterogeneity within the academic profession. For this research project, documents from each campus were reviewed in order to understand institutional differences that contextualized faculty work and understandings of their work and their professional identity.

Project: A Multisite Case Study: Subjective and Organizational Factors that Influence the Performance and Productivity of Faculty Members in Their Academic Functions within Three Different Higher Education Institutions in the U.S.

This research project was carried out by Professor John S. Levin, as member of the Graduate School of Education of the University of California, Riverside, in collaboration with professors of the Universidad Autónoma del Estado de Morelos who were involved in the research design, data collection, data analysis, and publication of results. This project sought to explore full-time faculty members' professional behavior patterns and understandings of productivity and research collaboration. Although the original data included interviews with faculty from three institutions, in this book we employed data from twenty faculty members from two public universities (a research university and a comprehensive master's university). The interviews from a community college were not included. The interviewees were academic professionals in one of the following areas: economics, chemistry, sociology, biochemistry, anthropology, chemistry, physics and astronomy, biochemistry, politics, biology, and psychology. This group of interviewees also included women and men, and included faculty from different ranks.

Project: Long-term Part-time Faculty's Professional Life at Public Comprehensive Universities in California

This research project was conducted by Ariadna Isabel López Damián as part of the requirements of the Higher Education Administration and Policy doctoral program at the University of California, Riverside. The project had as its aim the exploration and explanation of the professional life of part-time off-the-tenure-track faculty, who worked more than five years at their particular campus in the United States. The question that guided this inquiry was: What are the ways in which long-term part-time faculty understand their role in their profession and in the context of public comprehensive master's universities? This research was qualitative in nature and was framed by work engagement theory, identity theory, and institutional theory. For data collection, the author interviewed fifty-one part-time faculty members in three public comprehensive master's universities in California. Although the dissertation findings focused on the responses of twenty-nine long-term part-time faculty, in this book, the fifty-one interviews inform chapter 2.

Project: Managers or Academics? Department Chairs at Public Universities

This research project was designed and conducted by the authors of this book in collaboration with other members of the California Community College Collaborative at the University of California, Riverside. The purpose of this investigation was to explain the work of department chairs or department heads at higher education institutions in the United States. As such, it responded to three questions: In what way do department chairs organize their work? In what ways do they understand their role at the university and their relationships with faculty members? And, in what ways do department chairs characterize their profession?

The research included six universities from two institutional types (three research universities and three comprehensive universities), in three states (California, Arizona, Oregon). We interviewed and collected data from forty-nine department chairs. The department chairs or heads interviewed included both women and men and they were affiliated, collectively, with diverse fields (for example, linguistics, physiology, anthropology, mathematics, education, theatre and arts, political sciences, and communications). All of these interviews were used to inform chapter 3.

Project: Academic Deans in the Neoliberal University

This project was the doctoral dissertation research of Marie C. Martin as part of the requirements of the Higher Education Administration and

Policy doctoral program at the University of California, Riverside. This phenomenological qualitative field investigation explored the experiences of academic deans at four public research universities in the University of California system. The research sought to explain how academic deans at research universities enact neoliberal behaviors and reconcile neoliberal logics with academic logics through the maintenance of an academic identity. The data included multiple interviews (38) with twenty academic deans from diverse academic fields in the sciences, social sciences, and the liberal arts. Both men and women were interviewed and other data from their campuses, departments, and their university system were collected for this project. The thirty-eight interviews inform chapter 4.

Project: Institutional Sectoral Change and Faculty Work and Professional Identity

This investigation was conducted by Professor John S. Levin in the UK as a qualitative field research project. The purpose of this research project was to identify and explain if and the ways in which faculty have undergone professional role and identity change, including changes to their professional practices in the particular context of sectoral change (the change from one institutional type to another). Data were drawn from eleven in-depth qualitative interviews that illustrate our opening arguments in the Introduction.

Table 1. Data sets' characteristics

Project name	Data collection period	Population	Sample	Used in
Faculty members' professional identity	December 2010– January 2011	Full-time tenured and tenure-track faculty at three public higher education institutions in southern California	50 interviewees • 10 from a community college (these were not used in this book) • 19 from a comprehensive master's university ◊ 12 women ◊ 7 men • 21 from a research university ◊ 6 women ◊ 15 men	Introduction and Chapter 1

Project name	Data collection period	Population	Sample	Used in
A multi-site case study: Subjective and organizational factors that influence the performance and productivity of faculty members in their academic functions within three different higher education institutions in the U.S.	March–May 2013	Full-time tenured and tenure-track faculty at a public research university and a comprehensive master's university in southern California	20 interviewees • 5 women • 15 men • 11 from a research university • 9 from a comprehensive master's university • 4 Associate • 4 Assistant • 12 Professor	Chapter 1
Long-term part-time faculty's professional life at public comprehensive universities in California	November 2015–April 2016	Part-time off the tenure track faculty members at three comprehensive master's universities in California	51 interviewees • 34 women • 17 men • 29 with more than 5 years of experience • 22 newer faculty • 9 faculty of color • Higher degree: 27 doctoral degree, 21 master's degree	Chapter 2
Managers or academics? Department chairs at public Universities	October 2016–April 2017	Department chairs at six public comprehensive and master's universities in Arizona, California and Oregon	49 interviewees • 16 women • 33 men • 28 from a research university • 21 from a comprehensive master's university • 13 Associate professors • 34 full professors	Introduction Chapter 1 2 3
Academic deans in the neoliberal university	June 2016–December 2016	Academic deans at three campuses in the University of California system	20 interviewees • 7 women • 13 men	Introduction Chapter 1 4
Institutional sectoral change and faculty work and professional identity	June 2016	Full-time faculty at a university that has undergone sectoral change in the United Kingdom	11 interviews • 8 women • 3 men	Introduction

In following what we consider preferred practice, we caution the reader about some of the limitations of our data. First, data included here are not a representative, or a probabilistic, sample of members of the academic profession in the United States. Second, most of our data are derived from faculty and academic administrators in a number of western U.S. public universities. Third, faculty and academic administrators of color are not incorporated in sufficient numbers in these research projects to identify or explain as a category in this book. Finally, due to space limitations, we focused on data communicated by participants and excluded contextual data about the diverse universities in which they work. Regardless of these limitations, data from the six projects provide insights into the academic profession, academics, and academic administrators' everyday experiences, as well as changes over time in the academy, which have resulted in a more managed profession than in earlier periods noted by scholars in the latter part of the twentieth century. By describing the characteristics of our data sets and indicating these sets' limitations, we have a twofold aim: (1) to provide scholars with accurate information about our empirical evidence, and (2) to offer guidance for future research.

References

AFT Higher Education. (2009). *American academic: The state of the higher education workforce 1997–2007*. New Jersey: American Federation of Teachers Higher Education.

AFT Higher Education. (2010). *American academic: A national survey of part-time/adjunct faculty*. New York, NY: American Federation of Teachers Higher Education.

Allen-Meares, P. (1997). Serving as dean: A public university perspective. *New Directions for Higher Education, (98)*, 83–88.

Alvesson, M., & Spicer, A. (2016). (Un)conditional surrender? Why do professionals willingly comply with managerialism? *Journal of Organizational Change Management, 29*(1), 29–45.

American Association of University Professors. (2017). *Visualizing change: The annual report on the economic status of the profession, 2016–17*. Retrieved from AAUP Reports and Publications: https://www.aaup.org/report/visualizing-change-annual-report-economic-status-profession-2016-17.

Antony, J. S., & Hayden, R. A. (2011). Job satisfaction of American part-time college faculty: Results from a national study a decade later. *Community College Journal of Research and Practice, 35*(9), 689–709.

Antony, J. S., & Valadez, J. R. (2002). Exploring the satisfaction of part-time college faculty in the United States. *The Review of Higher Education, 26*(1), 41–56.

Archer, L. (2008). Younger academics' constructions of "authenticity," "success," and professional identity. *Studies in Higher Education, 33*(4), 385–403.

Archibald, R. B., & Feldman, D. (2011). *Why does college cost so much?* New York, NY: Oxford University Press.

Assemi, M., Yu, J., Liu, S., Corelli, R. L., & Hudmon, K. S. (2017). Educational attainment and academic profile of deans and chairs at US pharmacy schools. *American Journal of Pharmaceutical Education, 81*(7), 5928. http://doi.org/10.5688/ajpe8175928.

Austin, E. A. (1990). Faculty cultures, faculty values. *New Directions for Institutional Research, (68)*, 61–74.

Austin, A. E. (2002). Preparing the next generation of faculty: Graduate school as socialization to the academic career. *The Journal of Higher Education, 73*(1), 94–122.

Aziz, S., Mullins, M. E., Balzer, W. K., Grauer, E., Burnfield, J. L., Lodato, M. A., & Cohen-Powless, M. A. (2005). Understanding the training needs of department chairs. *Studies in Higher Education, 30*(5), 571–593.

Baldridge, J. V., Curtis, D. V., Ecker, G. P., & Riley, G. (2000). Alternative models of governance in higher education. In M. C. Brown (Ed.), *Organization and governance in higher education* (5th ed., pp. 128–142). Boston, MA: Pearson Custom Publishing.

Baldwin, R. G., & Wawrzynski, M. R. (2011). Contingent faculty as teachers: What we know; what we need to know. *American Behavioral Scientist., 55*(11), 1485–1509.

Baldwin, R., & Chronister, J. (2001). *Teaching without tenure. Policies and practices for a new era.* Baltimore, MD: The John Hopkins University Press.

Ball, S. J. (2003). The teacher's soul and the terrors of performativity. *Journal of Education Policy, 18*(2), 215–228.

Ball, S. J. (2012a). *Global education inc.: New policy networks and the neo-liberal imaginary.* New York, NY: Routledge.

Ball, S. J. (2012b). Performativity, commodification and commitment. An I-spy guide to the neoliberal university. *British Journal of Educational Studies, 6*(1), 17–28.

Ball, S. J. (2015). Accounting for a sociological life: Influences and experiences on the road from welfarism to neoliberalism. *British Journal of Sociology of Education, 36*(6), 817–831.

Bare, A. C. (1986). Managerial behavior of college chairpersons and administrators. *Research in Higher Education, 24*(2), 128–138.

Becher, T. (1989). *Academic tribes and territories.* Milton Keynes, UK: SRHE and Open University Press.

Benjamin, E. (2002). How over-reliance on contingent appointments diminishes faculty involvement in student learning. *Peer Review,* 4–10.

Besharov, M., & Smith, W. K. (2014). Multiple institutional logics for organizations: Explaining their varied nature and implication. *Academy of Management Review, 39*(3), 364–381.

Bettinger, E., & Long, T. (2004). Do college instructors matter? The effects of adjuncts and graduate assistants on students' interests and success. Retrieved from National Bureau of Economic Research: http://www.nber.org/papers/w103. *National Bureau of Economic Research.*

Billot, J. (2010). The imagined and the real: Identifying the tensions for academic identity. *Higher Education Research & Development, 29*(6), 709–721.

Birnbaum, R. (1988). *How colleges work: The cybernetics of academic organization and leadership.* San Francisco, CA: Jossey-Bass.

Birnbaum, R. (1989). The latent organizational functions of the academic senate: Why senates do not work but will not go away. *The Journal of Higher Education, 6*(4), 424–443.

Birnbaum, R. (2000). *Management fads in higher education: Where they come from, what they do, why they fail.* San Francisco, CA: Jossey-Bass.

Blackmore, J. A. (2005). A critical evaluation of peer review via teaching observation within higher education. *International Journal of Educational Management, 19*(3), 218–232.

Bleiklie, I., Enders, J., Lepori, B., & Musselin, C. (2011). New public management, network governance and the university as a changing professional organization. In T. Christensen & P. Laegried (Eds.), *The Ashgate research companion to new public management* (pp. 161–176). Farnham, UK: Ashgate.

Bloch, C. (2002). Managing the emotions of competition and recognition in academia. *The Sociological Review 50*(52), 113–131.

Bok, D. (2003). *Universities in the marketplace: The commercialization of higher education.* Princeton, NJ: Princeton University Press.

Bothma, F. C., Lloyd, S., & Khapova, S. (2015). Work identity: Clarifying the concept. In P. G. W. Jansen & G. Roodt (Eds.), *Conceptualising and measuring work identity* (pp. 23–51). Dordrecht: Springer.

Bourdieu, P. (1998). The essence of neoliberalism. *Le Monde diplomatique.* Retrieved from htttp://mondediplo.com/1998/12/08bourdieu.

Bousquet, M. (2008). *How the university works. Higher education and the low-wage nation.* New York, NY: New York University Press.

Bowen, H. R., & Schuster, J. H. (1986). *American professors: A national resource imperiled.* New York, NY: Oxford University Press.

Bradley, G. (2004). Contingent faculty and the new academic labor system. *Academe, 90*(1), 28–31.

Brennan, G. (2011). What's to be explained? And is it so bad? In M. Thornton (Ed.), *Through a glass darkly: The social sciences look at the neoliberal university.* Canberra: The Australian National University ANU Press.

Briggs, A. R. (2007). Exploring professional identities: Middle leadership in further education colleges. *School Leadership and Management, 27*(5), 471–485.

Bright, D. F., & Richards, M. P. (2001). *The academic deanship: Individual careers and institutional roles. The Jossey-Bass Higher and Adult Education Series.* San Francisco, CA: Jossey-Bass.

Brint, S. (1994). *In an age of experts: The changing role of professionals in politics and public life.* Princeton, NJ: Princeton University Press.

Brons, L. (2015). Othering, an analysis. *Transcience, 6*(1), 69–90.

Brown, M. C. (2000). *Organization and governance in higher education: An ASHE reader* (5th ed.). Needham Heights, MA: Pearson Custom.

Burke, P. J. (1991). Identity processes and social stress. *American Sociological Review, 56*(6), 836–849. doi: 10.2307/2096259.

Burke, P. J., & Stets, J. E. (2009). *Identity theory*. Oxford: Oxford University Press.

Butterwork, S., & Dawson, J. (2005). Undone business: Examining the production of academic labor. *Women's Studies International Forum, 28*, 51–65.

Campbell, J. (1968). *Masks of God: Creative mythology*. New York, NY: Viking Press.

Campbell, J., & Pedersen, O. (2001). Introduction: The rise of neoliberalism and institutional analysis. In J. Campbell & O. Pedersen (Eds.), *The rise of neoliberalism and institutional analysis* (pp. 2–23). Princeton, NJ: Princeton University Press.

Cannizzo, F. (2018). "You've got to love what you do": Academic labour in a culture of authenticity. *The Sociological Review, 66*(1), 91–106.

Cantwell, B. I., & Kauppinen, I. (Eds.). (2014). *Academic capitalism in the age of globalization*. Baltimore, MD: Johns Hopkins University Press.

Carroll, J. B. (1991). Career paths of department chairs: A national perspective. *Research in Higher Education, 32*(6), 669–688.

Carroll, J. B., & Gmelch, W. H. (1992). A factor-analytic investigation of role types and profiles of higher education department chairs. Paper presented at the Annual Meeting of the American Educational Research Association. San Francisco, CA, April 20–24.

Casey, C. (2002). *Critical analysis of organizations: Theory, practice, revitalization*. Thousand Oaks, CA: Sage.

Castells, M. (1997). *The power of identity*. Malden, MA: Blackwell.

Clark, B. (1987). *The academic life: small worlds, different worlds*. Princeton, NJ: The Carnegie Foundation for the Advancement of Teaching.

Clark, B. (1998). *Creating entrepreneurial universities: Organisational pathways of transformation*. Oxford: Pergamon.

Clarke, C. A., Knights, D., & Jarvis, C. (2012). A labour of love? Academics in business schools. *Scandinavian Journal of Management, 28*, 5–15.

Clegg, S. (2008). Academic identities under threat? *British Educational Research Journal, 34*(3), 329–345.

Clegg, S., & McAuley, J. (2005). Conceptualising middle management in higher education: A multifaceted discourse. *Journal of Higher Education Policy and Management, 27*(1), 19–34.

Cohen, M. D., & March, J. G. (1974). *Leadership and ambiguity: The American college president*. Hightstown, NJ: McGraw-Hill.

Collini, S. (2013). Sold out. *London Review of Books, 35*(20), 3–12.

Corson, J. (1960). *Governance of colleges and universities*. New York, NY: McGraw-Hill.

Cross, J. G., & Goldenberg, E. N. (2009). *Off-track profs: Nontenured teachers in higher education*. Cambridge, MA: The MIT Press.

Crouch, C. (2011). *The strange non-death of neoliberalism*. Malden, MA: Polity Press.

Davies, C. (2002). Managing identities: workers, professions and identity. *Nursing Management, 9*(5), 31–34.

Davies, B. (2005). The (im)possibility of intellectual work in neoliberal regimes. *Studies in the Cultural Politics of Education, 26*(1), 1–14.

Davies, W. (2014a). Neoliberalism: A bibliographic review. *Theory, Culture, Society, 31*(7/8), 309–317.

Davies, W. (2014b). *The limits of neoliberalism: Authority, sovereignty and the logic of competition.* Thousand Oaks, CA: Sage.

Davies, B., & Bansel, P. (2010). Governmentality and academic work: Shaping the hearts and minds of academic workers. *Journal of Curriculum Theorizing, 26*(3), 5–20.

Deem, R. (1998). "New managerialism" and higher education: The management of performances and cultures in universities in the United Kingdom. *International Studies in Sociology of Education, 8*(1), 47–70.

Deem, R. (2004). The knowledge worker, the manager-academic and the contemporary UK university: New and old forms of public management? *Financial Accountability & Management, 20*(2), 107–128.

Deem, R., & Brehony, K. J. (2005). Management as ideology: The case of "new managerialism" in higher education. *Oxford Review of Education, 31*(2), 217–235.

Deem, R., & Hillyard, S. (2002). Making time for management: The career lives of manager academics in UK universities. In G. Crow, & S. J. Heath (Eds.), *Social conceptions of time.* (pp. 126–143). Basingstoke: Palgrave.

Deem, R., Hillyard, S., Reed, M. (2007). *Knowledge, higher education, and the new managerialism: The changing management of UK universities.* Oxford: Oxford University Press.

Degn, L. (2015). Identity construction and sensemaking in higher education—A case study of Danish higher education department heads. *Studies in Higher Education, 40*(7), 1179–1193.

Del Favero, M. (2006a). Disciplinary variation in preparation for the academic dean role. *Higher Education Research & Development, 25*(3), 277–292.

Del Favero M. (2006b). An examination of the relationship between academic discipline and cognitive complexity in academic deans' administrative behaviors. *Research in Higher Education, 47*(3), 281–315.

Dill, D. (1984). The nature of administrative behavior in higher education. *Educational Administrative Quarterly, 20*(3), 66–99.

DiMaggio, P., & Powell, W. (1983). The iron cage revisited: Institutional isomorphism and collective rationality in organizational fields. *American Sociological Review, 48*, 147–160.

Dobbie, D., & Ian, R. (2008). Reorganizing higher education in the United States and Canada: The erosion of tenure and the unionization of contingent faculty. *Labor Studies Journal, III*(2), 117–140.

Donoghue, F. (2008). The erosion of tenure. In F. Donoghue, *The last professors. The corporate university and the fate of the humanities* (pp. 55–82). New York, NY: Fordham University Press.

Donoghue, F. (2008). *The last professors. The corporate university and the fate of the humanities.* New York, NY: Fordham University Press.

Dunsire, A. (1973). *Administration: The word and the science*. Great Britain: John Wiley & Sons.

Ehrenberg, R. G., & Zhang, L. (2005). Do tenured and tenure-track faculty matter? *The Journal of Human Resources, 40*(3), 647–659.

Enders, J., & Musselin, C. (2008). Back to the future? The academic professions in the 21st century. *Higher Education to 2030, Volume 1: Demography* (pp. 125–150): OECD.

Etzkowitz, H. (2001). The second academic revolution and the rise of entrepreneurial science. *IEEE Technology and Society Magazine, 20*(2), 18–29.

Fayol, H. (1949). *General and industrial management*. London: Pitman.

Feen-Calligan, H. (2005). Constructing professional identity in art therapy through service-learning and practica. *Art Therapy: Journal of the American Art Therapy Association, 22*(3), 122–131.

Feldman, D. C., & Turnley, W. H. (2001). A field study of adjunct faculty: The impact of career stage on reactions to non-tenure-track jobs. *Journal of Career Development, 28*(1), 1–16.

Financial Times. (2015). Short tenure of deans signals leadership void. Retrieved from https://www.ft.com/content/8af77ab4-e442-11e4-9039-00144feab7de.

Finkelstein, M. (2017). The American academic profession at risk. *International Higher Education*, (89), 10–11.

Finkelstein, M., Ju, M., & Cummings, W. K. (2011). The United States of America: Perspectives on faculty governance. In W. Locke, W. K. Cummings, & D. Fisher (Eds.), *Changing governance and management in higher education. The perspectives of the academy* (pp. 199–222). New York, NY: Springer.

Finkelstein, M. J., Martin Conley, V., & Schuster, J. H. (2016). *The faculty factor: Reassessing the American academy in a turbulent era*. Baltimore, MD: Johns Hopkins University Press.

Firmin, M. W. (2008). Transitioning from administration to faculty: Addictions to break. *Journal of Practical Leadership, 3*, 144–148.

Flew, T. (2014). Six theories of neoliberalism. *Thesis Eleven, 122*(1), 49–71.

Foster, B. L. (2006). From faculty to administrator: Like going to a new planet. *New Directions for Higher Education, 134*, 49–57.

Freidson, E. (2001). *Professionalism: The third logic*. Chicago, IL: The University of Chicago Press.

Gaffikin, F., & Perry, D. C. (2009). Discourses and strategic visions: The U.S. research university as an institutional manifestation of neoliberalism in a global era. *American Educational Research Journal, 46*(1), 115–144.

Gane, N. (2012). The governmentalities of neoliberalism: Panopticism, post-panopticism and beyond. *The Sociological Review, 60*, 611–634.

Gappa, J. M. (2000). The new faculty majority: Somewhat satisfied but not eligible for tenure. *New Directions for Institutional Research, 105*, 77–86.

Gappa, J. M., & Leslie, D. W. (1993). *The invisible faculty: Improving the status of part-timers in Higher education.* San Francisco, CA: Jossey-Bass.

Gappa, J. M., Austin, A. E., & Trice, A. G. (2007). *Rethinking faculty work: Higher education's strategic imperative.* San Francisco, CA: Jossey-Bass.

Garcia, P., & Hardy, C. (2007). Positioning, similarity and difference: Narratives of individual and organizational identities in an Australian university. *Scandinavian Journal of Management, 23,* 363–383.

Gee, J. P. (2000–01). Identity as an analytical lens for research in education. *Review of Research in Education, 25,* 99–125.

Gill, R. (2009). Breaking the silence: The hidden injuries of neo-liberal academia. In R. Flood & R. Gill (Eds.), *Secrecy and silence in the research process: Feminist reflections* (pp. 228–244). London: Routledge.

Giroux, H. A. (2002). Neoliberalism, corporate culture, and the promise of higher education: The university as a democratic public sphere. *Harvard Educational Review, 72*(4), 425–462.

Giroux, H. A. (2014). *Neoliberalism's war on higher education.* Chicago, IL: Haymarket Books.

Gmelch, W. H. (1991). Paying the price for academic leadership: Department chair trade-offs. Paper presented at the Annual Meeting of the American Education Research Association. Chicago, IL, April 3–7.

Gmelch, W. H. (1999). Building leadership capacity for institutional reform. Proceedings of the inaugural conference of the global consortium of higher education and research for agriculture. Ames, IA: Iowa State University, 77–84.

Gmelch, W. H. (2000a). Leadership succession: How new deans take charge and learn the job. *Journal of Leadership and Organizational Studies, 7*(3), 68–87.

Gmelch, W. H. (2000b). Rites of passage: Transition to the deanship. Paper presented at the 56th Annual Meeting of the American Association of Colleges for Teacher Education. Chicago, IL, February 25–28.

Gmelch, W. H. (2004). The department chair's balancing acts. *New Directions for Higher Education,* (126), 69–84.

Gmelch, W. H., & Burns, J. S. (1991). Sources of stress for academic department chairs: A national study. Paper presented at ASHE Annual Meeting. Boston, MA, November.

Gmelch, W. H., & Burns, J. S. (1993). The cost of academic leadership: Department chair stress. *Innovative Higher Education, 17*(4), 259–270.

Gmelch, W. H., & Carroll, J. B. (1991). The three Rs of conflict management for department chairs and faculty. *Innovative Higher Education, 16*(2), 107–123.

Gmelch, W. H., & Mishkin, V. D. (1995). *Chairing an academic department: Survival skills for scholars.* Thousand Oaks, CA: Sage.

Goffman, E. (1974). *Frame analysis: An essay on the organization of experience.* Cambridge, MA: Harvard University Press.

Goldberg, S. H. (2014). A dean for all seasons. *Pace L. Rev., 35*, 1128.

Goldstein, L. (2005). *College & university budgeting* (3d ed.). Washington, DC: NACUBO.

Goldstene, C. (2012). The politics of contingent labor. *Thought & Action, 28*, 7–15.

Gonzales, L., Martinez, E., & Ordu, C. (2014). Exploring faculty experiences in a striving university through the lens of academic capitalism. *Studies in Education, 39*(17), 1097–1115.

Goodman, P. (1962). *The community of scholars*. New York, NY: Random House.

Gornally, L., & Salisbury, J. (2012). Compulsive working, "hyperprofessionality," and the unseen pleasure of academic work. *Higher Education Quarterly, 66*(2), 135–154.

Gould, E. (2003). *The university in a corporate culture*. New Haven, CT: Yale University Press.

Griffith, J. C. (2006). Transition from faculty to administrator and transition back to the faculty. *New Directions for Higher Education, 134*, 67–77.

Gu, J., & Levin, J. S., (2016). Tournament in academia: A comparative analysis of faculty evaluation systems in research universities in the U.S. and China. Research paper for the Annual meeting of the Association for the Study of Higher Education Conference. Columbus, OH, November.

Gumport, P. J. (2000). Academic restructuring: Organizational change and institutional imperatives. *Higher Education, 39*, 67–91.

Hamann, T. (2009). Neoliberalism, governmentality, and ethics. *Foucault Studies* (6), 37–59.

Harari, Y. N. (2014). *Sapiens: A brief history of humankind*. London: Secker.

Harvey, D. (2005). *A brief history of neoliberalism*. New York, NY: Oxford University Press.

Haviland, D., Alleman, N. F., & Allen, C. C. (2017). "Separate but not quite equal": Collegiality experiences of full-time non-tenure-track faculty members. *The Journal of Higher Education, 88*(4), 505–528.

Hecht, I. W. D., Higgerson, M. L., Gmelch, W. H., & Tucker, A. (1999). *The department chair as academic leader*. Phoenix, AZ: The Oryx Press.

Henkel, M. (2005). Academic identity and autonomy in a changing policy environment. *Higher Education, 49*, 155–177.

Hines, E. (2000). The governance of higher education. In J. Smart & W. Tierney (Eds.), *Higher education: Handbook of theory and research, XV* (pp. 105–155). New York, NY: Agathon Press.

Hinings, B. (2012). Connections between institutional logics and organizational culture. *Journal of Management Inquiry, 21*(1), 98–101.

Hogg, M. A. (2001). A social identity theory of leadership. *Personality and Social Psychology Review, 5*(3), 184–200. doi: 10.1207/S15327957PSP R0503_1.

Hogg, M. A., & Ridgeway, C. L. (2003). Social identity: Sociological and social psychological perspectives. *Social Psychology Quarterly, 66*(2), 97–100.

Hoyt, J. E. (2012). Predicting the satisfaction and loyalty of adjunct faculty. *The Journal of Continuing Higher Education, 60*(3), 132–142.

Humphreys, M., & Brown, A. D. (2002). Narratives of organizational identity and identification: A case study of hegemony and resistance. *Organization Studies, 23*(3), 421–447.

Ibarra, H. (1999). Provisional selves: Experimenting with image and identity in professional adaptation. *Administrative Science Quarterly, 44*(4), 764–791. doi: 10.2307/2667055.

Isaac, C. (2007). *Women deans: Patterns of power.* Lanham, MD: University Press of America.

JBL Associates Inc. (2008). *Reversing the course: The troubled state of academic staffing and path forward.* Washington, DC: American Federation of Teachers.

Jeffrey, R. C. (1985). A dean interprets the role and powers of an ideal chair. *Association for Communication Administration, 52*, 15–16.

Jencks, C., & Riesman, D. (1968). *The academic revolution.* Garden City, NY: Doubleday.

Keller, G. (1983). *Academic strategy: The management revolution in American higher education.* Baltimore, MD: Johns Hopkins University Press.

Kezar, A. J. (Ed.). (2012). *Embracing non-tenure track faculty.* New York, NY: Routledge.

Kezar, A. J., & Sam, C. (2011). *Non-tenure-track faculty in higher education: Theories and tensions. ASHE Higher Education Report, 36*(5). San Francisco, CA: Jossey-Bass.

Kirp, D. L. (2003). *Shakespeare, Einstein, and the bottom line.* Cambridge, MA: Harvard University Press.

Knight, D., & Clarke, C. A. (2014). It's a bittersweet symphony, this life: Fragile academic selves and insecure identities at work. *Organization Studies, 35*(3), 335–357.

Knight, P. T., & Trowler, P. R. (2001). *Departmental leadership in higher education.* Philadelphia, PA: Open University Press.

Kok, S-K, Douglas, A., McClelland, & Bryde, D. (2010). The move towards managerialism: Perception of staff in "traditional" and "new" UK universities. *Tertiary Education and Management, 16*(2), 99–113.

Kupiec Clayton, M. (1991). Writing as outsiders: Academic discourse and marginalized faculty. *College English, 53*(6), 647–60.

Labaree, D. F. (2017). *A perfect mess: The unlikely ascendancy of American higher education.* Chicago, IL: The University of Chicago Press.

Layton, L. (2014). Some psychic effects of neoliberalism: Narcissism, disavowal, perversion. *Psychoanalysis, Culture & Society, 19*(2), 161–178.

Leaming, D. R. (2007). *Academic leadership: A practical guide to chairing the department.* Bolton, MA: Anker.

Lechuga, V. (2006). *The changing landscape of the academic profession. The culture of faculty at for-profit colleges and universities.* New York, NY: Routledge.

Lee, J. J. & Rhoads, R. A. (2004). Faculty entrepreneurialism and the challenge to undergraduate education at research universities. *Research in Higher Education*, 45(7), 739–760.

Lefebvre, L. A. (2008). Demographics, employment, motivations, and roles of part-time faculty in virtual universities. *New Directions for Higher Education*, (143), 37–44.

Lethabo King, T. (2015). Post-indentitarian and post-intersection anxiety in the neoliberal corporate university. *Feminist Formations*, 27(3), 114–138.

Levin, J. S. (2000). The practitioner's dilemma: Understanding and managing change in the academic institution. In A. Hoffman & R. Summers (Eds.), *Managing colleges and universities: Issues for leadership* (pp. 29–42). Westport, CT: Greenwood.

Levin, J. S. (2006). Faculty work: Tensions between educational and economic values. *The Journal of Higher Education*, 77(1), 62–88.

Levin, J. S. (2017). *Community colleges and new universities under neoliberal pressures: Organizational change and stability*. New York, NY: Palgrave MacMillan.

Levin, J. S. (2018a). "Who am I?": Institutional sectoral change and academic professional identity. Paper presented at the British Educational Research Association, Newcastle, UK, September.

Levin, J. S. (2018b). *Full-time tenure track faculty: stability within an insecure professional identity*. Paper presented at the American Educational Research Association (AERA-J), New York, NY, April.

Levin, J. S. (2018). Personal communication, confidential source.

Levin, J. S., & Aliyeva, A. (2015). Embedded neoliberalism within faculty professional identity. *The Review of Higher Education*, 38(4), 537–563.

Levin, J. S., Haberler, Z., Walker, L., & Jackson-Boothby, A. (2014). Community college culture and faculty of color. *Community College Review*, 42(1), 55–74.

Levin, J. S., López Damián, A., I., Martin, M. C., & Morales Vázquez, E. (2017). *Managers or academics? Department chairs at public universities*. Unpublished manuscript. University of California, Riverside. Riverside, CA.

Levin, J. S., & Montero-Hernandez, V. (2014). Divided identity: Part-time faculty in public colleges and universities. *The Review of Higher Education*, 37(4), 531–558.

Levin, J. S., & Shaker, G. (2011). Arrested development, undervalued teaching, and personal satisfaction: The hybrid identity of full-time nontenure-track faculty in U.S. universities. *American Behavioral Scientist*, 55(11), 1461–1484.

Levin, J., Shaker, G., & Wagoner, R. (2011). Post neoliberalism: The professional identity of faculty off the tenure-track. In Brian Pusser, Ken Kempner, Simon Marginson, & Imanol Ordorika (Eds.), *Universities and the public sphere: Knowledge creation and state building in the era of globalization* (pp. 197–217). New York, NY: Routledge.

Levin, J. S., Walker, L., Haberler, Z., & Jackson-Boothby, A. (2013). The divided self: The double consciousness of faculty of color at community colleges. *Community College Review, 41*(4), 311–329.

Locke, W., & Bennion, A. (2011). The United Kingdom: Academic retreat or professional renewal? In W. Locke, W. K. Cummings, & D. Fisher (Eds.), *Changing governance and management in higher education. The perspectives of the academy* (pp. 175–197). New York, NY: Springer.

Lockwood, G., & Davies, J. L. (1985). *Universities: The management challenge.* Windsor, Berks.: NFER-NELSON.

López Damián, A. I. (2017). Long-term part-time faculty's professional life at public comprehensive master's universities in California. (Unpublished doctoral dissertation), University of California, Riverside, Riverside, CA.

Lorenz, C. (2012). If you're so smart, why are you under surveillance? Universities, neoliberalism, and new public management. *Critical Inquiry, 38*(3), 599–629.

March, J., & Cohen, M. (1974). *Leadership and ambiguity: The American college president.* New York, NY: McGraw-Hill.

Marginson, S. (2009). University rankings, government and social order: Managing the field of higher education according to the logic of the performative present-as-future. In M. Simons, M. Olssen, & M. Peters (Eds.), *Re-reading education policies: A handbook studying the policy agenda of the 21st century* (pp. 584–604). Rotterdam: Sense.

Marginson, S., & Considine, M. (2000). *The enterprise university: Power, governance, and reinvention in Australia.* New York, NY: Cambridge University Press.

Mars, M. M., & Rios-Aguilar, C. (2010). Academic entrepreneurship (re)defined: Significance and implications for the scholarship of higher education. *Higher Education, 59*(4), 441–460. doi: 10.1007/s10734-009-9258-1.

Martin, J. L. (1993). Academic deans: An analysis of effective academic leadership at research universities. Paper presented at the Annual Meeting of the American Educational Research Association. Atlanta, GA, April.

Martin, M. C. (2018). Double agents: The dual logics and dual identities of academics in the neoliberal university. *UC Riverside.* ProQuest ID: Martin_ucr_0032D_13392. Merritt ID: ark:/13030/m5k985fp. Retrieved from https://escholarship.org/uc/item/4zg7r85b.

Martin, M. C., Levin, J. S., & López Damián, A. (2014). There are things that need doing: Faculty socialization to participate in committee work. Research paper presentation for the annual meeting of the Association for the Study of Higher Education, Washington, DC, November.

Martin, M., López-Damián, A. I., Levin, J. S., & Montero Hernández, V. (2015). Academia in transition: Academics' professional identity and the pursuit of productivity in the new world of neoliberalism. Research paper for the Annual meeting of the Association for the Study of Higher Education Conference. Denver, CO, November.

Martinez Alemán, A. M. (2014). Managerialism as the "new" discursive masculinity in the university. *Feminist Formations, 26*(2), 107–134.

Massy, W. (2016). *Reengineering the university: How to be mission centered, market smart, and margin conscious.* Baltimore, MD: Johns Hopkins University Press.

McClure, K. R. (2016). Building the innovative and entrepreneurial university: An institutional case study of administrative academic capitalism. *The Journal of Higher Education, 87*(4), 516–543.

McClure, K. R., & Teitelbaum, K. (2016). Leading schools of education in the context of academic capitalism: Deans' responses to state policy changes. *Policy Futures in Education, 14*(6), 793–809.

Meixner, C., Kruck, S. E., & Madden, L. T. (2010). Inclusion of part-time faculty for the benefit of faculty and students. *College Teaching, 58,* 141–147.

Mendoza, P., & Berger, J. B. (2008). Academic capitalism and academic culture: A case study. *Education Policy Analysis Archives, 16,* 1–27.

Mintzberg, H. (1975). The manager's job: Folklore and fact. *Harvard Business Review,* July–August, 56–62.

Mintzberg, H. (1979a). The professional bureaucracy. In Henry Mintzberg, *The structuring of organizations—A synthesis of research.* Englewood Cliffs, NJ: Prentice-Hall.

Mintzberg, H. (1979b). *The structuring of organizations—A synthesis of research.* Englewood Cliffs, NJ: Prentice-Hall.

Mintzberg, H. (1983). *Power in and around organizations.* Englewood Cliffs, NJ: Prentice-Hall.

Mintzberg, H. (1989). *Mintzberg on management: Inside our strange world of organizations.* New York, NY: The Free Press.

Mintzberg, H. (1991). The professional bureaucracy. In M. Peterson (Ed.), *Organization and governance in higher education.* Needham Heights, MA: Simon & Schuster.

Mintzberg, H. (1992). *Structure in fives: Designing effective organizations.* Upper Saddle River, NJ: Prentice-Hall.

Monks, J. (2007). The relative earnings of contingent faculty in higher education. *Journal of Labor Research, 28,* 487–501. doi:10.1007/s12122-007-9002-5.

Moore, W. J., Newman, R. J., & Turnbull, G. K. (2003). Internal markets for department chairs: Comparative advantage, life-cycle, and jury duty. *Journal of Labor Research, 24*(4), 669–682.

Moore, K. M., Salimbene, A. M., Marlier, J. D., & Bragg, S. M. (1983). The structure of presidents' and deans' careers. *The Journal of Higher Education, 54*(5), 500–515.

Morales Vázquez, E. (2019). *Humans behind intellectuals: Narratives, identities, and emotions of the academic profession in the neoliberal era* (Unpublished doctoral dissertation), University of California, Riverside, Riverside, CA.

Morgan, G. (2006). *Images of organization.* Thousand Oaks, CA: Sage.

Mountz, A., Bonds, A., Mansfield, B., Loyd, J. M., Hyndman, J., Walton-Roberts, M., Curran, W. (2015). For slow scholarship: A feminist politics of resistance through collective action in the neoliberal university. *ACME: An International Journal for Critical Geographies, 14*(4), 1235–1259.

National Center of Education Statistics (NCES). (2016). Characteristics of postsecondary faculty. Retrieved from: http://nces.ed.gov/programs/coe/indicator_csc.asp.

Ochoa, A. (2011). Contingent faculty: Helping or harming students? *The Journal of the Professoriate, 6*(1), 136–151.

Olssen, M., & Peters, M. A. (2005). Neoliberalism, higher education, and the knowledge economy: From the free market to knowledge capitalism. *Journal of Education Policy, 20*(3), 313–345.

O'Meara, K., & Campbell, C. M. (2011). Faculty sense of agency in decisions about work and family. *The Review of Higher Education, 34*(3), 447–475.

Owen-Smith, J., & Powell, W. W. (2003). The expanding role of university patenting in the life sciences: Assessing the importance of experience and connectivity. *Research Policy, 32*(9), 1695–1711.

Ozga, J. (1998). The entrepreneurial researcher: Re-formations of identity in the research marketplace. *International Studies in the Sociology of Education*, (2), 143–153.

Palm, R. (2006). Perspectives from the dark side: The career transition from faculty to administrator. *New Directions for Higher Education, 134*, 59–65.

Perlmutter, D. D. (2018, April 22). How to be both a professor and a dean. *The Chronicle of Higher Education*. Retrieved from https://www.chronicle.com/article/How-to-Be-Both-a-Professor-and/243168?cid=cp199.

Purcell, M. (2007). "Skilled, cheap, and desperate": Non-tenure-track faculty and the delusion of meritocracy. *Antipode, 39*(1), 121–143.

Pusser, B., & Marginson, S. (2013). University rankings in critical perspective. *The Journal of Higher Education, 84*(4), 544–568.

Pusser, B., Kempner, K., Marginson, S., & Ordorika, I. (Eds.). (2011). *Universities and the public sphere: Knowledge creation and state building in the era of globalization*. New York, NY: Routledge.

Quinn, K. (2007). Exploring departmental leadership: How department chairs can be transformative leaders. *InterActions: UCLA Journal of Education and Information Studies, 3*(1). Retrieved from https://escholarship.org/uc/item/66t8h5k7.

Readings, B. (1997). *The university in ruins*. Cambridge, MA: Harvard University Press.

Reay, T., & Hinings, C. R. (2009). Managing the rivalry of competing institutional logics. *Organization Studies, 30*(6), 629–652.

Rhoades, G. (1998). *Managed professionals: Unionized faculty and restructuring academic labor*. Albany, NY: State University of New York Press.

Rhoades, G. (1990). Change in an unanchored enterprise: Colleges of education. *The Review of Higher Education, 13*(2), 187–214.

Rhoades, G. (2008). The centrality of contingent faculty to academe's future. *Academe, 94*(6), 12–15.

Rhoades, G., & Maitland, C. (2008). Bargaining for full-time non-tenure-track faculty: Best practices. *The NEA 2008 Almanac of Higher Education* (pp. 67–73). Washington, DC: National Education Association.

Roach, K. D. (1991). University department chairs' use of compliance-gaining strategies. *Communication Quarterly, 39*(1), 75–90.

Rosinger, K. O., Taylor, B., J., Coco, L., & Slaughter, S. (2016). Organizational segmentation and the prestige economy: Deprofessionalization in high- and low-resource departments. *The Journal of Higher Education, 87*(1), 27–53.

Saunders, D. (2014). Exploring a customer orientation: Free-market logic and college students. *The Review of Higher Education, 37*(2), 197–219.

Saunders, D., & Blanco Ramirez, G. (2017). Against "teaching excellence": ideology, commodification, and enabling the neoliberalization of postsecondary education. *Teaching in Higher Education, 22*(4), 396–407.

Scharff, C. (2015). The psychic life of neoliberalism: Mapping the contours of entrepreneurial subjectivity. *Theory, Culture & Society*, 1–16. doi: 10.1177/0263276415590164.

Schipper, S. (2017). Social movements in an era of post-democracy: How the Israeli J14 tent protests of 2011 challenged neoliberal hegemony through the production of place. *Social and Cultural Geography, 18*(6), 808–830.

Schuster, J. K., & Finkelstein, M. J. (2006). *The American faculty: The restructuring of academic work and careers.* Baltimore, MD: Johns Hopkins University Press.

Scott, W. R. (2014). *Institutions and organizations* (4th ed.). Thousand Oaks, CA: Sage.

Seddon, T., Ozga, J., & Levin, J. S. (2013). Global transitions and teacher professionalism. In T. Seddon & J. S. Levin (Eds.), *World Yearbook of Education 2013. Educators, professionalism and politics: Global transitions, national spaces, and professional projects* (pp. 3–24). London: Routledge.

Sennett, R. (2006). *The culture of the new capitalism.* New Haven, CT: Yale University Press.

Shaker, G. G. (2008). Off the track: The full-time nontenure-track faculty experience in English (PhD dissertation). Indiana University, Bloomington, IN. Retrieved from Dissertations and Theses @ CIC Institutions. (Publication No. AAT 3387054).

Shore, C. (2008). Audit culture and the politics of accountability. *Anthropological theory, 8*(3), 278–298.

Slaughter, S., & Leslie, L. (1997). *Academic capitalism, politics, policies, and the entrepreneurial university.* Baltimore, MD: Johns Hopkins University Press.

Slaughter, S., & Rhoades, G. (2000). The neo-liberal university. *New Labor Forum, Spring/Summer*, 73–79.

Slaughter, S., & Rhoades, G. (2004). *Academic capitalism and the new economy: Markets, state, and higher education.* Baltimore, MD: Johns Hopkins University Press.

Snow, C. P. (1961). *The two cultures and the scientific revolution*. Cambridge: Cambridge University Press.

Speck, B. W. (2003). The role of doctoral programs in preparing faculty for multiple roles in the academy. *New Directions for Higher Education, 124*, 41–55.

Spenceley, L. (2006). "Smoke and mirrors": An examination of the concept of professionalism within the F.E. system. *Research in Post-Compulsory Education, 11*(3), 289–302.

Standifird, S. S. (2009). From faculty to administrator: The time management challenge. *The Journal of Academic Administration in Higher Education, 5*(1), 23–28.

Stern, M. (2012). "We can't build our dreams on suspicious minds": Neoliberalism, education policy, and the feelings left over. *Cultural Studies—Critical Methodologies, 12*(5), 387–400.

Stets, J. E., & Burke, P. J. (2000). Identity theory and social identity theory. *Social Psychology Quarterly, 63*(3), 224–237.

Stets, J. E., & Burke, P. J. (2003). A sociological approach to self and identity. In M. Leary & J. Tangney (Eds.), *Handbook of self and identity* (pp. 128–152). New York, NY: Guilford Press.

Stryker, S., & Burke, P. J. (2000). The past, present, and future of an identity theory. *Social Psychology Quarterly, 63*(4), 284–297.

Taylor, F. W. (1911). *Principles of scientific management*. New York, NY: Harper and Row.

Thedwall, K. (2008). Non-tenure track faculty: Rising numbers, lost opportunities. *New Directions for Higher Education, 143*, 11–19.

Thornton, P. H., Jones, C., & Kury, K. (2005). Institutional logics and institutional change in organizations: Transformations in accounting, architecture, and publishing. *Transformations in Cultural Identities, 23*, 125–170.

Thornton, P. H., & Ocasio, W. (2008). Institutional logics. *The Sage handbook of organizational institutionalism, 840*, 99–128.

Thornton, P. H., Ocasio, W., & Lounsbury, M. (2012). *The institutional logics perspective: A new approach to culture, structure, and process*. New York, NY: Oxford University Press.

The California State University. (2019). *CSU Faculty, Fall 2017*. Retrieved from CSU Employee profile: https://www2.calstate.edu/csu-system/faculty-staff/employee-profile/csu-faculty.

The Coalition on the Academic Workforce. (2012). *A portrait of part-time faculty members*. Retrieved from The coalition on the Academic Workforce research and reports: http://www.academicworkforce.org/CAW_portrait_2012.pdf.

Thirolf, K. Q. (2013). How faculty identity discourses of community college part-time faculty change over time. *Community College Journal of Research and Practice, 37*(3), 177–184.

Tierney, W. G. (2006). *Trust and the public good: Examining the cultural conditions of academic work*. New York, NY: Peter Lang.

Tierney, W. G. (2008). Trust and organizational culture in higher education. In J. Välimaa & O. Ylijoki (Eds.), *Cultural perspectives on higher education* (pp. 27–42). New York, NY: Springer.

Tierney, W. G., & Rhoads, R. A. (1993). *Enhancing promotion, tenure and beyond: Faculty socialization as a cultural process. ASHE-ERIC Higher Education Report No. 6.* ASHE-ERIC Higher Education Reports. Washington, DC: The George Washington University.

Tight, M. (2014). Collegiality and managerialism: A false dichotomy? Evidence for the higher education literature. *Tertiary Education and Management, 20*(4), 294–306.

Townsend, R. B. (2003). Changing relationships, changing values in the American classroom. *New Directions for Higher Education, 2003*(123), 23–32.

Trede, F., Macklin, R., & Bridges, D. (2012). Professional identity development: A review of the higher education literature. *Studies in Higher Education, 37*(3), 365–384.

Tuchman, G. (2009). *Wannabe U: Inside the corporate university.* Chicago, IL: University of Chicago Press.

Tucker, A. (1984). *Chairing the academic department.* New York, NY: Macmillan.

Tucker, A., & Brian, R. A. (1991). *The academic dean: Dove, dragon, and diplomat.* New York, NY: Macmillan.

Umbach, P. (2007). How effective are they? Exploring the impact of contingent faculty on undergraduate education. *The Review of Higher Education, 30*(2), 91–123.

Veblen, T. (1918). *The higher learning in America: A memorandum on the conduct of universities by business men.* Retrieved from http://www.elegant-technology.com/resource/HI_LEARN.PDF.

Walker, J. (2009). Time as the fourth dimension in the globalization of higher education. *The Journal of Higher Education, 80*(5), 483–509.

Waltman, J., Bergom, I., Hollenshead, C., Miller, J., & August, L. (2012). Factors contributing to job satisfaction and dissatisfaction among non-tenure-track faculty. *The Journal of Higher Education, 83*(2), 411–434.

Wang, S. (2018). The micro-foundation of academic entrepreneurship: Faculty entrepreneurial motivation and identity. Research proposal. The University of California, Riverside, Riverside, CA.

Ward, S. C. (2012). *Neoliberalism and the global restructuring of knowledge and education.* New York, NY: Routledge.

Weick, K. E. (1976). Educational organizations as loosely coupled systems. *Administrative Science Quarterly, 21*(1), 1–19.

Welch, A. P. (2000). Globalisation, post-modernity, and the state: Comparative education facing the third millennium. *Comparative Education, 37*(4), 475–492.

Whitchurch, C. (2006). Who do they think they are? The changing identities of professional administrators and managers in UK higher education. *Journal of Higher Education Policy and Management, 28*(2), 159–171.

Wilshire, B. (1990). *The moral collapse of the university: Professionalism, purity, and alienation*. Albany, NY: State University of New York Press.

Winter, R. (2009). Academic manager or managed academic? Academic identity schisms in higher education. *Journal of Higher Education Policy and Management, 31*(2), 121–131.

Wolverton, M., Ackerman, R., & Holt, S. (2005). Preparing for leadership: What academic department chairs need to know. *Journal of Higher Education Policy and Management, 22*(7), 227–238. doi:10.1080/13600800500120126.

Wolverton, M., & Gmelch, W. (2002). *College deans: Leading from within*. Westport, CT: Oryx Press.

Wolverton, M., Gmelch, W. H., Montez, J., & Nies, C. T. (2001). The changing nature of the academic deanship: ASHE-ERIC Higher Education Research Report. San Francisco, CA: Jossey-Bass.

Wolverton, M., & Gonzales, M. J. (2000). Career paths of academic deans. Paper presented at the Annual Meeting of the American Educational Research Association. New Orleans, LA, April.

Wolverton, M., Wolverton, M. L., & Gmelch, W. H. (1999). The impact of role conflict and ambiguity on academic deans. *The Journal of Higher Education, 70*(1), 80–106.

Ylijoki, O-H. (2005). Academic nostalgia: A narrative approach to academic work. *Human Relations, 58*(5), 555–576.

Index